Asia: The Next Higher Education Superpower?

Previous Titles in the Global Education Research Reports Series

Women in the Global Economy: Leading Social Change

Latin America's New Knowledge Economy: Higher Education, Government, and International Collaboration

Developing Strategic International Partnerships: Models for Initiating and Sustaining Innovative Institutional Linkages

Who Goes Where and Why?: An Overview and Analysis of Global Educational Mobility

Innovation through Education: Building the Knowledge Economy in the Middle East

International India: A Turning Point in Educational Exchange with the U.S.

Higher Education on the Move: New Developments in Global Mobility

U.S.-China Educational Exchange: Perspectives on a Growing Partnership

Asia: The Next Higher Education Superpower?

9th in the series of Global Education Research Reports,
supported by IIE and AIFS Foundation

Edited by Rajika Bhandari and Alessia Lefébure

INSTITUTE OF
INTERNATIONAL
EDUCATION

New York

IIE publications can be purchased at: www.iiebooks.org

The Institute of International Education
809 United Nations Plaza, New York, New York 10017

Library of Congress Control Number: 2015931101

Series Editor: Daniel Obst

Managing Editor: Jon Grosh
Copy Editors: Teresa Barensfeld, Jon Grosh
Cover Design and Layout: Pat Scully Design
Cover Image: Amy Cheng, amychengstudio.com

Table of Contents

Figures and Tables

Figures

Tables

Forewords

By Allan E. Goodman

As the latest data shows, Asia is a major player in student mobility. It comprises over 40 percent of globally mobile students and is now attracting international students at unprecedented rates, with China as the third-largest hosting country. Both outbound and inbound students, however, make up only a small proportion, less than 2 percent, of the region's massive student population. As these countries continue to develop and to invest in the establishment of more world-class universities, sheer numbers indicate that higher education in Asia will begin to reshape the global educational landscape.

With nine local offices and affiliates, IIE is already deeply engaged in the region, and it has been throughout its 95-year history. Chinese students were the biggest cohort of international students in the United States when IIE started counting in the early 1920s. Today, the United States still welcomes more Chinese students than any other nationality and has become the fifth leading study abroad destination for U.S. students. In 1946, China was the first country to sign a bi-national agreement to participate in the Fulbright Program, which we are honored to assist the U.S. government in implementing in cooperation with the Chinese and other partner governments around the world.

The second country to sign a Fulbright agreement was also in Asia. A newly independent Myanmar joined a month after China, 15 years before conflict and military rule took hold of the country. Today, international education is playing an important role in Myanmar's reform, and IIE is at the front of this effort, setting up international partnerships and leading delegations to support education reform and development in the country. What we are seeing in Myanmar is reminiscent of what I witnessed as a professor in Hanoi a generation after the Vietnam War, and what seems to be a rule for post-isolationist countries: international education is a significant first step to reform.

International education carries other benefits, as governments in the region are keenly aware. Many countries have set ambitious goals to increase international education, including China's aim to host 500,000 international students by 2020 and Malaysia's plan to attract 200,000. Japan's 2020 target is 300,000, and, it has financed internationalization programs in 37 universities in an effort to have at least 10 universities in the list of the world's top 100. Governments in Asia see internationalization of their colleges and universities as a means to capitalize on rapid globalization and remain competitive in the global marketplace. Their progress in these regards will define Asia's future involvement with the world and possibly redefine the way the world engages in higher education.

This publication, edited by two leading experts in higher education, is intended to help readers understand how governments, universities, and multilateral organizations are applying innovations in higher education to meet the diverse challenges across Asia. We hope this resource will help educators and policymakers adapt to new developments and create more productive and mutually beneficial educational relationships.

Allan E. Goodman
President & CEO, Institute of International Education

By William L. Gertz

All signs point toward Asia growing in importance and influence in the field of international education.

While the Times Higher Education World University Rankings show only six of the world's top 50 universities located in Asia, Asian higher education systems are predicted to progress and expand in the next ten years. Many leading universities from Asia have seen significant improvements in their 2012-2013 rankings gaining ground on the United States and the United Kingdom.

The British Council estimates that 2,000 more universities will be built in South Asia alone by 2024. As the demand for higher education increases both domestically and abroad, Asian institutions are poised to enroll students in growing numbers. Furthermore, U.S. colleges and universities, along with government iniatives such as 100,000 Strong Educational Exchange Initiatives, are fueling the increase of U.S. students studying in China.

In addition to an increase in higher education domestically, there has been a sharp increase of Asian students studying abroad. The sheer mobility of Asian students is impressive; high school and college students from Asia are studying abroad more than ever before. According to the Chinese Ministry of Education, the number of Chinese students who studied abroad increased by 17.7 percent from 2011 to 2012—a total of 399,600 students. Of this number, nearly 380,000 were self-sponsored. This willingness to invest financially in education suggests that Chinese families are seeing greater value in international education. Governments in Asia are also investing more, as they increasingly regard internationalization as a valuable component of economic growth and development—a dynamic unlikely to change.

At AIFS, we have seen a significant increase in the number of students from Asia attending our variety of pre-college programs—such as the Summer Institute for the Gifted, which holds classes at U.S. universities such as Yale and Princeton—as well as growth in Academic Year in America, our program enabling foreign high school students currently from China, Korea, Thailand, and Malaysia to study in America while living in volunteer homestays. We also have many students from Asia on the J-1 cultural exchange program, Au Pair in America. In addition, we recently developed a new summer study abroad program in China and are exploring several more opportunities for student programs in that region.

We hope you will find this book provocative as we continue to learn more about this fascinating and rapidly growing region in the ever changing landscape that is international education.

William L. Gertz
President and CEO, American Institute For Foreign Study (AIFS)
Trustee, AIFS Foundation

Higher Education in Asia and the Search for a New Modernity: An Introduction

RAJIKA BHANDARI, INSTITUTE OF INTERNTIONAL EDUCATION, UNITED STATES

ALESSIA LEFÉBURE, COLUMBIA UNIVERSITY, UNITED STATES

> *To familiarize oneself with the unfamiliar, to open oneself to the different, one must exercise the courage to leave the familiar and to throw oneself into the unknown.*
> — JOHN DEWEY, 1933

> *The unknown makes it necessary to imagine and possible to create the new.*
> — EDMUND PHELPS, 2014

No region has undergone as profound a transformation as Asia during the past half-century, from the 1970's to the present. The unprecedented economic growth has driven major social and demographic changes and institutional reforms and, in most countries, has brought about greater political stability. The advent of a large middle class, coupled with the openness driven by economic imperatives, has contributed to greater interconnectedness among Asian states and between them and the rest of the world. Higher education was not estranged from these dynamics. On the contrary, at a time when economic growth seems to be related to knowledge production and advanced skills, Asian governments and citizens expect higher education institutions (HEIs) to create the conditions for the development of their countries and to train the future generation to be innovative and creative and to pursue sustainable growth.

This acknowledgement and clear shift toward prioritizing higher education are not unique to Asia, though the means and pace of reform are. Despite national differences—including varied political and institutional settings, historical legacies, and local constraints—reform of the higher education sector across Asia has been largely state-driven and publicly funded. In other regions, the state gradually withdrew from investments in higher education, which encouraged private investments and market competition.

After several years of sustained high economic growth in several Asian countries, most governments in the region succeeded in driving major reforms of their higher education system. These reforms often took inspiration from overseas, while also addressing local issues. China, Japan, South Korea, Taiwan, as well as ASEAN members and India have regularly referenced Western models and practices—most often those of the Unites States, but also Europe.

Asia's presence is growing in the international education landscape. When we look at its rise through the lens of academic mobility, a clear pattern emerges: many of the Asian faculty who return to their country of origin to take leadership positions have studied in the United States and obtained their PhD at a U.S. or European university; many post-secondary students in Asia plan to at some point continue their education overseas, likely in the United States or Australia. The most recent *Open Doors* 2014 statistics once again point to the surge in mobility *out* of Asia and well as *into* Asia. Students from Asia make up 64 percent of the total international student body in the United States, particularly from China, India and South Korea. Asian students are now a strong presence on many U.S. campuses, with faculty and administrators having to rethink their assumptions about the cultural, historical, and academic backgrounds of their student population. Although U.S. students are still relatively less mobile than their peers in the rest of the world, they are drawn to Asia in growing numbers for shorter-term study experiences as well as for full degree study.

Given this overall expansion of international academic mobility, most Asian governments decided to join the competition with the clear ambition to have their higher education system play at the top. Yet, if there is a power shift, it is more about redeployment rather than a rebalance. American and European research-based universities are still influential and highly attractive in Asian emerging countries. What happens in major research-based universities in the "old Western World" still matters and still has an impact on the rest of the world, including on Asia. North American and European universities invest considerable financial resources and energy in trying to establish a presence in Asia by creating branch campuses, platforms of services, local representative offices, strategic alliances, dual degree programs, and large networks.

By attracting a more diversified student body and actively appealing to international audiences, Asian universities are now, like their western counterparts, making commitments to offer portable skills and to train leaders capable of adapting their talents to a variety of institutional and regional settings. In the midst of this profound transformation of their ecosystem, they are progressively moving beyond the narrow confines of academia and becoming central to any political narrative about development and economic growth. Higher education today is one of the most convenient and critical arenas to establish consensual cooperative engagements and partnerships, despite the persistence of divergences and disagreements.

As Asian countries forge ahead to embrace new developments within their systems and beyond, they open the debate about the possibility of reconciliation between the ancient traditions of learning that have existed within the region for centuries and the new emerging models of learning. Among Asian countries are some of the world's oldest and largest universities, such as Nalanda in India, which dates back to the 5th century AD. The period of western colonialism in the 19th and 20th century further complicated or diluted these ancient systems. Today, professional accomplishments of institutions and faculty are based on a system of merit that is largely western-based, with western criteria and metrics that often place non-western systems at a disadvantage, especially those Asian countries where English—the lingua franca of scientific innovation and enterprise—is not one of the dominant languages.

Nonetheless, the heritage of colonialism in the region has not prevented Asian governments and institutions from experimenting with alternate and perhaps more authentic approaches to higher education development. As a consequence, in contemporary Asia today, traditions coexist with new models of higher education either imported directly from the west or shaped after a notion of what it means to be world class. Hence it is possible that we are seeing the emergence of a unique Asian model of higher education that selectively borrows from the west, yet freely draws upon its own solid academic traditions.

Why a Book on Higher Education in Asia?

In this book we attempt to show that the challenge in the 21st century is not about who is going to win the race. There is no race; there is no single superpower when it comes to education. What we see is greater mobility, growing interconnectedness, increased dialogue, and many more bridges rather than barriers. Higher education in Asia is interacting with this dynamic in new and different ways. And this engagement is continuously enhancing all players, leading to new forms of strategic alliances.

To give a complete picture of the developments in this region, this book, in addition to analyzing global trends in higher education, also looks at domestic transformations occurring within systems not engaged with other countries or regions.

Higher education institutions in Asia, like elsewhere, are facing a new kind of competition. Foundations and large non-profit organizations outside academia are often better positioned strategically to achieve civic and political objectives than universities, political parties, and governmental organizations. Questioning whether higher education is the only relevant scale for action could feasibly limit academia's power, as resources are channeled elsewhere.

International rankings, global competition, and marketing constraints also pose new challenges to academia in Asia. These conditions push university leaders to engage in a race to the top, collectively taking on a service-provider role. HEIs are finding that they cannot devote resources to human development projects, such as promoting digital literacy or focusing on climate change imperatives and the development of the civil societies, since these projects would not directly impact their academic ranking and reputation. The story is well known and documented. Higher education increasingly became a global market in the 1990s, allowing more students to select colleges outside their resident countries. Students therefore needed global comparisons and benchmarking. International rankings appeared in the early 2000s and have gained influence and strength since then. HEIs are trying to appeal to a worldwide audience, and historical prestige and reputation is no longer the only indicator of excellence and quality. International rankings have introduced new metrics, such as peer competition, research achievements of the faculty, and quality of services, that give a comparative advantage to new comers and to universities able to invest in brand development. Ranking systems have transformed the research-based university and Ivy League model into the world-class university standard, making it impossible to reach without the underlying business model. U.S. research universities rely financially upon endowments and tuition revenues that are not easily transposable in other parts of the world. Private donors, the tradition of legacy, and student loans are very specific to the U.S. social structure.

By looking at the most recent developments in Asian higher education, the book contributes to a new definition of excellence. While many of our authors, including Kishore Mahbubani and Tan Eng Chye, allude frequently to global rankings as one way to assess the quality and excellence of a country or region's HEIs, others point to the ability of higher education to adequately serve the aspirations of a growing domestic population as a key indicator. In India, limited higher education opportunities push a large number of domestic students overseas. Greater access to higher education is crucial even for other growing Asian economies not primarily focused on improving their global positioning, as they also seek to bolster their domestic sectors and talents, including through articulation of vocational and technical education.

There are many unique challenges that must be addressed, especially given the fact that Asia as a whole is home to a large number of developing countries whose educational needs are distinctly different from those of more developed countries. Countries like India, which otherwise has one of the largest and fastest growing college-aged cohorts in the world, has remained relatively disengaged in international education and the globalization of its higher education sector. A common arguement is that this type of engagement makes sense only if it helps address the country's existing domestic education issues, which are primarily those of adequate access and quality. Our book attempts to address the critical question: How do developing Asian countries respond to global changes and the imperative to be outward-facing, while also remaining focused on their very real domestic education challenges?

The book offers a review of both regional trends and local initiatives, converging around the idea that universities should become incubators of talents, capable of developing the best and the brightest in each country and from all over the world. The book features prominent higher education scholars and experts who have been asked to discuss the major evolutions and trends in education and research policies throughout Asia. Through an interdisciplinary and comparative approach, they investigate the origin, design, implementation, and effects of different policy responses to development problems and challenges. By analyzing precise reforms and measures adapted since the 1990s, the authors show how higher education decisions have reflected the national development goals of states and nations. Given the pace and the scale of change, Asian higher education can be regarded as a laboratory for studying and improving our comprehension of a multitude of worldwide evolutions. Indeed, in the past decade, the study of higher education policies has not been limited to education specialists, but has been progressively incorporated into a larger theoretical debate on the analysis of public policies and their instruments.

While Asia has been understood in its broadest geographic sense, including the Far East, Southeast Asia, and South Asia, the book focuses primarily on countries whose higher education systems have either undergone a transformation or are part of the global competition. Nonetheless, our book is not just about the "big players"; it is as much about the smaller, rapidly emerging economies in Asia, including Malaysia, Vietnam, and Thailand. These countries have experienced strong economic growth in the past decades and have undertaken steps towards an internationalization of their HEIs.

What we intend to convey in the book is that in Asia, as anywhere else in the world, higher education is about raising talents; it is about encouraging the best in students and helping them grow as responsible citizens in this global world. A cross-cultural dialogue and an international dimension are doubtlessly crucial to achieving this objective. Not only are HEIs in Asia upgrading and scaling up, but they are also becoming interlocutors, partners, and peers for universities in other parts of the world. A new relation seems to be about to emerge, offering students in Asia and in other parts of the world the possibility to move from one system to another, to experience new environments, to push themselves out of their comfort zone, and to embrace the differences and opportunities that this brings.

Despite the rapid growth of higher education in Asia, the issue of quality is paramount. Are the sheer quantity of HEIs and enrollments occurring at the cost of quality? Assuring consistent quality remains a key issue for many Asian countries which otherwise might have large higher education sectors. This quality issue becomes even more important, as many Asian countries are seeing a large growth in the number of private institutions that are not regulated by a government body. Altbach highlights the same situation for India, where despite valiant efforts on the part of the higher education sector and the government to implement reforms, there remains widespread and endemic corruption, and educational quality suffers.

Overview of the Book

The focus of the book reflects our personal and professional experience of the region and of the higher education sector. It draws inspiration from the extensive research on higher education mobility carried out at IIE's Center for Academic Mobility Research and Impact, and from our teaching at Columbia University's School of International and Public Affairs and at Teachers College. Our contributors were chosen for their expertise in the topics addressed by their respective chapters. In selecting authors for the book, we included researchers, academics, and practitioners based in Asia as well as those outside Asia so as to fully reflect voices and perspectives *from* the region as well as those *about* the region.

The first part of the book includes four chapters that situate the current Asian higher education landscape within a wider global context by raising critical questions about competitiveness, educational quality, and excellence. In Chapter One, **Kishore Mahbubani** and **Tan Eng Chye** argue with a sense of optimism that Asia is indeed poised to become the next higher education superpower, but that there are challenges that must be overcome. Presenting a different point of view, **Miguel Lim** questions whether Asian higher education is at the level where it can compete with other higher education superpowers and world-class institutions, especially when global university rankings are used as a yardstick. Lim also introduces the idea of world-class institutions and the knowledge economy, a relationship that is developed in greater detail in Chapter Three by **Chaya Jain,** in which she examines in detail the intersections between knowledge economies, higher education sectors, and economic growth in Asian nations. Chapter Four by **Simon Marginson** addresses the systemic and national-level challenges in Asia that continue to impede educational quality and global competitiveness.

Chapters Five and Six address from different angles the internationalization of higher education in Asia. **Futao Huang**'s chapter identifies distinctive characteristics of higher education internationalization in Asia, which has drawn upon internationalization in other countries and yet has evolved with its own, distinctly Asian flavor. This is followed by **Jack Lee**'s chapter on the role of cross-border education—and education hubs in particular—in Singapore, Malaysia, and Hong Kong, and the motivations, economic benefits, and outcomes of these types of arrangements.

The second portion of the book focuses on how the cross-cutting, region-wide issues raised in the first four chapters are reflected at the local level in four Asian economies: India, Malaysia, Vietnam, and Japan. **Philip Altbach**'s chapter analyzes a few of the current trends within the Indian higher education system and highlights the continuing challenges associated with rapid massification and poor educational quality. Chapter Eight by **Mohd. Ismail Abd Aziz** and **Doria Abdullah** explores the role of Malaysia in the ASEAN regional integration process, while also providing an overview of current developments within the Malaysian higher education sector. This is followed by a chapter on Vietnam, in which **Pham Thi Ly and Martin Hayden** explore the challenges for a country with a rapidly growing economy and higher education system, yet one that is grappling with systemic issues that prevent it from achieving its full potential. In Chapter Ten, **Takao Kamibeppu** traces the evolution of internationalization within Japanese higher education and explores the relevance of European mobility schemes and regional harmonization schemes for Japan and whether such initiatives work in the Japanese context.

The final chapter by **Jouko Sarvi** highlights the potential role for donor agencies such as the Asian Development Bank in addressing some of the current higher education challenges in Asia, and what the future might hold both in terms of a shift in development strategy and in higher education growth within the region.

Chapter One

Is Asia the Next Higher Education Superpower?

Kishore Mahbubani, National University of Singapore

Tan Eng Chye, National University of Singapore

Introduction

The 21st century will be the Asian century. This is overdue and inevitable. A surge of investment in higher education is already taking place in Asia, which will accompany the emergence of the Asian century. Asia has already overtaken both North America and Europe in the number of universities and university graduates. Asian universities need only to improve their quality in order to catch up with the West. As Asia struggles to make these advances, it also must meet new challenges presented by its rapidly changing educational landscape. In short, success is not guaranteed. Leaders of Asian universities must be bold and innovative if they want to move up in the global rankings.

This chapter consists of three main sections. The first section, "Asian Optimism," explains why optimism over the future of higher education in Asia is justified. The second section, "The Asian Experience in Context," draws out the diversity of the Asian experience, given that the Asian continent is far more varied than either

North America or Europe. The third section, "Future Challenges," touches on new challenges that Asian universities must overcome.

ASIAN OPTIMISM

A few leading indicators explain why optimism is justified for the future of Asian higher education. First, the outstanding performance of Asian students in leading global universities, especially in postgraduate science and engineering disciplines, indicates that Asian minds can perform as well as the rest of the world, if not outperform them, on a level playing field in higher education. A recent study examining two nationally representative cohort longitudinal surveys provided strong evidence that Asian Americans have an academic advantage over their peers (Hsin & Xie, 2014), apparently due to a tendency to exert more effort in their academics. In fact, Asian Americans constitute only 6 percent of the U.S. population, but compose 12–18 percent of the student body at Ivy League schools (Chen, 2012). In 2013, 8,549 Chinese students were enrolled in Ivy League schools, constituting 27 percent of total enrollment (Lai, 2012).

Second, many Asians, especially Asian Americans, have risen to key leadership positions in leading global universities. The academic talent to nurture great Asian universities is growing worldwide. Third, and perhaps most importantly, many Asian countries have significantly stepped up their national budgetary allocations for both higher education and research and development in science and technology. Hence, at a time when the publicly funded universities in both North America and Europe face budgetary challenges in obtaining funding from shrinking state budgets, many Asian public universities are benefiting from increased funding.

As a result, more and more Asian universities are entering the list of the top 100 universities in the world. According to Quacquarelli Symonds (QS), out of the top 100 universities in the world list, 17 are from Asia (Quacquarelli Symonds, 2014a). The top 17 universities on the QS list are shown in Table 1.1.

TABLE 1.1: ASIAN UNIVERSITIES IN THE QS LIST OF TOP 100 WORLD UNIVERSITIES

QS Ranking	University
22	National University of Singapore (Singapore)
28	University of Hong Kong (Hong Kong)
31	The University of Tokyo (Japan)
31	Seoul National University (South Korea)
36	Kyoto University (Japan)
39	Nanyang Technological University (Singapore)
40	The Hong Kong University of Science and Technology (Hong Kong)
46	The Chinese University of Hong Kong (Hong Kong)
47	Tsinghua University (China)
51	KAIST (Korea Advanced Institute of Science and Technology; South Korea)
55	Osaka University (Japan)
57	Peking University (China)
68	Tokyo Institute of Technology (Japan)
71	Tohoku University (Japan)
71	Fudan University (China)
76	National Taiwan University (Taiwan)
86	Pohang University of Science And Technology (POSTECH) (South Korea)

Similarly, Times Higher Education also lists 11 Asian universities in its list of top 100 universities (Times Higher Education, 2014). Another reason for optimism is that there are 13 Asian universities in the list of top 50 universities under 50 years old (Quacquarelli Symonds, 2014b) as shown in Table 1.2.

TABLE 1.2: ASIAN UNIVERSITIES IN THE QS LIST OF TOP 50 UNIVERSITIES UNDER 50 YEARS OLD

QS Ranking	University
1	Nanyang Technological University (Singapore)
2	The Hong Kong University of Science and Technology (Hong Kong)
3	KAIST (South Korea)
4	Pohang University of Science and Technology (South Korea)
5	City University of Hong Kong (Hong Kong)
8	The Hong Kong Polytechnic University (Hong Kong)
13	University of Tsukuba (Japan)
18	National Yang Ming University (Taiwan)
20	Universiti Kebangsaan Malaysia (Malaysia)
30	Ben Gurion University of The Negev (Israel)
37	Hong Kong Baptist University (Hong Kong)
38	L.N. Gumilyov Eurasian National University
42	King Abdul Aziz University (Saudi Arabia)

Significantly, these top Asian universities come from a small group of Asian universities or territories, such as China, Hong Kong, Japan, Korea, Singapore, and Taiwan. Similarly, five other highly populated Asian countries, namely, Bangladesh (population: 155 million), Indonesia (population: 247 million), Pakistan (population: 179 million), the Philippines (population: 97 million), and Vietnam (population: 89 million), do not have any universities in the top 100 list. Figure 1 illustrates the state of tertiary education in several Asian countries.

FIGURE 1.1: GROSS ENROLLMENT RATIOS FOR BACHELOR'S DEGREE PROGRAMS BY COUNTRY OR TERRITORY, 1980–2011

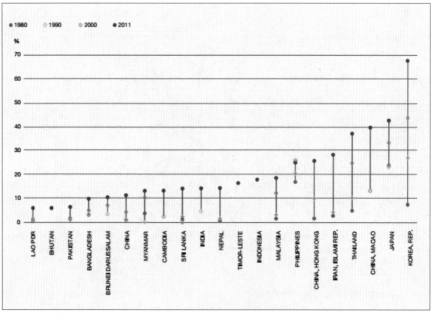

Source: UNESCO, 2014

All these differences emphasize the diversity of the Asian experience. The story of higher education of each Asian country can only be understood in the context of its national experience. To illustrate this diversity, this chapter will delve deeply into the experiences of Asia's two largest countries, China and India, and will explain the extraordinary success of universities in the smaller East Asian countries.

THE ASIAN EXPERIENCE IN CONTEXT

The China Story

Over time, volumes will be written on the story of higher education in China, because it is extraordinary in several ways. It will take some time before we can solve the mysteries behind some of the bold decisions made by Chinese leaders in this area. Consider the programs and initiatives described in the following sections.

University Expansion

It was an extraordinarily brave decision by Chinese leaders to launch the process of university expansion when it did. In the last 25 years, the rate of enrollment of young people going to college has grown 10-fold, from 3 percent of each cohort in 1990 to almost 30 percent in 2013 (World Bank, 2014). The year 1990 is significant. It was exactly one year after Chinese university students occupied Tiananmen Square and challenged the Chinese government. A more natural reaction of the Chinese government would have been to clamp down on university education in response to this political challenge from university students. Instead, it made the bold decision to expand it significantly.

Major Shifts

The Chinese higher education system made several major shifts in the 20th century. It initially followed the Western academic tradition, due to 19th-century reforms aimed at combining Chinese and Western knowledge. From 1952 to 1953, China adopted the Soviet model of higher education and centralized the educational bureaucracy. China nationalized existing higher education institutions, and Soviet-style specialized technical and research institutes were built. However, in 1998, China turned away from elite education and began a rapid drive toward mass higher education, based on the Chinese Ministry of Education's Action Plan to Vitalize Education Facing the Twenty-First Century (Pretorius & Xue, 2003). This plan stipulated that the gross enrollment ratio (GER) should reach 15 percent by the end of 2010. It has now far exceeded that goal, hitting a 27 percent GER in 2012 (World Bank, 2014). Table 1.3 indicates the expansion of the number of institutions and enrollments in China since 1949.

TABLE 1.3: SCALE OF REGULAR HIGHER EDUCATION IN CHINA BY PERIOD

Period	Year	No. Institutions	Undergraduate Enrollment
Reconstruction	1949	205	116,504
and 1st Plan	1957	229	441,181
Great Leap Forward	1958	791	659,627
and Adjustment	1960	1,289	961,623
	1965	434	674,436
Great Proletariat	1966	434	533,766
Cultural Revolution	1970	434	47,815
	1976	392	564,715
Reform and Opening Up	1978	598	856,322
	1983	805	1206,823
	1988	1075	2065,900
	1993	1065	2535,500
	1998	1022	3408,800

Source: Educational statistics published by Ministry of Education, China

Subsidization of Expansion

The Chinese government also heavily subsidized the massive expansion to ensure that university education remained affordable for the masses. As a result, the number of Chinese students graduating from Chinese universities, in terms of absolute numbers, has exploded from 614,000 in 1990 to almost 7 million in 2013 (National Bureau of Statistics of China, 2013). Figure 1.2 illustrates the scale and pace of expansion.

FIGURE 1.2: UNDERGRADUATES AND COLLEGE STUDENTS IN CHINA, 1978–2012

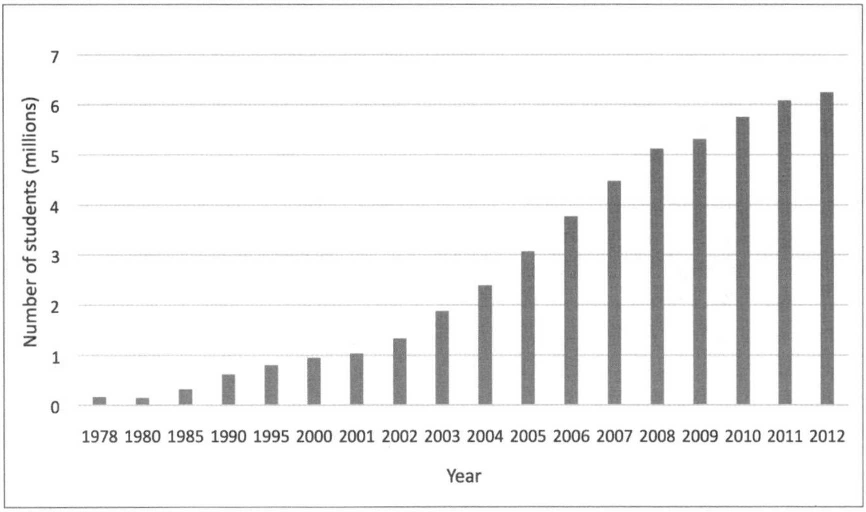

Source: National Bureau of Statistics of China, 2013

Chinese Initiatives

It was equally bold for the Chinese government to focus on improving the quality of university education as much as it focused on increasing the number of educational institutions. This is why the Chinese government launched several high-profile initiatives to attract to China both Chinese and foreign academics who were teaching or conducting research in American universities. It also invested more in leading Chinese universities.

The first big initiative by the Chinese government was the Thousand Talents initiative, launched in 2008. This high-profile scheme was aimed at luring back top talents to boost the country's innovative capacity and international competitiveness. This ambitious plan aims to attract more than 2,000 leading researchers who have held professorship or equivalent at renowned universities or institutes abroad. In some cases, the Chinese government was spectacularly successful in attracting back world-class talent. One good example was Professor Shi Yigong, who left Princeton University to head the Department of Life Sciences in Tsinghua University in 2009, and Professor Andrew Yao, a Taiwanese American computer scientist and computational theorist, who, after teaching at Stanford and Princeton, moved to Tsinghua to head the Institute for Theoretical Computer Science in 2004.

IIE/AIFS Foundation Global Education Research Reports
ASIA: THE NEXT HIGHER EDUCATION SUPERPOWER?

7

The second big initiative was launched in 2012 by the Chinese Ministry of Human Resources and Social Security, in collaboration with four other ministries. Again, this was aimed at implementing China's long-term plan of importing expert talent from abroad. Under this new measure, all foreigners who are eligible for "Highly Qualified" status are granted privileges, which include relaxation of the visa rules on entry into China and easier regulations for the granting of permanent residencies (Dezan Shira & Associates, 2012).

The third big initiative by China was the 2009 creation of the *C9 League*, an alliance of the top nine universities in China, to boost their global standing. In this alliance, the nine institutions would recognize each other's course credits, share resources, and allow students to attend courses on each other's campuses. In 2013, these nine leading research universities signed the Hefei Statement, which was jointly drawn up with the League of European Research Universities (LERU), Australia's Group of Eight Universities, and the Association of American Universities to uphold academic freedom in research and development (Heron, 2013).

As a result of attracting back world-class academic talent and increased investment, the Chinese universities have been climbing up in the global ranking of universities. In the latest QS ranking of top Asian universities in 2013, China had six universities in the top 100.

Autonomy

Even though the state remains dominant in China, the Chinese government has been trying to provide greater autonomy to Chinese university administrations. Surprisingly, even though both a university president and a party secretary lead each Chinese university, the administrations of Chinese universities are leaner than American universities. Two leading scholars, Devesh Kapur and Elizabeth J. Perry, have written a brilliant paper entitled "Higher Education Reform in China and India: The Role of the State." They stated, "China's commitment to reduce the size of academic administration stands in stark contrast to higher education trends in other parts of the world. In the United States, the number of administrators and professional staff at universities and colleges has doubled in the past 25 years—a rate of increase more than twice that of student enrollments in the same period" (Kapur & Perry, 2014).

At the same time, China has invested heavily in developing world-class university administrators. For several years running, Yale University, led by the then-president Richard Levin, hosted a two- to three-week seminar for university leaders from leading Chinese universities. Clearly, managing a university is very different from managing a government department or a multinational corporation. Hence, China has invested seriously in developing the next generation of university leaders (Jiangsu

Education, 2011).[1] As a result, Chinese university leaders have greater freedom than their Indian counterparts to match leading global salaries in attracting the best academic talent back to China.

Despite these remarkable advances and bold experiments, it would be a mistake to assume that Chinese universities have achieved nirvana. Many of them are still new institutions. As the third section of this essay will document, the "massification" of the Chinese university system has introduced new challenges for China to contend with.

The India Story

All over Asia, modern universities are a Western import (Kapur & Perry, 2014). Even though, in the last 10 years of the Cold War, India was closer to the Soviet Union, and China drew closer to the United States, India has had a deeper and longer engagement with the West. It was colonized by the British for over a century. Even after independence, Indians used to revere London as a cultural capital, before they discovered the magic of the American dream. Hence, hundreds of thousands of young Indians studied in leading Western universities long before the young Chinese students arrived in the West. This may also explain why Indians significantly outnumber Chinese in leading positions in American universities. For example, it is remarkable how many Indians have become deans of leading American business schools. They include Nitin Nohria, dean of the Harvard Business School; Soumitra Dutta, dean of the Samuel Curtis Johnson Graduate School of Management at Cornell University; and Sunil Kumar, dean of the University of Chicago Booth School of Business.

Against this historical backdrop, it would have been natural to assume that India would have provided a more promising soil for the nurturing of Western-style universities than China. Surprisingly, the opposite has happened. While China has six universities in the QS list of top 100, India has none, despite that fact that India, like China, has had a significant "massification" of its higher education system. In 1990, the GER was 3 percent in China and 6 percent in India. Despite this initial lag, China quickly overtook India, achieving a 27 percent GER in 2012, while India raised its GER to 20 percent (Government of India, 2013). In 2011, India had around 4 million graduates (Nandakumar & Sabharwal, 2011), while China had 6 million graduates (National Bureau of Statistics of China, 2013). The expected number of graduates from India in 2014 is 5 million (NASSCOM, 2014), compared to 7 million in China (China Daily, 2014). Figure 1.3 shows the dramatic increase in university enrollment rates in China in the last three decades.

FIGURE 1.3: GROSS ENROLLMENT RATIOS IN CHINA AND INDIA, 1980–2012

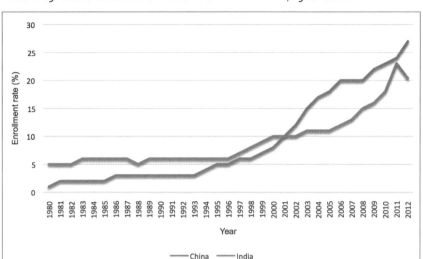

The article by Kapur and Perry (2014) mentioned earlier provides some of the reasons why the Indian universities have lagged behind China. They pointed out that in the case of India,

> in contrast to China—and indeed relative to its own pre-independence past—Indian higher education is highly centralized, politicized, and paradoxically anti-intellectual. The prevailing political ideological climate in which elite institutions are seen as anti-democratic, finds its natural response in political control to influence admissions policies, internal organization, and the structure of courses and funding (Kapur & Perry, 2014, p. 17).

They also added that "higher education in India suffers from political, administrative, and regulatory interference on virtually every aspect of higher education—be it admissions policies, internal organization, fees and salaries, and the structure of courses and funding" (Kapur & Perry, 2014, p. 17). Given that public-sector universities in India face serious constraints, private-sector initiatives have been growing. Kapur and Perry further noted:

> In contrast to China, most of the growth in enrollments in higher education in India has taken place through the establishment of new private colleges in the last decade, with the bulk of expansion in professional and technical education like engineering, business,

pharmacy, and the like. Between 2000–2001 and 2011–2012, the number of colleges in India increased from 12,800 to 35,500, which meant an average of nearly six new colleges *a day* for more than a decade (p. 9).

This may well be India's greatest hope: that the dynamic private sector will make up for the weaknesses of the Indian state in developing world-class institutes of higher education. The Indian School of Business provides a good illustration of how private-sector initiatives can work well. Established in 2001, it has grown rapidly and now has two campuses: one in Hyderabad and one in Mohali. The good news is that India represents the norm rather than the exception. Private education has been expanding in many other Asian countries besides India, as shown in Figure 1.4.

FIGURE 1.4: ENROLLMENT IN PRIVATE HIGHER EDUCATION INSTITUTIONS AS A PERCENTAGE OF TOTAL HIGHER EDUCATION ENROLLMENT BY COUNTRY OR TERRITORY, 2011 OR MOST RECENT YEAR AVAILABLE

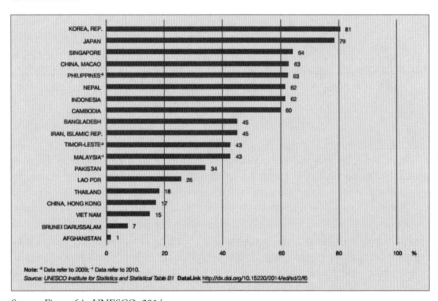

Source: Figure 6 in UNESCO, 2014

The Advanced Asian Economies

In contrast to China and India, which have recently increased their university enrollments, the advanced Asian economies of Japan, South Korea, Taiwan, Hong Kong, and Singapore have been investing heavily in higher education for several decades.

Universities, unlike corporations like Google and Microsoft, cannot succeed overnight. They require some nurturing. Hence, it is not surprising that most of the leading Asian universities are found in the advanced Asian economies.

Japan was the first Asian country to modernize (after the Meiji restoration), and it has the highest number of universities in the list of top 50 universities in Asia. Globally, in the 2013–14 QS World University Rankings, the highest-ranked Japanese universities are the University of Tokyo in 32nd place, Kyoto University in 35th place, and Osaka University in 55th place. Similarly, South Korea, which is the second Asian country after Japan to join the OECD (Organization for Economic Cooperation and Development), had for a long time a higher education landscape that had been dominated by the SKY universities: Seoul National University, Korea University, and Yonsei University. However, the intense competition in Korea has led to the creation of an "upstart" university, the Korea Advanced Institute of Science and Technology (KAIST). In the latest QS ranking, KAIST has emerged as the number two university in Asia after National University of Singapore (NUS), and it has come third in the ranking of the world's 50 universities under 50 years old (QS, 2014).

Among the universities in the advanced Asian universities list, the story of the NUS is particularly inspiring. Established in 1905 as the Straits and Federated Malay States Government Medical School (NUS, n.d.), NUS has climbed its way up to emerge as the top university in Asia in QS world ranking of global universities in 2013–14 (Davie, 2014).

This success was a result of several factors. First, as Singapore joined the league of advanced economies with a per capita income that exceeds those of many OECD member states, its government realized that Singapore could only compete in the advanced league of economies if it invested heavily in higher education. Second, a major effort has been made to emulate leading American universities. Hence, when Shih Choon Fong, a Singaporean academic who taught at Brown University, was appointed to lead NUS in 1997, his title was changed from Vice Chancellor to President. This was more than a symbolic change. It was a signal that NUS would adopt best practices from leading global universities, including the tightening of promotion and tenure procedures. Third, the Singapore government wisely decided to grant greater autonomy to its universities. NUS was incorporated as a not-for-profit company limited by guarantee. The government remained committed to funding NUS, even while it provided maximal autonomy for NUS to chart its own course and deploy its resources as they deemed fit. This allowed NUS to become very nimble and was a critical factor in its surge ahead. Fourth, NUS also succeeded because it was supported by a positive eco-system. A dynamic and globally competitive economy generated a strong demand for its graduates and researchers. The Singapore economy was ranked second in the World Economic Forum Global Competitiveness Report 2014–2015 (World Economic Forum, 2014) and ranked seventh in the 2014

Global Innovation Index (Cornell University, INSEAD, and WIPO, 2014). Singapore was also ranked number three in the world in the 2014 QS list of "Best Student Cities," reflecting on the open cosmopolitan environment of Singapore (Quacquarelli Symonds, 2013).

Hong Kong, a former British colony like Singapore, shares many of these competitive attributes. Hence, it also has several leading universities. Hong Kong University, like NUS, has always done well in the global rankings. The Hong Kong University of Science and Technology and the Nanyang Technological University in Singapore have both done well in the list of top 50 under 50 years old.

Southeast Asia

The Association of Southeast Asian Nations (ASEAN) countries today represent the ninth largest economy in the world with a gross domestic product of U.S. $2 trillion. ASEAN Vision 2020 calls for investments to be made in the development of a knowledge economy.

University enrollment has improved in emerging Southeast Asian countries. According to World Bank Data, the GER in ASEAN countries (excluding Singapore) multiplied 2.5 times, from just over 10 percent in 1995 to almost 25 percent in 2010 (World Bank, 2014). Malaysia and Thailand are among the Southeast Asian middle-income countries that lead the region in the development of graduate education. Both countries have experienced rapid growth in undergraduate enrollment, and both have developed an extensive network of both public and private colleges and universities. In Malaysia, graduate enrollment increased fourfold (from about 21,100 in 2000 to 85,200 in 2010). Malaysia has also been active in developing its higher education system, aiming to produce 100,000 PhD holders by 2020 (including locally trained, overseas-trained, and split programs with foreign universities) and to increase its higher education participation rate from the current 40 percent to 50 percent by 2020. The development of higher education in smaller Southeast Asian countries has been promising. In Brunei, the enrollment rates increased from 10 percent in 1998 to 24 percent in 2012; Cambodia's enrollment rates increased from 1 percent in 1995 to 16 percent in 2011; and in Myanmar, the increase was from 5 percent in 1995 to 14 percent in 2011 (World Bank, 2014).

The number of higher education institutes in Southeast Asian countries has also been increasing, driven particularly by the growth of private higher education institutions. Across Asia, almost 40 percent of higher education students are enrolled in private institutions (UNESCO, 2014). For example, the Philippines higher education system has been characterized by rapid expansion in the last 10 years: The number of higher education institutions increased from 1,400 in 2001 to 1,800 in 2010, growing by an annual average of 45 new institutions, or 3 percent. Only 12 percent of these institutions are public and 88 percent are private (Asian Development Bank [ADB], 2012). In Cambodia, 44 out of 73 higher education institutions are private, and as many as 16 of these private institutions were established in 2002–2003 alone (ADB, 2012).

However, the level and quality of development across the region has been diverse, particularly due to the rise of these private higher education institutions. While Indonesia, Malaysia, Philippines, and Thailand have been developing their quality systems in the higher education sector for decades now, countries like Laos, Vietnam, and Cambodia have only recently started to pursue strategies to improve quality in their national strategic plans (UNESCO, 2006). For example, in 2004, Cambodia issued a regulation to create a quality assurance unit in every higher education institution to undertake self-assessment (ADB, 2012). Regionally, ASEAN created the ASEAN Quality Assurance Network (AQAN), which has the aim of promoting and building a common and harmonious language of quality assurance in higher education institutions across Southeast Asia without losing individual country identity (AQAN, 2012). However, it will take some time before we know the impact of AQAN in improving the quality of higher education in Southeast Asia.

FUTURE CHALLENGES

Despite the many positive trends in the field of higher education in Asia, there remain many serious challenges to overcome. It would be a mistake for Asian governments to continue on a steady course of expansion and massive investments in the higher education sphere without paying attention to the changing education landscape.

The first challenge that Asian governments have to deal with is the result of the massification of higher education. China and India alone will account for 40 percent of all young people with a tertiary education in G20 and OECD countries by 2020 (Garcia de León, Heckmann, & González, 2012). Indeed, by 2020, four countries (China, India, United States, and Brazil) will account for more than half of global tertiary enrollments (ages 18–22). The current estimates are shown in Table 1.4.

TABLE 1.4: TERTIARY ENROLLMENT IN 2020 IN SELECTED COUNTRIES

Country	Tertiary enrollment by 2020 (millions)
China	37.4
India	27.8
United States	20
Brazil	9.2
Indonesia	7.7
Russia	6.3

Source: British Council, 2012

China has increased its number of university graduates significantly, from 3 percent of each cohort in 1990 to almost 30 percent in 2013 (World Bank, 2014). Now China is struggling to find jobs for this massive number of university graduates. Although the current unemployment rate in China is 4 percent (Statistica, 2014), the *New York Times* has reported a figure of 18 percent unemployment for this cohort of 7 million Chinese graduates (Fischer, 2014). As a result, China has significantly curtailed the expansion of its higher education system. This reduction also reflects the demographic decline in China.

By contrast, India is about to reap its demographic dividend, and the expansion of its higher education sector is likely to continue. The Modi government, which took office in June 2014, declared human resource development as one of its priorities, stating that it will invest more in higher education and support private-sector efforts to invest more in this area. In February 2014, Prime Minister Narendra Modi described education as "the only potent route to fight poverty," acknowledging that India should review its commitment to education. He said that the private sector should be given more leeway to develop education, and that the government should set up more major institutions, such as the Indian Institute of Technology and the Indian Institute of Management, in all states (IANS, 2014). In keeping with these beliefs, the new Modi government announced several measures to improve access to and quality of education and to institute educational reforms aimed at spurring growth in science and technology (Government of India, 2014).

Both South Korea and Taiwan, which have also carried out similar massification processes, have an oversupply of university graduates as well (Chong, 2013).[2] South Korea has among the highest university participation rates in the world, at around 80 percent compared with 15 percent to 40 percent for most advanced economies, but the number of "economically inactive" graduates has risen to more than 3 million (Sharma, 2014a), with an unemployment rate of about 6 percent.[3] Similarly, in Taiwan, the number of higher education institutions has increased to 165, with a total student enrollment of 1.3 million, representing a gross enrollment ratio of 79 percent.

However, Taiwan had an unemployment rate of 6 percent for university graduates in 2012 (Taipei Economic and Cultural Office, 2012).

The second challenge is one that is faced by all universities: the impact of new technology. The proliferation of online courses, such as massive open online courses (MOOCs), has raised profound questions about the future of universities. Some have suggested that, just as digital technology buried Kodak, universities face the same threat today. For example, University of Maryland professor Henry C. Lucas, Jr., has suggested that the American higher education systems will face the same fate as the three failed organizations of Borders, Kodak, and Blockbuster if they continue to embrace the status quo. He argued that only the top universities will survive because of their superior brands. The mass industry of brick-and-mortar universities will be replaced by MOOCs or their equivalent, as young people find cheaper and more innovative means of educating themselves (Lucas, 2013). These predictions of doom and gloom for traditional universities may be overblown, but it would be a mistake for traditional Asian universities to remain complacent in the face of this new challenge.

Third, the changing nature of work introduces new challenges. In the West, many see universities primarily as a place to nurture citizens, while in many Asian countries, universities are seen as agencies for developing a talented workforce. Of course, the picture is more nuanced. Asian countries are increasingly adopting Western models of education in order to produce a well-educated citizenry capable of innovative and critical thinking. For example, in 2001, Peking University introduced the Yuanpei Honors Program in 2001, a pilot program that immerses a select group of the most gifted Chinese students in a liberal arts environment (Levin, 2010). At the same time, Western universities are beginning to focus on students' employability and developing skills that are compatible with today's macroeconomic requirements. Two recent works explain the Western challenge well. A McKinsey Center for Government report, *Education to Employment: Getting Europe's Youth into Work* (Mourshed, Patel, & Suder, 2014), points out how higher education institutions must collaborate with employers to prepare young graduates in terms of "work readiness." This report also highlights the gap between universities and employers, which has led to the production of graduates who do not fit the employers' requirements. Similarly, an article on job polarization and rising inequality focusing on New York and New Jersey explains how technological change and globalization has led to the demand for a new kind of highly skilled workers, which are not being currently produced by universities (Abel & Deitz, 2012). What all this means for higher education is that universities will increasingly have to transform their curricula and prepare their students for a future of work that is dominated by infocomm technologies, robotics, big data, and supercomputing power. Even highly skilled professionals such as doctors, accountants, economists, and, yes, even university professors will not be spared. They will find themselves competing in increasingly winner-take-all markets. Although both reports focused mainly on the challenges of preparing today's youth in Europe and New York for the workplace, there can be no doubt that Asian countries will face similar challenges as they move up the ladder of economic development.

Anticipating these challenges, China has taken a major leap forward by recently announcing that it will turn at least half of its public universities into institutions of applied learning or polytechnics to produce more technically trained graduates to meet the competing demand for jobs. Lu Xin, vice minister in China's Ministry of Education said that in a "gradual transition to the dual system, the new applied institutions would focus on training engineers, senior technicians, and other highly skilled workers rather than pursuing over-academic, highly theoretical studies." (Sharma, 2014b). With more than 7 million graduates pouring into China's economy, China is taking concrete measures to address the issues of unemployment and economic instability through innovation in its education system. To combat unemployment, China recently took a transformational step toward increasing employability and diversity in the job market among university graduates by announcing its decision to turn 600 public universities into institutions of applied learning or polytechnics, intended to produce technically trained graduates. This reform of educational institutions aims to produce more technically trained graduates and increase their market relevance, which will transform the educational landscape of the Chinese higher education system.

Fourth, as Asian universities strive to move up the "global leagues," they will have to develop the same ability as leading Western universities in attracting the best international students. This has been one of the greatest strengths of the American higher education system. Each year, the United States attracts at least 800,000 foreign students to study in its campuses. China is by far the largest supplier of international students with more than 200,000 Chinese students. The next largest suppliers are India, South Korea, Saudi Arabia, and Canada (Institute of International Education, 2013).[4]

Several Asian countries are now attempting to emulate the United States in this field. Arguably, the most successful country in attracting international students has been China, which is surprising because both Japan and South Korea developed earlier than China and could have become the most favored destination for higher education in Asia. In 1999 China had a mere 44,700 international students. In 2011, China hosted a total of 292,600 foreign students from 194 countries, studying at 660 higher education institutions. This marked a more than 10 percent increase over the previous year (Kapur & Perry, 2014). Figure 1.5 shows the increase in foreign students in China from 1999 to 2010.

China's popularity among international students can be attributed to many factors. First, the rapid growth of the Chinese economy since 1978 increased the role of the market and substantially reduced government planning and direct control. Second, the economic success of China has benefited international students. Since 1997, China has relentlessly pursued many agreements and programs with more than

174 countries to facilitate the inbound mobility of students through scholarships and Chinese government grants, which, combined with low tuition, makes higher education in China more affordable than many Asian countries. Third, the quality of education provided by the Chinese universities has improved significantly. China has signed protocols with more than 34 countries in mutual recognition of academic degrees and qualifications. The fourth significant factor that makes China attractive to international students is the better prospects of being hired by foreign companies, who look for Chinese-speaking graduates, given China has gained recognition as the second largest economy in the world (UNESCO, 2013).

FIGURE 1.5: TOTAL NUMBER OF INTERNATIONAL STUDENTS IN CHINA

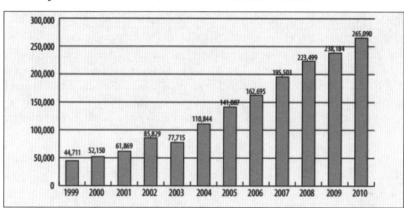

Source: National Bureau of Statistics of China, China Statistical Yearbook, 2011 (UNESCO, 2013)

As the evidence becomes increasingly clear that the 21st century will be the Asian century, it is natural that more and more international students will enroll in Asian universities to fulfill several goals simultaneously: attain a good university education, develop a good understanding of Asian cultures (which will enhance their competitiveness in global job markets), and develop their Asian networks. Hence, just as the American century led to a natural shift of international students studying in American universities, the dawn of the Asian century will see a similar shift of international students studying in Asian universities. In this spirit, *Forbes* published an article in 2014 with this provocative headline: "Why Go to Harvard When You Can Opt for an Asian Ivy League?" (Ni, 2014). The article proceeded to list the Asian equivalents of American Ivy League universities. The NUS was compared to Stanford for its entrepreneurial campus environment; the University of Hong Kong was deemed the Columbia of Hong Kong for its prestige and international orientation; Seoul National University was likened to University of Pennsylvania for its strong business programs;

Nanyang Technological University was compared to University of California, Berkeley, for its strong science, technology, engineering, and mathematics (STEM) majors and political activism; Peking University was likened to Yale University for its strong social sciences, humanities, and pure sciences programs; University of Tokyo was compared to Cornell University for its strong agricultural sciences and engineering programs; and Tsinghua was deemed the "MIT of Asia" for its strength in STEM fields.

It is not surprising that the two Asian giants are attracting more international students. However, it is surprising that small Persian Gulf countries are making huge investments in global campuses on their soil, such as the S.P. Jain School of Global Management in Dubai and Georgetown University School of Foreign Service in Qatar. Similarly, Malaysia has been successfully attracting Western universities to set up branch campuses on its soil.

The next big wave will not be the proliferation of passive branch campuses, but the creation of active new partnerships between leading Western and Asian universities. The innovative collaboration between Yale and NUS in setting up the Yale-NUS College in Singapore provides a glimpse into the future that is emerging as both Western and Asian universities realize the value of close collaboration. Such collaboration will, in turn, strengthen Asian universities, leading to the emergence of Asia as the next higher education superpower.

Despite having come a long way in less than half a century, Asians should not rest on their laurels. First, the harmonization of higher education systems among ASEAN countries—not to mention all of Asia—is far from complete, with the differing capacities of universities and different education systems proving a significant obstacle. Second, the increasing professionalization and changing needs of the job market are also a challenge for universities in Asia, which are responsible for training graduates with skills that are relevant to a rapidly evolving global market. Third, instead of trying to unquestioningly copy the best Western institutions and theories, Asian universities should gradually develop the confidence to find their own niches. They should cultivate the ability to complement Western-dominated research by starting their own research programs that do justice to Asia's own rich traditions of the sciences and humanities, as well as their high moral regard for education.

As President Tan Chorh Chuan, quoting Winston Churchill, said in a speech in November 2010 (Tan, 2010), "The empires of the future are the empires of the mind." He argued that Asian universities need to make a big shift from highly specialized education models to more broad-based ones, and develop strong global education programs and research centers that are among the leaders in the world. In doing so, Asian universities will be able to overcome their limitations and "leapfrog ahead to join the distinguished league of the world's leading universities."

REFERENCES

Abel, J. R., & Deitz, R. (2012). Job polarization and rising inequality in the nation and the New York–Northern New Jersey Region. *Current Issues in Economics and Finance, 18*(7).

Asian Development Bank (ADB). (2012). *Administration and governance of higer education in Asia: Patterns and Implications.* Mandaluyong City, Philippines: Author.

AQAN. (2012). About us—Message from the president. AQAN: Retrieved from ASEAN quality assurance network website, http://www.mqa.gov.my/aqan/aboutus_message.cfm

British Council. (2014, June 2). *The shape of things to come: Higher education global trends and emerging opportunities to 2020.* British Council. Retrieved from http://www.britishcouncil.org/sites/britishcouncil.uk2/files/the_shape_of_things_to_come_-_higher_education_global_trends_and_emerging_opportunities_to_2020.pdf

Chen, C. (2012, December 19). Asians: Too smart for their own good? *International Herald Tribune.* Retrieved from http://www.nytimes.com/2012/12/20/opinion/asians-too-smart-for-their-own-good.html?ref=contributors&_r=1&

China Daily. (2014, April 28). Expected salary of graduates hits 4-year low. *China Daily.* Retrieved from http://www.chinadaily.com.cn/china/2014-05/28/content_17547583.htm

Chong, D. (2013, March 19). Too many graduates devalue university, Taiwan warns. *South China Morning Post.* Retrieved from http://www.scmp.com/news/hong-kong/article/1193950/too-many-graduates-devalue-university-taiwan-warns

Cornell University, INSEAD, and WIPO. (2014). *The Global Innovation Index 2014: The Human Factor in Innovation.* Fontainebleau, Ithaca, and Geneva.: World Intellectual Property Organization (WIPO) and the Confederation of Indian Industry (CII).

Davie, S. (2014, May 13). NUS tops ranking of Asian universities for first time. *Straits Times.* Retrieved from http://www.straitstimes.com/news/singapore/education/story/nus-tops-ranking-asian-universities-first-time-20140513

Dezan Shira & Associates. (2012, November 7). Highly-qualified foreigners to face easier visa formalities in China. *China Briefing.* Retrieved from http://www.china-briefing.com/news/2012/11/07/highly-qualified-foreigners-to-face-easier-visa-formalities-in-china.html

Fischer, K. (2014, May 25). For some foreign students, U.S. education is losing its attraction. *International New York Times.* Retrieved from http://www.nytimes.com/2014/05/26/world/asia/for-some-foreign-students-us-education-is-losing-its-attraction.html

Garcia de León, P., Heckmann, C., & González, G. R. (2012). *Education indicators in focus no. 5: How is the global talent pool changing?:* Organization for Economic Cooperation and Development.

Government of India. (2013). *All India survey on higher education 2011–12 (provisional).* New Delhi, India: Ministry of Human Resource Development, Department of Higher Education.

Government of India. (2014, July). Key Features of Budget 2014-2015. Retrieved from Union Budget - Ministry of Finance: http://www.indiabudget.nic.in/ub2014-15/bh/bh1.pdf

Heron, L. (2013, October 15). Nine Chinese universities sign academic freedom pact. *South China Morning Post.* Retrieved from http://scholarsatrisk.nyu.edu/Events-News/Article-Detail.php?art_uid=4261

Hsin, A., & Xie, Y. (2014). Explaining Asian Americans' academic advantage over whites. *Proceedings of the National Academy of Sciences of the United States of America, 111*(23), 8416–8421. doi:10.1073/pnas.1406402111

IANS. (2014, February 9). Education will help eradicate poverty: Narendra Modi. *Times of India*. Retrieved from http://timesofindia.indiatimes.com/india/Education-will-help-eradicate-poverty-Narendra-Modi/articleshow/30102138.cms

Institute of International Education. (2014). *Open Doors 2014: International students in the United States and study abroad by American students are at all-time high*. Retrieved from Institute of International Education: http://www.iie.org/Research-and-Publications/Open-Doors

Jiangsu Education. (2011). *China-Yale University advanced seminar for university leaders starts at Zhejiang University*. Retrieved from Jiangsu Education: http://english.jsjyt.gov.cn/news/keynews/folder612/2013/04/2013-04-232697.html

Kapur, D., & Perry, E. (2014). *Higher education reform in China and India: The role of the state*. Paper presented at Changing Role of State in Asia II: Comparative Perspective, Asia Research Institute, Singapore. May 30-31, 2014.

Lai, A. (2012, November 26). Chinese flock to elite U.S. schools. *CNN*. Retrieved from http://edition.cnn.com/2012/11/25/world/asia/china-ivy-league-admission/

Levin, R. C. (2010, May/June). Top of the class: The rise of asia's universities. *Foreign Affairs*. Retrieved from http://www.foreignaffairs.com/articles/66216/richard-c-levin/top-of-the-class

Lucas, H. C. (2013, October 7). Can the current model of higher education survive MOOCs and online learning? *Educause Review*. Retrieved from http://www.educause.edu/ero/article/can-current-model-higher-education-survive-moocs-and-online-learning

Mourshed, M., Patel, J., & Suder, K. (2014). *Education to employment: Getting Europe's youth into work*. London, UK: McKinsey. Retrieved from http://www.mckinsey.com/insights/social_sector/~/media/mckinsey/dotcom/insights/social%20sector/education%20to%20employment%20getting%20europes%20youth%20into%20work/education%20to%20employment%20getting%20europes%20youth%20into%20work%20full%20report.ashx

Nandakumar, I., & Sabharwal, S. (2011, November 24). Number of tech graduates swells: Salaries at IT firms stay stagnant. *The Economic Times*. Retrieved from http://articles.economictimes.indiatimes.com/2011-11-24/news/30437637_1_engineering-colleges-engineering-and-technology-graduates

NASSCOM. (2014). *Human capital leadership: World's largest, most diverse talent pool*. Retrieved from National Association of Software and Services Companies: http://www.nasscom.in/knowledge-professionals

National Bureau of Statistics of China. (2011). *China statistical yearbook 2011*. Beijing, China: China Statistics Press.

National Bureau of Statistics of China. (2013). *China statistical yearbook*. Beijing, China: China Statistics Press.

National University of Singapore (NUS). (n.d.). *1905*. Retrieved from National University of Singapore, http://www.nus.edu.sg/about-nus/history/milestones/54-1905;

Ni, Z. (2014, June 6). Why go to Harvard when you can opt for an Asian Ivy League? *Forbes*. Retrieved from http://www.forbes.com/sites/zheyanni/2014/06/11/why-go-to-harvard-when-you-can-opt-for-an-asian-ivy-league/

Pretorius, S. G., & Xue, Y. Q. (2003). The transition from elite to mass higher education: A Chinese perspective. *Prospects, 33*(1), 89–101.

Quacquarelli Symonds. (2013, November 21). *Top 10 Student Cities 2014*. Retrieved from QS Top Universities: http://www.topuniversities.com/university-rankings-articles/qs-best-student-cities/top-10-student-cities-2014

Quacquarelli Symonds. (2014, September 16). *QS World University Rankings 2014/15*. Retrieved from QS Top Universities: http://www.topuniversities.com/university-rankings/world-university-rankings/2014

Quacquarelli Symonds. (2014b, September 24). QS University Rankings: Top 50 Under 50 2014. Retrieved from QS Top Universities: http://www.topuniversities.com/top-50-under-50/2014

Sharma, Y. (2014a, February 14). Rising unemployment—Are there too many graduates? *University World News*. Retrieved from http://www.universityworldnews.com/article.php?story=20140213153927383

Sharma, Y. (2014b, June 12). Major reform as 600 universities become polytechnics. Retrieved from University World News: http://www.universityworldnews.com/article.php?story=20140612080509913

Statistica. (2014). *China: Unemployment rate from 2004 to 2014.* Retrieved from Statistica: The Statistic Portal, http://www.statista.com/statistics/270320/unemployment-rate-in-china/

Taipei Economic and Cultural Office. (2012, August 10). Graduate degree holders face increased unemployment. *Taiwan Insights.* Retrieved from http://www.taiwaninsights.com/2012/08/10/graduate-degree-holders-face-increased-unemployment/

Tan, C. C. (2010). Opportunities and challenges facing Asian higher education. *1st Asian University Presidents Forum.* Guangzhou. Retrieved from http://president.nus.edu.sg/pdf/forum.pdf

Times Higher Education. (2014, October 2). World University Rankings 2014-2015. Retrieved from THE World University Rankings: http://www.timeshighereducation.co.uk/world-university-rankings/2014-15/world-ranking

UNESCO. (2013). *The international mobility of Students in Asia and the Pacific.* Paris, France: UNESCO Asia and Pacific Regional Bureau for Education, Bangkok Office.

UNESCO. (2014). *Higher education in Asia: Expanding out, expanding up.* Montreal, Canada: UNESCO Institute for Statistics.

UNESCO. (2006). *Higher Education in South East Asia.* Bangkok, Thailand

World Bank. (2014). Explore. Create. Share: Development data. Retrieved from World DataBank: http://databank.worldbank.org/

World Economic Forum. (2014). *The Global Competitiveness Report 2014–2015.* Geneva, Switzerland: World Economic Forum. Retrieved from World Economic Forum: http://www.weforum.org/reports/global-competitiveness-report-2014-2015

NOTES

[1] The China-Yale University Advanced Seminar for University Leaders is an education project organized by the Ministry of Education of China and Yale University. It is the first advanced seminar jointly held by the Chinese government and one of the most prestigious universities in the United States.

[2] A senior Taiwanese education official comments that the abundance of places had undermined the quality of degrees and created a skill mismatch in the job market. "We would not like to see low-ranking jobs that only require a high school education flooded by applicants with PhDs," he said.

[3] Based on calculating 3 million unemployed graduates out of a total of 50 million graduates.

[4] Data is from the Institute of International Education's *2014 Open Doors Report.* The United States achieved a record high 8 percent increase for international student intake to a record high of 886,052 students. China supplied 274,439 students to the United States.

Chapter Two

Global University Rankings: Determining the Distance Between Asia and "Superpower Status" in Higher Education

MIGUEL LIM, AARHUS UNIVERSITY, DENMARK

Introduction

This chapter aims to contribute to the understanding of international university rankings and how these increasingly popular instruments draw attention to higher education as a sector of importance for policymakers concerned about economic development. The rise in rankings frames the central question of this volume: whether Asia will become a higher education superpower. How well higher education institutions perform matters because of a central concern in policymaking circles: Nations and regions need greater competitiveness in the global knowledge economy. For many audiences—including some policymakers and members of the general public—rankings not only reflect the rise in prestige of some Asian higher education institutions but also show how far they have to go before attaining the status of education superpower.

The origins of international rankings can be traced to a set of policy events in China, starting with the Shanghai Jiao Tong Academic Ranking of World Universities (ARWU). Trends from the Shanghai rankings as well as Times Higher Education (THE) and

Quacquarelli Symonds (QS) rankings indicate the opportunities and challenges around Asia's possible future superpower status in higher education. More importantly, the dynamics among ranking organizations, public policymakers, and higher education institutions in Asia point out who is concerned about superpower status.

The "World-Class University" and the Knowledge Economy

The central question of this volume—whether Asia will be the next higher education superpower—stems from a growing conviction in policy circles that the production of knowledge and, by extension, the performance of the higher education sector matters to national and regional competitiveness in a global knowledge economy. While the definition of *knowledge economy* is disputed and sometimes critically discussed, there is research that finds that, for example, in the United Kingdom "higher education is particularly effective in generating GDP [gross domestic product] per capita, compared to several other sectors of the economy" (Kelly, McNicoll, & McLellan, 2004).

Research reports by international institutions such as the Organisation for Economic Co-operation and Development (OECD) and the National Research Council (NRC) in the United States link the research productivity of the higher education sector to economic output. Thus the role of the university in the context of global economic competition becomes ever more important (NRC, 2012; OECD, 2010, 2013). Being at "the nexus of science, scholarship and the new knowledge economy" (Altbach & Balán, 2007), the university becomes the central actor in the creation and dissemination of knowledge as well as in the formation of the knowledge workforce of the future.

For many countries, particularly advanced, industrialized ones, the common policy concern is to turn to the production of high-value knowledge goods in a world environment that is characterized by extreme competitiveness in lower-value manufacturing. The development of new products and technologies that can be quickly brought to market and serve as the foundation of even further technological advances is the Holy Grail that economic policymakers are pursuing. Central to the goal of high productivity in knowledge goods is the performance of the research university— described as the "central institution of the 21st century" (Altbach & Balán, 2007). Higher education as a whole is also accorded new value. A population that is highly educated may be costlier because more resources have to be invested in the higher education sector and because college graduates enter the workforce later. But it is commonly argued that this investment pays off eventually as students go on to contribute more to the economy, presumably in knowledge-intensive and innovation-related tasks, over the course of their working lives.

The link between the higher education sector and a country's or region's economic competitiveness, commonly accepted in policy circles, begs the question among Asian policymakers as to whether their countries, with their large populations and rapidly growing economies, are set to become the next higher education superpowers. The narrative of the rise of the emerging economies, popularized first in the realm of finance and economics with the coining of the acronym BRIC, for Brazil, Russia, India, and China, by economist Jim O'Neill of Goldman Sachs, appears to have led many observers to a tentative but likely conclusion. As Asian economies expand, and as more and more young people enter higher education, many assume that their climb upwards from labor-intensive to more knowledge-intensive production is also assured. At the heart of many public policies to support this transition is support for higher value research, such as in pharmaceuticals or high-technology industries, and development taking place in the region's top universities (Mohrman, 2013).

This narrative of Asia's rise is set against a higher education landscape in which the most important research universities are in the developed world. The grand story of the sector in the last couple of decades is the growth, or catch up, in prestige and output of some universities in the developing world and in particular in Asia. Yet to determine Asia's superpower status means to try and understand its higher education sector's position relative to other regions—particularly those of the advanced regions of Europe and North America. One instrument that has become the most popular basis for comparing higher education systems and institutions across countries is the international university ranking. Because more and more policymakers are using these ranking as inputs into their own policymaking processes (Hazelkorn, 2014; Rauhvargers, 2011), it is important to discuss the dynamics that underlie the most influential ranking organizations.

International University Rankings: Growing Influence

Rankings have increasingly become, in the popular imagination as well as in some policy circles, the arbiters as to what constitutes excellence in higher education and thus whether Asia is climbing the ladder of world-class higher education (Altbach & Balán, 2007). University rankings are not immodestly described by their makers as "exceptionally powerful" (Baty, 2012). Rankings have attained significance not only in the higher education sector but also at a geopolitical level (Hazelkorn, 2014, p. 14). While some rankings initially set out simply to help students make decisions regarding which university to attend, "the attention now being given to rankings by policy makers and decision-makers indicates that, in reality, rankings are much more about geo-political positioning, by nations and HEIs [higher education institutions]" (Hazelkorn, 2014, p. 14).

Rankings claim to offer some sort of evaluation of education and research quality; others then invoke the ranking results as markers of a country's competitiveness in the knowledge economy (European Commission, 2011). Many governments, concerned about the reputation of their education sectors, are anxious to ensure that their national "champions" appear at the top of these rankings. There are many examples of rankings becoming the object of national concern. In France, disappointment over the performance of French universities in the rankings led to "Shanghai Shock" and a wave of university policy reforms: "France's poor showing in the Shanghai rankings —it had only two universities in the first top 100—helped trigger a national debate about higher education that resulted in a new law, passed last month, giving universities more freedom" (Enserink, 2007, p. 1026). It was during France's rotating presidency of the European Union that the EU-supported U-Multirank project was launched as an alternative to other rankings that showed the dominance of Anglo-Saxon institutions.

In the greater Asian region, there has been no less concern over the university rankings. Malaysia, Singapore, and Taiwan have all used the rankings as part of their efforts to restructure their higher education sectors (Rauhvargers, 2013). The Russian 5/100 initiative aims to place five Russian universities in the top 100 of the rankings by 2020 (Alekseev, 2014). Under the moniker "Abeducation" (after Japanese Prime Minister Shinzo Abe), Japan's goal is aims to raise the number of Japanese universities in the top 100 of the rankings to 10 from the present 2 (Kakuchi, 2013). As a reaction to the 2014 THE Asian University Rankings, India's secretary for higher education, Ashok Thakur, said that

> the question of whether the country should go "full hog" for the global university rankings has mercifully been laid to rest by none other than the president of India, Pranab Mukherjee, who has made it clear that as a matter of policy, all institutions in the country have to participate wholeheartedly in the rankings process. The benefits of this commitment are obvious to all" (Thakur, 2014, p. 1).

There is an intense concern not only over achieving world-class status but also over not being left behind by Asian regional rivals.

The pressure of rankings is keenly felt on a national level, but even more so on an institutional level. Several higher education institutions set themselves their own targets in this regard. In China, Tsinghua University and Peking University are not only aiming to become world-class universities, but they also have set 2020 and 2016, respectively, as target dates to achieve this goal (Liu, 2007). It was a national drive to build world-class universities that led Shanghai Jiao Tong University to develop the first international university ranking. The Shanghai rankings, as they are popularly known, were first published in 2003. While *U.S. News & World Report* has published a ranking of colleges and graduate schools since 1983, these were limited only to comparisons between U.S. institutions. The Shanghai rankings were the first widely circulated systematic comparison of universities across nations.

The Story at Shanghai

The Shanghai rankings were a response to a specific Chinese higher education policy, named Plan 985. The policy originates from the centennial anniversary celebration of Peking University in May (the fifth month) of 1998—and thus the name Plan 985. Peking University together with Tsinghua University, both in Beijing, are widely considered to be the country's top higher education institutions. The goal of Plan 985 was to consolidate Peking University's success and to produce a larger number of world-class universities in order to fuel China's economic development. The plan allotted a significant sum of 32.9 billion yuan to build a set of world-class universities (Ying, 2011). The first phase lasted from 1999 to 2001 and was a crucial period in the development of the Shanghai ranking (Liu, 2009). In this period alone, Tsinghua and Peking Universities received $280 million (U.S. dollars; Li, 2012). The second phase took place in 2004–2007. A third phase is being planned (Liu, 2014). As a result of this plan, a group of nine leading Chinese universities (referred to as the C9) has emerged. They are the first recipients of Plan 985's support, and the C9 is seen within China as a group that aspires to the status of its counterparts in other countries such as the U.S. Ivy League and the UK Russell Group.

In response to Plan 985, Professor Nian Cai Liu and a group of academics at Shanghai Jiao Tong University, itself a member of the C9, aimed to develop a tool to benchmark their own institution against the Chinese government's ideal of a world-class university. The genesis of the ranking revolved around Liu's role as part of the university's strategic planning team (Liu, 2009). The ranking was an effort to answer several key questions brought up by the Plan 985 goal: "What is the definition of a world-class university? What are the positions of top Chinese universities in the world higher education system? How can top Chinese universities reduce their gap with world-class universities?" (Liu, 2009, p. 2).

The result of the efforts of Liu's team to answer these questions was a benchmarking of the top Chinese universities against U.S. universities. They turned largely to the U.S. research university model as an exemplar of world class and aimed to produce a metric of comparison based on objective data collected by disinterested third parties (Liu, 2010). This tool was the progenitor of the now well-known Shanghai Jiao Tong Rankings, also known as the Academic Ranking of World Universities (ARWU). Liu mentioned that they only publicized the ranking after interest from other scholars visiting the Graduate School of Education at Shanghai Jiao Tong reminded Liu that "not only in China, but also universities, governments, and other stakeholders in the rest of the world are interested in the ranking of universities" (Liu, 2009, p. 2). The group at Shanghai Jiao Tong proceeded to develop the tool, and in 2003, the first Shanghai rankings were released.

The Shanghai rankings were quickly followed by others. In 2004, a collaboration between the Times Higher Education Supplement and the data consultancy Quacquarelli Symonds released the Times Higher Education–Quacquarelli Symonds (THE-QS) rankings. In 2009, these two organizations decided to produce separate rankings, now known as the THE World University Rankings and QS World University Rankings, and the first rankings were released in 2010. Since then, numerous international rankings have been developed and circulated. Some examples include the Leiden University Rankings, the National University of Taiwan (NTU) Rankings (formerly known as HEEACT), the Webometrics Rankings, and the EU funded U-Multirank. The U-Multirank initiative, which was released in May 2014, is seen by some as an attempt to provide an alternative to the perceived underappreciation of the qualities of some leading European institutions in the other rankings (see Van Vught & Ziegele, 2012). Its first edition featured a large number of European higher education institutions and only a small number of Asian institutions, but it aims to continue collecting data on a wider number of global institutions.

Each of these rankings differs in some way from the others, but there are some general themes: There is a remarkable stability at the top of the tables, but lower down in the ranking list there is a trend showing that an increasing number of Asian institutions perform well vis-à-vis their global counterparts.

International Rankings and the Measure of World Class

The international rankings are much criticized. One line of critique holds that the ranking methodologies are flawed because the qualities described are not accurately captured by the corresponding indicator. Each ranking organization uses its own methodology, with its own particular criteria, to generate its ranking list. Critics argue that even when there is a correspondence between what rankers seek to measure and the "unit of measurement," there still exist better ways of obtaining and treating data. One early critique involved the difficulty of attributing citations properly to their institutions of origin and how to distribute scientific prizes among co-winners' institutions, given the importance Nobel prizes in the Shanghai ranking's methodology (Van Raan, 2005). See Table 2.1.

TABLE 2.1: WEIGHTINGS USED IN THE ACADEMIC RANKING OF WORLD UNIVERSITIES

Criteria	Indicator	Weight
Quality of education	Alumni of an institution winning Nobel Prizes and Fields Medals	10%
Quality of faculty	Staff of an institution winning Nobel Prizes and Fields Medals	20%
Quality of faculty	Highly cited researchers in 21 broad subject categories	20%
Research output	Papers published in Nature and Science Journals	20%
Research output	Papers indexed in Science Citation Index Expanded and Social Science Citation Index	20%
Per-capita performance	Per-capita academic performance of an institution	10%
Total		100%

Source: Shanghai Jiao Tong Academic Ranking of World Universities

The teams at Shanghai, as well as at other rankers, attempted to resolve concerns regarding the attribution of citations to the proper institutions by using the growing sophistication in bibliometric systems provided by data management firms Thomson Reuters and Scopus (Liu, Cheng, & Liu, 2005). However, even where perfect attribution is possible, a long-held critique of the Shanghai ranking is the proportion of the ranking's weight given to Nobel (and Fields) Prize winners. Almost a third of the ranking depends on this crucial measure, and according to the ranking's website, it is used as an indicator of the quality of education as well as the quality of the faculty at a given institution. While acknowledging this limitation, the Shanghai ranking maintains the value of the Nobel Prize as an objectively generated indicator of research quality.

These technical critiques are joined by those who argue that the entire ranking endeavor is flawed because it introduces a competitive dynamic into the higher education sector that at best distracts and at worst misleads universities from their diverse missions (Marginson & van der Wende, 2007). The weight given to research quality in most of the rankings provides an incentive for universities that wish to climb the rankings to prioritize research over other university functions such as teaching and other socially relevant missions that rankings find difficult to assess. Indeed, the danger lies in tempting policymakers "to judge all higher education in the world by the standards that rankings use to detect the top *research* universities, rather than applying … the 'fitness for purpose' principle" (Rauhvargers, 2011, p. 13, emphasis in the original).

These prevailing standards of quality and excellence matter when policymakers aim to understand whether Asia will take on the mantle of higher education superpower. The notions of what constitutes this "power" are shaped forcefully by rankings as instruments that policymakers can easily understand. If the Shanghai rankings, which give the most weight to research, are to be standards setters, then achieving superpower status will depend on winning many Nobel and Fields Prizes as well as publishing in the journals with the highest impact factor. Climbing up the THE and QS rankings will require not only an effort to increase both quantity and quality of research output but also an effort to improve the reputations of Asian institutions among their global peers and thus increase the proportion of international students and faculty at these institutions.

Asia's Quest for Higher Rankings

National performance in the university rankings matters on several levels. Rankings might only seem to be a media phenomenon, but there is much at stake. Hazelkorn (2011) described the "Matthew effect"—to those who have shall more be given—whereby those institutions that have better reputations (and are higher ranked) continue to improve and to consolidate their positions on the top of the list. The logic is simple: Well-ranked universities attract the attention of multiple audiences who reinforce each other and the position of the university overall. Good students seek to study at highly ranked institutions and, at the postgraduate level, contribute to the research output of that institution, which further cements its position in the rankings. These students also attract top-level academics, since they are crucial in supporting cutting-edge research. Academics who are able to critique the methodologies behind each ranking might be presumed to be better insulated from the rankings and thus pay less attention to ranking results. However, they cannot ignore that rankings are important in shaping student choices, and many academics will most likely seek to work at highly ranked institutions that attract ambitious students. Particularly in the case of rankings that incorporate reputational indicators (i.e., THE and QS rankings), there is a strong pattern of well-ranked universities doing better at reputational surveys, which then feed into the next period's rankings. This means that institutions that do well in one period gain more recognition and are likely to be judged as more reputable by respondents in the next period's survey. In this way, rankings can perpetuate existing hierarchies among the world's higher education superpowers and become self-fulfilling prophecies.

Where the Matthew effect is present, there will be relative stability among the institutions at the top of the rankings. Bowman and Bastedo (2011) found that there is indeed an anchoring effect of university reputation that contributes to the staying power of better-known universities at the top of the lists. Even among the world's best, there is a growing differentiation between the very top and the rest of the world-class universities. Phil Baty, the editor of the THE rankings, speaks of the six superbrands in the THE Reputation rankings. These include Harvard University; Massachusetts Institute of Technology; the universities of Cambridge and Oxford; the University of

California, Berkeley; and Stanford University (Baty, 2013). Better known and older universities, many of which are large and have relatively greater resources, fare so well in the world rankings that both the THE and QS produced new rankings of up-and-coming universities that include only institutions younger than 50 years old. In like manner, because universities from developed nations dominate their global editions of the rankings, the THE and QS also release regional rankings for Asia and Latin America. There is also now a ranking of institutions in the BRICS (Brazil, Russia, India, China, and South Africa) countries and other emerging economies.

The strong hierarchy at the top of the rankings is a considerable obstacle to Asia's (or any other region's) quest to become a higher education superpower. The rise of Asian universities in the rankings has been a slow and gradual process. They have made the most progress in the QS rankings, which are mostly student-oriented and give relatively greater weight to employability and the proportion of international students and faculty as measures of a university's excellence. In the QS rankings, the number of Asian institutions in the top 100 has climbed from 13 in 2004 to 20 in 2012, although they have not yet broken into the very highest ranks. In the THE rankings, which they produced separately from QS in 2010, this number has remained stable at 10 (in 2012). There are even fewer Asian institutions in the top 100 of the Shanghai rankings. There are only three Asian institutions (excluding Israel from the Asian region) in the top 100 of the ARWU 2013 ranking. All of these are from Japan. The highest ranked Chinese universities come in the 151–200 ranking band.

The underperformance of Asian institutions in the Shanghai rankings is perhaps not entirely unexpected, given that these rankings used top U.S. research universities as the gold standard. This implies that these same U.S. universities will continue to remain at the top until other institutions can arrive at a degree of congruence with Harvard (or any institution that acts as a standard), which will inherently be a long, drawn-out process. The reputation of Harvard, as well as Oxford and Cambridge, is so valuable that they are loosely described as "national treasures" (Baty, 2013). While Asian countries also have their own national treasure universities, they are still behind the non-Asian ones. The top-ranked Asian institutions based *only on reputation* as measured by the 2013 THE reputation survey (THE, 2013) are the University of Tokyo (ranked 9), National University of Singapore (22), Tsinghua University (35), the University of Hong Kong (36), and Seoul National University (41). See Table 2.2.

Country	Number of Top 100 Institutions	Top Institution	Top Institution Rank
United States	43	Harvard University	1
United Kingdom	9	University of Cambridge	3
Australia	6	University of Melbourne	39
Germany	5	Ludwig Maximilians University Munich	44
Japan	5	University of Tokyo	9
Netherlands	5	Delft University of Technology	51–60
France	4	University of Paris–Sorbonne	71–80
Canada	3	University of Toronto	16
Hong Kong	3	University of Hong Kong	36
Sweden	3	Karolinska Institute	61–70
Switzerland	2	Swiss Federal University of Technology (ETH) Zurich	=20
Republic of Korea	2	Seoul National University	22
China	2	Tsinghua University	35
Note: Apart from those listed above, the following countries or territories have at least one institution in the top 100 of the THE Reputation Rankings: Israel, Russian Federation, Turkey, Taiwan, Belgium, and Brazil.			

Source: THE 2013 Reputation Rankings

Even though some Asian universities are rising in these ranking tables, improvement has not been equal across different countries; only a small number of Asian countries have begun to climb the world-class ladder. In 2013–2014, China (excluding Hong Kong) managed to place its two top institutions, Peking University and Tsinghua University, within the top 50 in the THE World University Rankings (in which reputation is only one factor among others). However, there are no other mainland Chinese institutions in the top 200. There are a small number of universities from Japan, (5), South Korea (4), Hong Kong (3), Singapore (2), and Taiwan (1) that made the top 200 list, but even taken together, these are only a fraction of the number of world-class institutions found in the United States (77) and the United Kingdom (31). Thus, despite varying degrees of investment in their higher education sectors, Asian countries have only begun to see the start of improved visibility of their institutions at the top of the international rankings.

Chinese Efforts to Build World-Class Universities

In China, there is a strong drive to produce a set of world-class universities and also, with significant financial resources, a small number of institutions that can be included in reasonable comparison with the very top. These resources have produced a remarkable increase in Chinese research production: Peer-reviewed papers in China have risen 64-fold in the last 30 years (Yang and Welch, 2012). Chinese scientists have managed to publish in the top scientific journals, such as *Science, Nature, Cell,* and the *Lancet.* The number of researchers returning with doctorates from abroad is also increasing.

The state, however, has had to balance its drive to produce world-class universities with the imperative of improving the higher education sector across the board (Marginson, 2011). These two goals require different performance metrics and explain, to some extent, why the Chinese government neither endorses nor prohibits the rankings. While many governments use rankings, the Chinese government is a notable exception. It prefers instead a broad-based national policy of creating world-class universities without reference to international rankings; because of the state's important role in the governance of the higher education sector, an endorsement of any ranking could give rise to numerous problems. China's higher education sector involves governance at various levels, with many local and regional officials eager to safeguard their universities' prestige but also their ability to contribute to local and regional development. This could be due to a "classical fundamental Chinese principle of all things being nourished together without hurting one another and all courses being pursued without being conflictual or mutually exclusive" (Doctrine of the Mean, 30.3, in Li, 2012, p. 333). China's desire to maintain institutional diversity is at odds with the powerful standardizing logic that rankings could bring about.

Despite this ambivalent stance on the part of the government, it is clear that the top Chinese universities use the rankings in their own strategies and performance goals. Liu (2014) mentioned that the Shanghai rankings have now begun to appear in official Chinese public policy documents as higher education institutions report on their performance in the first phases of the Plan 985 project and refer to the rankings as a demonstration of tangible progress given the increased funding they received under the scheme.

Challenges: Research Productivity, Regional Imbalances, and Competition with Other Regions

Even where Asian universities are able to climb up the rankings, there is some concern over the associated costs. Academics at Chinese universities have increasingly been able to produce world-class research papers, a key indicator measured by the rankings, yet there is some concern over the productivity of Asian research institutions and whether the sums spent on Chinese universities are indeed producing research commensurate to the investment. The cost per highly cited paper at the top Chinese universities seems to be higher than expected (Mohrman, 2013). For example, Tsinghua spends more to produce an article in a Thomson Reuters Web of Science (formerly ISI Web of Knowledge) journal than Oxford or other top-ranked European universities such as ETH Zurich and University of Paris-06 (Mohrman, 2013). Nevertheless, on the whole, Asian universities may be beginning to make their mark, although this is not yet visible at the very top.

The absence of institutions from other parts of Asia is another sign that the region is a long way off from establishing itself as a superpower. The Shanghai rankers note that there are several countries that are largely unrepresented in the list given their national GDP and GDP-per-capita figures. These countries include Indonesia, Thailand, Malaysia, the Philippines, the United Arab Emirates, Kuwait, and Kazakhstan (Liu, 2010). The THE's "BRICS & Emerging Economies Rankings" (which exclude developed economies) show that large economic powerhouses such as Indonesia do not even have one institution in this ranking's top 100 (THE, 2014).

The logic of competitive comparison means that no institution or region can stand still. Thus, for Asia, it is not simply a question of self-improvement, but improved performance relative to established incumbents and other ambitious regions. In Europe, for instance, many higher education institutions have been affected by the financial crises. Nevertheless, the European Commission has just launched its Horizon 2020 project—representing a significant increase in its research budget to close to 80 billion euros from 2014 until 2020. This increase in research funding has taken place despite decreases in other budget areas and a general environment of government constraint. The message for Asia or any other aspirant higher education superpower is that other countries and regions are not standing still. Given the developed regions' other advantages, it clearly still has some way to go before it can achieve superpower status.

The comparisons presented by rankings highlight geopolitical contests among countries and among institutions. It is precisely this intense pressure that has led to critiques that rankings have begun to affect the behavior of policymakers and institutions to focus on measured performance at the expense of other performance factors such as teaching quality and social mission initiatives. A broader question is whether poorer countries should engage in the race at all. Hazelkorn (2011) estimated the necessary budget to run a world-class university at €2 billion per annum. Even for richer countries, there is the question of whether the national prestige of a few institutions at the expense of the wider system justifies the costs. These questions cannot be answered here, but they are raised to show the numerous choices public policymakers face when designing policies to build better higher education systems.

Conclusion

Rankings shape university governance and the flow of international students in the growing industry of higher education. While some countries have had national ranking systems for some time, systematic rankings of universities at an international level have only recently been developed.

Rankings are invoked by some public policymakers as markers of the country's competitiveness in the knowledge economy (Baty, 2012). Governments concerned about the reputation of their education sectors are anxious to ensure that their national champions appear at the top of these rankings. They steer resources in particular ways to enhance university performance in the rankings, which lead, in some instances, to redefinitions of not only university missions but also entire university configurations.

Rankings have many critics. Some point out the technical limitations of the rankings exercise and the difficulty of capturing the variety of factors that constitute research and institutional excellence. Others argue, disapprovingly, that rankings are another step toward the commoditization of higher education (Kehm, 2014) and the hollowing of the academe. One particular critique has been that rankings draw attention only to certain measurable aspects of university performance at the expense of other factors. Rankings have increased the pressure for universities to produce top-level research at the expense of other goals such as teaching quality. For some universities, with missions to contribute to national development by permitting wide access, being sensitive to concerns over student inclusion is at odds with allocating resources to pursue a higher place in the rankings.

Some argue that rankings have their uses, such as the attention they bring to such issues as research productivity or, at the very least, another contribution to the contentious discussion of quality in higher education (Hazelkorn, 2014). Despite the critiques laid against them, there is a widespread belief that rankings are here to stay.

Asian countries have been particularly interested in rankings as they strive to improve their standing in the knowledge economy. The performance of the higher education sector is seen as a crucial factor in stepping up to produce higher value goods and greater competitiveness. There has been intense attention given to university rankings in several Asian countries, and many have put ambitious plans into place to promote the emergence of world-class universities in the region. An example of such an initiative, China's Plan 985, was a crucial factor in the production of the first Shanghai Jiao Tong Academic Ranking of World Universities in 2013, whose results now inform many policies, not only in higher education but also in other policy fields around the world.

Asian institutions have begun to climb the ladder of world university rankings, but they have yet to reach the very top. Even where they have made progress, there is concern over the cost involved in producing the research papers and student-to-staff ratios as well as other factors that are used by organizations such as Shanghai Jiao Tong, QS, and THE to produce their rankings. Rankings may also lead some universities to aspire to the standard of a comprehensive research-focused model that may be inappropriate in some cases across the Asian region. These problems, among several others, all raise questions for university leaders and policymakers regarding which trade-offs they will need to make in order to improve their institutions. Whether they are able to make the right choices will ultimately determine whether Asia becomes the next higher education superpower.

REFERENCES

Alekseev, O. (2014). First steps of Russian universities to Top-100 global university rankings. *Higher Education in Russia and Beyond, 1*(Spring). 6-7.

Altbach, P. G., & Balán, J. (2007). *World class worldwide: Transforming research universities in Asia and Latin America.* Baltimore, MD. JHU Press.

Baty, P. (2012, October). Global university rankings: Great responsibility. Retrieved from THE 2012-2013 World University Rankings, http://www.timeshighereducation.co.uk/world-university-rankings/2012-13/world-ranking/analysis/global-university-rankings

Baty, P. (2013). *Beyond the super-brands, universities are strengthening their positions.* Retrieved from THE World Reputation Rankings 2013, http://www.timeshighereducation.co.uk/world-university-rankings/2013/reputation-ranking/analysis/super-brands

Bowman, N. & Bastedo, M. (2011). Anchoring effects on world university rankings: Exploring biases in reputation scores. *Higher Education, 61*, 431–444.

Enserink, M. (2007). Who ranks the university rankers? *Science, 317*(5841), 1026–1028.

European Commission. (2011). *Supporting growth and jobs: An agenda for the modernisation of Europe's higher education systems.* Retrieved from http://ec.europa.eu/education/library/policy/modernisation_en.pdf

Hazelkorn, E. (2011). *Rankings and the reshaping of higher education the battle for world-class excellence.* Basingstoke: Palgrave Macmillan.

Hazelkorn, E. (2014). Reflections on a decade of global rankings: What we've learned and outstanding issues. *European Journal of Education, 49*(1), 12–28.

Kakuchi, S. (2013, June 27). Abeducation—A new push for higher education internationalization, *University World News*, issue no. 278. Retrieved from http://www.universityworldnews.com/article.php?story=20130627113411208

Kehm, B. M. (2014). Global university rankings—Impacts and unintended side effects. *European Journal of Education, 49*(1), 102–112.

Kelly, U., McNicoll, I., & McLellan, D. (2004). *The economic impact of UK higher education institutions* (Report). Glasgow, UK: University of Strathclyde.

Li, J. (2012). World-class higher education and the emerging Chinese model of the university. *Prospects, 42*(3), 319–339.

Liu, N. C. (2007). Research university in China: Differentiation, classification, and future world-class status. In P. G. Altbach & J. Balán (Eds.), *World class worldwide: Transforming research universities in Asia and Latin America* (pp. 54–69). Baltimore, MD: JHU Press.

Liu, N. C. (2009). The story of the academic ranking of world universities. *International Higher Education, 54*, 2–3.

Liu, N. C. (2010, July 2). *Shanghai ranking* (Presentation). Retrieved from http://www.slideshare.net/KentBusinessSchool/paper-1-shanghai-ranking-liu-nian-cai

Liu, N. C. (2014, May 13). Transforming Shanghai Jiao Tong University (SJTU) into a world-class university: Past experiences and future challenges. Lecture conducted at Institute of Education. CHES 2013–14 Seminar Series, London, UK.

Liu, N. C., Cheng, Y., & Liu, L. (2005). Academic ranking of world universities using scientometrics—A comment to the "Fatal Attraction." *Scientometrics, 64*(1), 101–109.

Marginson, S. (2011). Higher education in East Asia and Singapore: Rise of the Confucian model. *Higher Education, 61*, 587–611.

Marginson, S., & van der Wende, M. (2007). To rank or to be ranked: The impact of global rankings in higher education. *Journal of Studies in International Education*, 11(3–4), 306–329.

Mohrman, K. (2013). Are Chinese universities globally competitive? *China Quarterly, 215*, 727–743.

National Research Council (NRC). (2012). *Improving measurement of productivity in higher education*. Washington, DC: National Academies Press.

OECD. (2010). *Governance and quality guidelines in higher education: A review on governance arrangements and quality assurance guidelines*. Paris: OECD Press.

OECD. (2013). *The state of higher education 2013*. Paris: OECD Press.

Rauhvargers, A. (2011). *Global university rankings and their impact*. EUA Report on Rankings 2011. Retrieved from http://www.eua.be/pubs/global_university_rankings_and_their_impact.pdf

Rauhvargers, A. (2013). *Global university rankings and their impact*. EUA Report II. Brussels: EUA.

Shanghai Jiao Tong University Academic Ranking of World Universities. (2012). *Methodology*. Retrieved from Academic Ranking of World Universities website, http://www.shanghairanking.com/ARWU-Methodology-2012.html

Thakur, A. (2014, June 25). Ten Indian universities in top 100 of THE Asia rankings. Hindustan Times. Retrieved from http://www.hindustantimes.com/hteducation/greatcareers/ten-indian-universities-in-top-100-of-the-asia-rankings/article1-1233422.aspx

Times Higher Education (THE). (2013). *THE 2013–2014 World Reputation Rankings*. Retrieved from http://www.timeshighereducation.co.uk/world-university-rankings/2013/reputation-ranking Retrieved from http://www.timeshighereducation.co.uk/world-university-rankings/2013-14/world-ranking

Times Higher Education (THE). (2014). *THE 2014 BRICS & emerging economies rankings*. Retrieved from http://www.timeshighereducation.co.uk/world-university-rankings/2014/brics-and-emerging-economies

Van Raan, A. F. J. (2005). Fatal attraction: Ranking of universities by bibliometric methods. *Scientometrics, 62*(1), 133–143.

Van Vught, F. A., & Ziegele, F. (Eds.). (2012). *Higher Education Dynamics Series: Vol. 37. Multidimensional ranking: The design and development of U-Multirank*. . Dordrecht: Springer.

Yang, R., & Welch, A. (2012). A world-class university in China? The case of Tsinghua. *Higher Education, 63*(5), 645–666.

Ying, C. (2011). A reflection on the effects of the 985 Project. *Chinese Education & Society, 44*(5), 19–30.

Chapter Three

The Knowledge Economy and the Transformational Dynamics of Education in Asia's Emergent Economic Growth

Chaya R. Jain, Virginia State University, United States

Introduction

This chapter examines the knowledge economy (KE) and its role in economic growth for the developing nations in the Asian region. In support of the observation of Kuznets (1965, pp. 85-87) that "useful knowledge" is a key mechanism of modern economic growth, this chapter posits that knowledge in itself is not as useful an economic resource until applied, shared, and transferred for competitive advantage toward an intended or specific purpose. Thus, the chapter uses a generic definition of knowledge as a measurable commodity (i.e., innovation) and a key component toward value creation, productivity, and economic growth. Accordingly, with Asia as the focus, this theoretical discourse offers an analysis and a comparative synthesis of the global KE dynamics. The framework takes into consideration three contemporary corollaries of the KE within the global and Asian context: (1) collaborative academic output with regard to research and publications, (2) national investment commitment for research and development (R&D), and (3) impact of the integrated KE manifestations and mechanisms on a country's overall preparedness to compete in the KE sector.

The KE concept regards education and knowledge as tradable commodities for economic gain. This perspective is rooted in innovative intellectual products and services that can be disseminated for a high-value return. KE is inherently prone to provincial context and, therefore, subject to differing governance-related practices and policies, which in turn influence intellectual property rights, knowledge, capital investments, organizational character, management structure and size, and mission of the stakeholders. This multiplicity adds to global competition, further affecting transformations in the characters, roles, and relationships among the economy's key stakeholders: industry, corporations, government, and communities. Although expansion of knowledge parallels human existence itself, the genesis of modern KE is arguably embedded in the industrial revolution and the subsequent global colonial expansion (Jacob 2014).

The Historical Context

Evidence of collaboration among academicians and industries on marketable projects can be traced back to the industrial revolution (Mokyr, 2002; Quah, 2000). However, the impact of the industrial revolution dynamic between Western Europe and Asia is subject to a rigorous debate with divergent views. Among these are Eurocentrism and Orientalism. Eurocentrism asserts a worldview focused on Western civilization, developed during the height of the European colonial empires since the Middle Ages. Orientalism, as interpreted by Edward Said (1979) in his book by the same title, distinguishes among various Western and Eastern precepts including art, culture, politics, power, and scholarship through illumination of the West's Eurocentric prejudices regarding the Eastern societies. Expanding the debate on this divide, Michael Parenti's four decades of incisive depictions of the Western and Northern nations' (primarily European colonial nations and the "imperialist" United States; Parenti, 2011) exploitations of the non-Western societies (nations of Asia, Africa, and Latin America) further illustrate the divergences between the developed and the so-called developing nations.

Juxtaposing the notions of Eurocentrism and Orientalism, proponents of the "California School"[1] (Frank, 1998; Goldstone, 2008[2]; Lee & Wang, 2009; Pomeranz, 2000; Wong, 1997) contend that there are no distinguishable differences in the post–industrial revolution period among the socioeconomic aspects of European and Asian societies. On the other hand, proponents of the "Postdevelopment School"[3] question the Western and Northern notion of development altogether and instead emphasize acknowledgment of the diverse cultural perspectives and priorities from the viewpoint of indigenous societies. Scrutinizing the issue, Arturo Escobar (1992, 27) suggests an alternative to development as "local culture and knowledge; a critical stance toward established scientific discourses, and the defense and promotion of localized, pluralistic grassroots movements."

Knowledge Economy: The Post-Modern Initiatives

With due recognition of these divergent viewpoints highlighting critical subtleties of the complex historical context, this discussion's framework will best be served by the author's deference to Mignolo's "decoloniality"[4] perspective, which seeks forward-looking intercultural dialogue. Accordingly, perhaps the pioneering initiative of the United States offers a stable although somewhat elite model of the KE's postmodern evolution in the post-World War II era for three reasons. First, it transformed academe's deployment of innovation capacity through university–industry collaborations. Second, it initiated a ground-breaking step to advance the KE for higher-value return through public policy (i.e., government's commitment to research and development [R&D]). Third, it set the stage for the newly ex-colonized nations in modeling their KE agenda as a strategy for economic growth.

President Franklin Roosevelt's letter of November 17, 1944,[5] to Vannaver Bush, director of the U.S. Office of Scientific Research and Development, established the context for the post-modern transformation that continues until this day. It began with Roosevelt seeking profitable employment of scientific knowledge in times of peace by asking four specific questions: (1) How can the U.S. government develop scientific talent? (2) How can the U.S. government stimulate scientific research? (3) How can the U.S. government best diffuse the scientific knowledge developed during World War II? (4) How can the U.S. government use science in the struggle against disease? Bush's response, a 35-page report, informally called the Bush Report (Bush, 1945),[6] offered several recommendations including, the creation of the National Research Foundation. It also suggested support for collaboration among government, university, and industry to foster innovation through R&D. The report's ambitious agenda included an increasing dominance of corporate R&D that would integrate knowledge workers with knowledge management (Duderstadt, 2005).

Incorporating recommendations of the Bush Report, the government sought to overhaul the system of higher education. Instead of building separate research institutes, the Bush Report recommended the federal government's renewed support for a partnership among government, universities, and industry, implementing a competitive system for faculty to conduct basic research under the so-called linear model.[7] It also extended contracts to industrial R&D laboratories to expand applied research with specific goals, such as the national defense. The federal assistance was thus channeled through various governmental research agencies such as the National Science Foundation and the National Institutes of Health, as well as mission agencies such as the Department of Defense, the Department of Energy, and the Department of Agriculture. This creative and collaborative capitalization of knowledge through an interlinking of academia, industry, and government—what Henry Etzkowitz (1993; Etzkowitz & Leydesdorff, 1997) called the "triple helix interaction"—became a popular network strategy to create research-driven high-technology clusters within the United States. It also set a trend that continues to be a popular practice around the world today.

Throughout the second half of the 20th century, the U.S. model of establishing and advancing profitable employment of scientific knowledge continued to gain worldwide recognition and acceptance. Among other important developments during the same period, in July 1944, the World Bank began its effort to bridge the economic disparity between developed and developing nations. During the mid-1990s, the World Bank initiated a paradigmatic shift in its policy by making higher education a key priority as a development strategy among the developing nations. It created a benchmarking tool called the Knowledge for Development Program to help countries identify the challenges and opportunities they face in making the transition to a knowledge-based economy. The World Bank also developed an interactive tool called Knowledge Assessment Methodology, which consists of 148 structural and qualitative variables for 146 countries to measure their performance on the four KE pillars.

Although KE manifestations and mechanisms induce greater potential for countries to strengthen their economic and social development, a review of the contemporary trends reveals two opposing opinions on the benefit or detriment of the colonial legacy. On the one hand, data trends (Giebel, 2013; The World Bank, 2013) show a global knowledge divide, which, considering that almost 80 nations secured autonomy from colonial powers in the 20th century (a vast majority during the middle four decades alone), warrants further inquiry though beyond the scope of this chapter. The task of gauging the KE capital from each side of the divide is rather complex; and requires a basic understanding of the contemporary dynamics between developed and developing nations as well as a focus on equity as opposed to the hegemonic inequity of the past.

For most ex-colonized nations, the KE evolution has been a challenging endeavor depending upon a country's postcolonial conditions concerning infrastructure involving political, economic, social, cultural, and other germane aspects of indigenous ecology. By the very design, sustained colonial hegemony prevented indigenous technological advancements that did not benefit the imperial crowns. For many, the decades immediately following postcolonial self-rule inevitably turned out to be multifarious experimentations to establish respective autonomy as a nation first—a long, drawn-out process, particularly for large nations such as China and India. For most, the loss of traditional bearings of self-governance under centuries of colonial occupation, combined with having to chart a new course amid an increasingly segregated global society of advanced and developing nations led to daunting challenges on numerous fronts. Further complicating the matter is the reality that, for some nations, self-governance continues to be a long reign of equally oppressive, dictatorial, authoritarian, or corrupt regimes and leaders.

On the other hand, the impact of colonial legacy is viewed as a positive influence by some. Mawusse Okey's (2014) assessment of the colonial legacies, analyzing econometric data from 47 African countries—18 former British colonies, 20 former French colonies, and 9 former non-British and non-French colonies—from 1994 to 2009, renders a favorable view. Arguing a positive impact of the persistent legacy on contemporary science, Okey contended that for most African nations the variety of research and education policies have been strongly influenced by former colonial powers in a positive way. He found that these legacies helped to establish efficient, open, and dynamic research models backed by comparative language advantages and political and economic institutions that support higher education policies.

Knowledge Economy: The Emergent Paradigm Shift

Beginning in the 1990s however, three evolving changes in the global landscape have advanced, and continue to advance, the role of higher education and research in the worldwide KE, especially in Asia. Moreover, they have also served somewhat of a catalyst role in narrowing the astringencies associated with the colonized/colonial dichotomy and the East-West divide. First of these is the global technological interconnectedness, which has helped standardize curriculum across nations in spite of the indigenous sociopolitical, economic, and cultural contexts. Second is the annual comparative rankings of global education institutions, which have encouraged students to seek admission to Western universities—primarily in the United States—which continue to dominate the world's highest rankings of higher education institutions, with 52 of the top 100 according to the Academic Ranking of World Universities (ARWU).[8] The 2013 *Open Doors Report on International Educational Exchange* notes that U.S. colleges and universities have 40 percent more international students than a decade ago, with a steady rise in the rate during the past three years (Institute of International Education, 2013). The *Open Doors* report also cites China, India, and South Korea as representing nearly half (49 percent) of the total 819,644 students in U.S. universities for 2012–13. Third, recognizing the role of higher education and research with regard to higher-value KE returns, governments have begun initiating plans and policies to incorporate education and research as entrepreneurial commodity. Together, these three influences are affecting a paradigm shift in institutions of higher education from teaching and learning to centers of research and innovation.

Conceptual Framework, Rationale, Methodology and Definitions

Conceptual Framework

Advancing the view that the KE is one of the key indicators of a nation's potential for economic growth, this discussion's conceptual framework incorporates a review and analysis of KE's three key corollaries used by the World Bank Group (2011): (1) collaborative academic output with regard to research and publications, (2) a nation's investment in R&D, and (3) the KE indices representing a country's overall preparedness to compete within the global KE regime. As one of the fundamental components of KE, academic output integrates the knowledge, research, and innovation achieved through any combination of inter- and intra-university and university–industry research relationships. Such partnerships enable the involved entities to sustain growth in their respective areas. Companies count on academic researchers for product innovations, and faculty gain prestige through increased competition for external research funds. Similarly, a nation's scientific progress and investment greatly depends upon public support of the R&D as well because the decisions by policy-makers can greatly influence the outcome, including international convergence and cooperation. The KE indices involve a nation's economic and institutional regimes and regulatory requirements involving tariff/nontariff constraints, and rule of law that ultimately indicate a nation's global competitive preparedness.

The Rationale

The integrated KE conceptual framework outlined above serves as a rational mechanism to analyze nations' potential for economic growth for numerous reasons. KE manifestations involve links between science and technology, innovation, global connectivity, and a nation's capacity and capability to advance R&D and information and communication technology (ICT). All of which induce economic stimulus and international competition. An integrated KE also requires acquisition or creation and dissemination of knowledge more effectively for greater economic and social development. Because of these characteristics, the very concept of KE is recognized as a key indicator to measure growth in the global economic context.

Methodology

Recognizing that an objective method to measure the KE is difficult to operationalize, the World Bank's Knowledge Assessment Methodology (KAM)[9] provides a reasonable assessment mechanism to evaluate a nation's standing amid the world's KE stage. It takes into consideration four key corollaries of the KE (Figure 3.1): economic incentive, innovation and technology, education and training, and ICT. Together, these help provide a viable comparative instrument, particularly for the Asian nations, which range from lumbering democracies such as India to government-controlled economic regimes such as China.

The KE indices include two indicators to measure a country's ability to generate, adopt, and diffuse knowledge: (1) the Knowledge Index (KI) and (2) the Knowledge Economy Index (KEI). The KI represents a simple average of the *normalized*[10] performance scores of a country or region on the key variables in three KE pillars: education and human resources, the innovation system, and ICT.

The KEI takes into consideration whether the environment is conducive for knowledge to be used effectively for economic development. It is an aggregate index that represents the overall level of development of a country or region toward the KE. The KEI is calculated based on the average of the normalized performance scores of a country or region on all four pillars related to the KE: (1) economic incentive and institutional regime (EIR) (2) education, (3) innovation, and (4) ICT index. The KI measures a country's ability to generate, adopt, and diffuse knowledge. Together, the KI and KEI provide an indication of the overall potential of knowledge development in a given country. Data from the National Science Foundation and the World Bank for 2011-2014 are used as applicable.

FIGURE 3.1: CRITERIA TO DETERMINE THE KEI AND KI RANKINGS

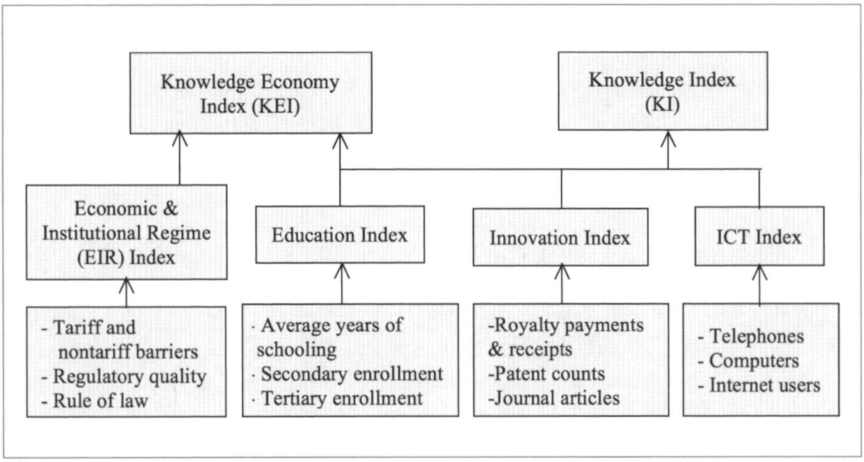

Source: The World Bank Group (2011)

Definitions

Academic output includes academic and research publication output for all disciplines. In addition to measuring the impact, the data also include overall collaborative publication output, interuniversity collaborative publication output, and university–

industry co-publication output. Such distinctions are relevant for a couple of reasons. In addition to being measurable indicators of knowledge and learning, they help to assess innovation and discovery potential, whether as creative adaptations of the exiting knowledge or new scientific knowledge. Data indices, collected by world's leading research institutions, such as the Netherlands' Center for Science and Technology Studies (CWTS) and the U.S. National Science Foundation, will be analyzed here.

R&D investment is one of the strongest and fastest-growing corollaries of the economic sector and includes a nation's public and private investment and sponsorship of research and development.

Information Communication Technology (ICT) represents the innovation strength of a nation's human resources that encompass educated, trained, and highly qualified people in technical, managerial, and interdisciplinary roles and responsibilities.

Innovation is a direct outcome of R&D. Traditionally, government actions initiate steps in creating a favorable climate to maintain and advance innovation through laws, incentives, and development and implementation of public policy. However, government-initiated public policies are a complex undertaking requiring consideration of the "indigenous ecology," which could include various challenges and constraints involving government structure, institutions, economy, and politics, as well as social, cultural, and structural norms. The Global Innovation Index (GII) composite will be analyzed to determine the global innovation output.

Knowledge Economy: The Global Trends and Asia as a Rising Power

Academic Output

The Center for Science and Technology Studies (CWTS) 2014 Report[11] provides a ranking of the world's top 500 leading academic institutions' collaborative academic output for 2009–2012. Among its top 10 universities (Table 3.1), the United States (Harvard University) and Canada (University of Toronto) rank as the top two. Third is Japan's Tokyo University, whose collaborative publication volume is significant. Among the CWTS list of 500 top academic institutions, United States ranks highest at 166 universities and 38 (8 percent) for Japan. Considering that Japan's education system was devastated in World War II, its academic advancement over the past 70 years demonstrates remarkable progress by any standards.

TABLE 3.1: GLOBAL COLLABORATIVE ACADEMIC OUTPUT 2009–2012 (ALL SCIENCES)

Rank	University	Country	P	P (collab)	P (inter-collab)	P (UI collab)
1	Harvard University	USA	56,018	47,994	23,385	3,756
2	University of Toronto	Canada	31,971	25,192	15,330	1,607
3	Tokyo University	Japan	29,341	23,033	9,136	2,291
4	Univ of Washington–Seattle	USA	26,768	20,864	8,862	1,998
5	Johns Hopkins University	USA	25,715	20,551	9,872	1,989
6	University of Michigan	USA	28,660	20,437	9,166	1,709
7	Univ of California, Los Angeles	USA	26,840	20,268	9,572	2,101
8	University College of London	UK	24,163	19,950	13,694	1,208
9	Oxford University	UK	25,244	19,787	15,073	1,595
10	Stanford University	USA	25,777	19,301	9,404	2,429

Notes: P = number of overall publications; P (collab) = collaborative publications;
P (intercollab) = interuniversity collaborative publications;
P (UI collab) = university–industry collaborative publications.

Source: Center for Science and Technology Studies (CWTS), Leiden University, 2014

Within the Asian region, five nations: Japan, China, Singapore, South Korea, and Taiwan have established themselves as dominant nations for the KE's academic output (Table 3.2).

TABLE 3.2: ASIA'S COLLABORATIVE ACADEMIC OUTPUT 2009–2012

Rank	University	Country	P	P (collab)	P (inter-collab)	P (UI collab)
1	University of Tokyo	Japan	29,341	23,033	9,136	2,291
2	Seoul National University	S. Korea	21,508	16,369	5,887	1,755
3	Kyoto University	Japan	21,501	15,824	6,208	1,661
4	National Univ of Singapore	Singapore	18,177	13,240	9,883	774
5	National Taiwan Univ	Taiwan	16,739	13,120	4,616	560
6	Osaka University	Japan	17,375	13,085	4,659	1,681
7	Peking University	China	17,296	12,592	6,547	494
8	Tohoku University	Japan	16,835	12,487	5,086	1,724
9	Zhejiang University	China	19,213	11,768	5,207	547
10	Shanghai Jiao Tong Univ	China	17,825	11,319	4,660	651

Notes: P = number of overall publications; P (collab) = collaborative publications;
P (intercollab) = interuniversity collaborative publications;
P (UI collab) = university–industry collaborative publications.

Source: Center for Science and Technology Studies (CWTS), Leiden University, 2014

Research and Development

Since university–industry collaborative academic output is a strong indicator of a nation's potential for R&D, these rankings are significant for reasons that will be discussed. The global ranking of the world's 10 regions as measured by R&D spending for 2011 by various sources shows a fast rise by East and Southeast Asia (Table 3.3). Although the United States continues to maintain its global dominance, China is closing the gap for two reasons: the U.S. federal spending's focus on defense and aerospace priorities and China's consistent adherence to its 2011–2015 Five-Year Plans. Long-term projections by the U.S. National Science Foundation (2014) and the Battelle Memorial Institute (2014) show that China is expected to continue its two-decade trajectory in R&D investment. China's research intensity is projected to increase to 1.95 percent of gross domestic product (GDP) by 2014, and Five-Year Plans are aimed at achieving 2.2 percent of GDP by 2015. This rate of growth is expected to continue through the end of the decade as China strives to transition from a manufacturing to an innovation-driven economy by 2020. At current rates of R&D investment and economic growth, China is projected to surpass the United States in total R&D spending by 2022 (Battelle Institute, 2014).

TABLE 3.3: GLOBAL R&D EXPENDITURES, BY REGION, 2011

Region	Billions of U.S. PPP dollars	Percent
North America	461.6	32.2
East and Southeast Asia	456.0	31.8
Europe	344.6	24.0
South America	35.5	2.5
South Asia	36.2	2.5
Central Asia	35.4	2.5
Middle East	30.6	2.1
Australia and Oceania	23.6	1.6
Africa	11.2	0.8
Central America & Caribbean	0.6	< 0.1
World total	1,435.3	100.0
Note: PPP = purchasing power parity		

Source: National Science Foundation (2014)

Also, although the rankings of the world's top 10 R&D-spending countries remain mostly unchanged over the past five years, in 2011 China surpassed Japan for the number two position. During the first decade of the 21st century, China has led a dramatic shift in research as well as in the way funds are spent. Although China's assertive stance on economy and politics presents both challenges and opportunities for the nations of Southeast Asia, as the world's largest region for research investments, it promises a potential that is expected to continue over the upcoming decades. Cognizant of China's emergent stature as a powerful neighbor, Southeast Asian nations are also eager to establish economic prosperity, security, and peace in the region (Baviera, 1999; Tong & Chong, 2010). China and the Association of Southeast Asian Nations (ASEAN, which includes Brunei, Burma, Cambodia, Indonesia, Laos, Malaysia, Philippines, Singapore, Thailand, and Vietnam) made an agreement in November 2004, which became effective January 1, 2010, to gradually remove tariffs and create the world's largest free-trade area. The China-ASEAN Free Trade Area (CAFTA) agreement is expected to have significant, long-term trade and development implications for the Southeast Asia region.

According to the U.S. National Science Foundation (2014), the worldwide R&D performance data for 2011 show Asia (including China, Taiwan, Japan, India, and South Korea) leading at 34 percent ($492 billion), followed by North America (United States, Canada, and Mexico) at 32 percent ($462 billion) and Europe, including (but not limited to) the European Union at 24 percent ($345 billion). China by itself is among the highest in the world at 16 percent. Japan was third at 10 percent and $146.5 billion. Combined, the top 10 countries, five of which (including the Russian Federation) are from Asia, accounted for approximately 80 percent of the world spending of $1.62 trillion invested in R&D (Table 4.4). The estimates for gross R&D expenditure for the years 2012–2014 project India ranking in eighth place, outranking the Russian Federation and replacing Taiwan (Battelle Memorial Institute, 2013) among the world's top 10 nations.

As Asia seeks to leverage global scientific knowledge and capabilities, the region's collaborations with U.S. and European technology firms and research organizations are also increasing. Combined investments by the United States, China, and Japan account for more than half of the world's total. The United States, by far the largest R&D performer at $429 billion in 2011 and accounting for just below 30 percent of the global total, has declined from 37 percent in 2001.

TABLE 3.4: INTERNATIONAL COMPARISONS OF GROSS DOMESTIC EXPENDITURES ON R&D AND R&D SHARE OF GROSS DOMESTIC PRODUCT (GDP), 2011

	Country	GERD (PPP in millions dollars)	GERD/GDP (%)
1	United States	$429,143.0	2.85
2	China	$208,171.8	1.84
3	Japan	$146,537.3	3.39
4	Germany	$93,055.5	2.88
5	South Korea	$59,890.0	4.03
6	France	$51,891.0	2.24
7	United Kingdom	$39,627.1	1.77
8	Russian Federation	$35,045.1	1.09
9	Taiwan	$26,493.1	3.02
10	Brazil	$25,340.2	1.16

GERD = gross expenditure on R&D
GERD/GDP = R&D share of gross domestic product
PPP = purchasing power parity

Source: National Science Foundation (2014)

Innovation

The Global Innovation Index (GII) composite uses 81 indicators to gauge innovation capacity, competitiveness, and the strength of national innovation networks. It is published by Cornell University, the European Institute for Business Administration (INSEAD), and the World Intellectual Property Organization. The GII ranks innovation capabilities of 183 countries and economies with two sub-indices, the Innovation Input Sub-Index and the Innovation Output Sub-Index, each built around five key pillars. These pillars capture elements of the national economy that enable innovative activities: (1) institutions, (2) human capital and research, (3) infrastructure, (4) market sophistication, and (5) business sophistication. Two output pillars capture actual evidence of innovation outputs: (1) knowledge and technology outputs and (2) creative outputs.

The 2014 GII Report focused human contribution behind the innovation process. Each pillar is divided into sub-pillars and each sub-pillar is composed of individual indicators (81 in total). Sub-pillar scores are calculated as the weighted average of individual indicators; pillar scores are calculated as the weighted average of sub-pillar scores. Four key KE indicators from the 2014 Global Innovation Index: R&D, Innovation, Education, and Information Communication Technology (ICT), also rank the Asian nations at 20 percent or better among the world's top ten nations, as shown in Table 3.5.

TABLE 3.5: THE GLOBAL INNOVATION INDEX 2014

	Innovation	Education	R&D	ICT
1	Switzerland	China	Korea, Republic	Korea
2	United kingdom	UA Emirates	USA	Netherlands
3	Sweden	Macedonia	Finland	Singapore
4	Finland	Finland	Denmark	United Kingdom
5	Netherlands	Lesotho	Sweden	USA
6	USA	New Zealand	Japan	Finland
7	Singapore	Demark	Israel	Sweden
8	Denmark	Estonia	Australia	Hong Kong, China
9	Luxemburg	Portugal	Switzerland	Australia
10	Hong Kong, China	Cyprus	Germany	Japan

Source: The Global Innovation Index 2014

Economic Incentive Regime

Although the Great Recession of 2007-2009 tested the economic strength and caused stagnation in total global output of commercial KI service industries, the growth rates for developed and developing countries were different. Developed countries' output was flat at –0.1 percent, but it grew by 4 percent in developing countries, thus shifting an increasing share of world output to the developing world. Double-digit growth in China was largely responsible for the difference, aided by India's rapid increase in output. The 2010 recovery, with 8 percent growth of global output, was also led by double-digit increases in most major developing economies, continuing the shift in global share from developed to the developing countries. During this period, both U.S. and Japanese output grew by 5 percent (NSF, 2014).

In 2010, Japan's share of commercial KI service industries—business, financial, and communications—was $900 billion, followed by China with $700 billion. From 1995 to 2010, the value-added KI of developing countries grew far faster than in the developed world more than quadrupled, from $500 billion to $2.3 trillion, whereas value-added KI of developed countries more than doubled, from $3.9 trillion to $8.6 trillion. Faster growth of KI services industries in developing countries during the last 15 years resulted in their share of global output rising from 12 percent to 21 percent. China's output rose sevenfold, tripling its world share from 2 percent to 6 percent.

Among the World Bank Group's 2012 rankings of the world's top ten economies (Table 3.6), the Asian nations represent 20 percent or better for each of the four sub-indices. The 2012 Competitive Index, an annual assessment of the long-term business environment and performance of the 146 nations for Organisation for Economic Co-operation and Development (OECD) member countries, lists Singapore at the top of the Economic Incentive Regime hierarchy. It shows Hong Kong (China) climbing

11 positions since 2000 to 5th place in the EIR rankings for 2012. Switzerland leads the innovation ranking due to its lead in number of Science and Engineering journal articles published per million people: 1,218, the highest of any country (2012, 5). In the ICT rankings, Asia's Bahrain climbed 39 levels, from 40th to first, primarily due to tenfold increase in the usage of telephone and the Internet.

TABLE 3.6: RANKING OF THE TOP TEN WORLD ECONOMIES, 2012

	Economic Incentive Regime	Innovation	Education	Information Communication Technology
1	Singapore	Switzerland	New Zealand	Bahrain
2	Finland	Sweden	Australia	Sweden
3	Denmark	Finland	Norway	Luxembourg
4	Sweden	Singapore	S. Korea	United Kingdom
5	Hong Kong, China	Demark	Greece	Netherlands
6	Switzerland	USA	Sweden	Finland
7	Canada	Netherlands	Iceland	Switzerland
8	Norway	Israel	Taiwan, China	Germany
9	Luxembourg	Taiwan, China	Ireland	Taiwan, China
10	Austria	Canada	Spain	Hong Kong, China

Source: World Bank, 2012

A review of the statistical trends lead to two emerging patterns: first, that globalization of the world economy and a vigorous pursuit of national innovation policies are creating new centers of high-technology manufacturing and knowledge-intensive societies. Second, Asia is on the upswing with China, Japan, South Korea, Singapore, and Taiwan representing emergent growth within the global and regional knowledge community.

Conclusion

This chapter set out to examine the higher education's evolving transformational role as value-added entrepreneurial commodity (i.e., the knowledge economy) in regard to economic growth of developing Asian nations within the global context. The analysis comprised of three key corollaries of the knowledge economy: collaborative academic output (research and publications); national investment for research and development (R&D); and impact of the integrated KE manifestations and mechanisms (national policy) on a country's overall preparedness to compete in the KE sector. With due recognition of the historical context concerning the East-West/colonized-colonial divide, the argument was that three evolving changes—the global technological inter-connectedness; the impact of the annual comparative rankings of global education institutions bolstering Asian students' admissions to Western (primarily, American) academic institutions; and governments' support of plans and policies to incorporate education and research as entrepreneurial priority—have helped level the field thus facilitate Asia's ascent to economic growth.

Statistical trends for the past two decades reveal two patterns. First, there is a positive correlation between the Asian nations' fast economic growth and their vigorous pursuit of national innovation policies to create new centers of high-technology manufacturing and knowledge-intensive societies. Second, although global trends confirm U.S. preeminence in science and engineering, there is a decided shift in the previously established norms and expectations. During 1995–2011, Asia's KE share has risen to nearly one-third, mostly because of China's rapid R&D growth, as opposed to the traditional front-runners: the United States and the European countries. The doubling of the researcher community in South Korea, Taiwan, China, and Singapore from 16 percent to 31 percent during 1990–2005 adds to the shifting role of the KE in the 21st century. The dynamics of economic development for the Asian region are also creating new global partnerships and collaborations, which bode well not only for the developing societies but also the world at large.

Asia's evolving patterns and trends demonstrate the importance of the higher education KE in advancing socioeconomic development. However, this transformation also signifies multidimensional manifestations on societies, whether democratic or government-controlled political systems. While the contemporary "virtual theatre" connectivity has helped dissipate the complex, historical East-West/colonized-colonial dichotomy discussed earlier, debate about the term "development" has given rise to new questions about the role of higher education in transforming the Asian economies. A case in point is the matter of some East Asia nations' fast economic ascent in spite of their general disregard for "good" governance principles. In that regard, Ray Kiely's (1999, 2007) argument that development is about choices with outcomes that may be positive, negative, or questionable, invites further inquiry. Should intensification of economic gains be the prerequisite for advancement, or should the principles of good governance advocating democracy, transparency, the rule of law, and human rights? On the other hand, the recent political sea change in India, a paradoxical example of a lurching democracy with 65 percent of its population under the age of 35, promises a continuing experiment involving higher education's KE dynamics toward Asia's still emergent economic growth.

REFERENCES

Baviera, Aileen, S. P. (1999). *China's relations with Southeast Asia: Political security and economic interests.* PASCN Discussion Paper No. 99-17. Retrieved from http://hilo.hawaii.edu/uhh/faculty/tamvu/documents/baviera.pdf

Brattelle Memorial Institute. (2014). *2014 Global R&D Funding Forecast.* The Business of Innovation. Retrieved from http://www.battelle.org/docs/tpp/2014_global_rd_funding_forecast.pdfBlack

Bush, V. (1945). *Science, the endless frontier. A report to the president on a program for postwar scientific research.* Washington, DC: Office of Scientific Research and Development. Reprinted in 1990 by the U. S. National Science Foundation. Retrieved from http://www.nsf.gov/od/lpa/nsf50/vbush1945.htm

Center for Science and Technology Studies, Leiden University. (2014). *CWTS Leiden Ranking 2014.* Retrieved from http://www.leidenranking.com/

Cheah, P. (2006, November). *The limits of thinking in decolonial strategies.* Retrieved from http://townsendcenter.berkeley.edu/publications/limits-thinking-decolonial-strategies

Cowen, R. (2005, January 10–11). *Universities and the KE.* Paper presented at the Advancing Knowledge and the KE Conference. Washington, DC. Retrieved from http://www.merit.unu.edu/publications/rmpdf/2005/rm2005-027.pdf

Duderstadt, J. J. (2007). The Midwest Region and the Knowledge Economy A: Roadmap to the Future. Retrieved from http://milproj.ummu.umich.edu/pdfs/Midwest%20Media%20Project.pdf

Escobar, A. (1992).Imagining a Post-Development Era? Critical Thought, Development and Social Movements. *Social Text*, No. 31/32, pp. 20-56. Durham, NC: Duke University Press.

Etzkowitz, H. (1993). Technology transfer: The second academic revolution. *Technology Access Report*, Vol. 6, p. 7-9.

Etzkowitz, H., & Leydesdorff, E., Eds.. (1997). *Universities and the global knowledge economy: A triple helix of university-industry-government relations.* London, UK: Cassell Academic.

Frank, A. G. (1998). *ReOrient: Global economy in the Asian age.* Berkeley: University of California Press.

Giebel, M. (2013). Digital Divide, Knowledge and Innovations. *Journal of Information, Information Technology, and Organizations*, Vol. 8, p 1-24.

Goldstone, J. A. (2008). Capitalist origins, the advent of modernity, and coherent explanation: A response to Joseph M. Bryant. *The Canadian Journal of Sociology, 33*(1), 119–133.

Institute of International Education. (2013, November 11). *Open doors 2013: International students in the United States and study abroad by American Students are at all-time high* [Press release]. Retrieved from http://www.iie.org/Who-We-Are/News-and-Events/Press-Center/Press-releases/2013/2013-11-11-Open-Doors-Data

Jacob, M. C. (2014). *The first KE human capital and the European economy, 1750–1850.* New York, NY: Cambridge University Press.

Kiely, R. (1999). The last refuge of the noble savage? A critical assessment of post-development theory. *The European Journal of Development Research, 11,* 30–55.

Kiely, R. (2007). *The new political economy of development: Globalization, imperialism, hegemony.* Basingstoke: Palgrave Macmillan.

Kuznets, S. (1965). *Economic growth and structure.* New York, NY: WW Norton.

Lee, J. Z., & Wang, F. (2009). *One Quarter of the Humanity.* Cambridge, Mass: Harvard University Press.

Letter from President Franklin D. Roosevelt to Vannevar Bush, Director, Office of Scientific Research and Development, November 17, 1944, retrieved from: http://www.nsf.gov/od/lpa/nsf50/vbush1945.htm#letter

Mignolo, W. D. (2002). The geopolitics of knowledge and the colonial difference. *South Atlantic Quarterly, 101*(1), 57–96.

Mokyr, J. (2002). *The gifts of Athena: Historical Origins of the Knowledge Economy.* Princeton, NJ: Princeton University Press. Retrieved from http://www.nes.ru/NES10/cd/materials/Mokyr-2chapters.pdf

National Science Foundation. (2014). *Science and engineering indicators 2014.* Arlington, VA. Retrieved from http://www.nsf.gov/statistics/seind14/index.cfm/chapter-4/c4h.htm

Okey, Mawusse, K. N. (2014). The scientific research wealth of African Nations: Do colonial origins matter? *International Journal of Education Economics and Development, 5*(1), 113–125.

Parenti, M. (2011). *The face of Imperialism.* Boulder, CO: Paradigm.

Pomeranz, K. 2000. *The great divergence: China, Europe, and the making of the modern world economy.* Princeton, NJ: Princeton University Press.

Quah, D. (2000). *Cross-country growth comparison: Theory to empirics* (CEP discussion paper 442). London, UK: Centre for Economic Performance, London School of Economics and Political Science.

Said, E. W. (1979). *Orientalism.* New York: Vintage Press.

The Global Innovation Index 2014: The Human Factor in Innovation. *The 2014 Country Rankings.* Retrieved from https://www.globalinnovationindex.org/content.aspx?page=data-analysis

The World Bank Group (2013). *Digital Divide.* Retrieved from http://web.worldbank.org/WBSITE/EXTERNAL/TOPICS/EXTEDUCATION/0,,contentMDK:20640041~menuPK:617592~pagePK:148956~piPK:216618~theSitePK:282386,00.html

The World Bank Group. (2012). *Knowledge Economy Index Rankings.* Retrieved from http://siteresources.worldbank.org/INTUNIKAM/Resources/2012.pdf

The World Bank Group. (2012). *Normalization Procedure.* Retrieved from http://web.worldbank.org/WBSITE/EXTERNAL/WBI/WBIPROGRAMS/KFDLP/EXTUNIKAM/0,,contentMDK:20584281~menuPK:1433234~pagePK:64168445~piPK:64168309~theSitePK:1414721,00.html

Tong, S. Y., & Chong, C. S. K. (2010). *China-ASEAN Free Trade Area in 2010: A regional perspective.* EAI Background Brief No. 519. Retrieved from http://www.eai.nus.edu.sg/BB519.pdf

Wong, R. B. (1997). *China transformed: Historical change and the limits of European experience.* Ithaca, NY: Cornell University Press.

NOTES

[1] A number of historians and historical sociologists identified as the "California School" have opposed the Eurocentrism view. Advancing their viewpoint, Goldstone (2008) suggested that whatever their institutional and cultural differences, there was in fact no significant divergence of material in living standards in Europe from those in the advanced Asian societies until much later, circa 1800. For further details, see Goldstone's (2008) article.

[2] See Goldstone's response to Bryant, J. T. (2006) article, The West and the Rest Revisited: Debating Capitalist Origins, European Colonialism, and the Advent of Modernity, *The Canadian Journal of Sociology*, 31(4): 403-444.

[3] The Postdevelopment School argues "development" to be unjust and unworkable in the "developing" societies, as it represents the Western concepts of development with total disregard to indigenous cultural, economic, and social ecology. Among its key proponents are A. Escobar, G. Esteva, M. Rahnema, W. Sachs, J. Ferguson, S. Latouche, Ashis Nandy, G. Rist, F. Sabelli and several others.

4 Cheah (2006) offered a succinct summary of Walter Mignolo'a (2002) "decoloniality": "*it involves two key gestures: first, the re-embodiment and relocation of thought in order to unmask the limited situation of modern knowledges and their link to coloniality, and second, another thinking that calls for plurality and intercultural dialogue.*"

5 See Bush, V. (1945), *Science–the Endless Frontier.* Washington, DC: Government Printing Office, pg. 3 at http://www.nsf.gov/od/lpa/nsf50/vbush1945.htm#letter

6 A public policy intellectual and an avid inventor, Bush is considered to be the first science policy advisor to a president of the United States.

7 A linear model defines the roles played by different actors and institutions regarding R&D and funding. It refers to a general idea that basic R&D provides the foundational knowledge for applied R&D, which provides the foundational knowledge for innovation, which then becomes a good to be diffused to users. The process is linear, with one stage feeding the next, and it is unidirectional. In this model, the role of universities is to do the basic R&D, thereby providing the foundational knowledge, information, data, instrumentation, and so on (Cowen, 2005).

8 The 2014 Academic Ranking of World Universities (ARWU) is compiled by the Center for World-Class Universities at Shanghai Jiao Tong University, China.

9 Knowledge Assessment Methodology, as used by the World Bank Group (2011), utilizes variables that are measured in different units and on different scales. Methodology details to calculate the KEI and KI are available at the World Bank Group website: http://go.worldbank.org/SDDP3I1T40

10 To calculate aggregate knowledge economy indices, as well as to simplify graphic representation of countries' comparative performance, all the indicators are brought to the same standard of measurement through the process known as *normalization.*

11 The CWTS Leiden university annual Global University Ranking is based exclusively on bibliometric data from the Web of Science database of Thomson Reuters (Scientific), Inc., Philadelphia, Pennsylvania, USA.

Chapter Four

Systemic Challenges to Educational Quality and Global Competitiveness

Simon Marginson, UCL Institute of Education, United Kingdom

Introduction

This chapter focuses on higher education and research in three regions: South Asia, Southeast Asia, and Northeast Asia (hereinafter, Northeast Asia will be referred to as simply "East Asia"). The chapter discusses the processes, growth and challenges, and the strengths and limits of national systems. Higher education in South, Southeast, and East Asia combines instances of remarkable progress with great unevenness and continued constraints. However, the strengths and limits of the post-Confucian model of higher education and science in Sinic East Asia and Singapore will compose the main discussion in the chapter.

Education and Modernization

Everywhere the world nations have achieved or are moving to high-participation tertiary education[1] systems, enrolling more than half of those leaving secondary school. Nations are at different points on the trajectory. Participation expands in fits and starts. But as Table 4.1 suggests, all except very poor countries are on this path. The growth of tertiary participation is broadly consistent with economic growth but does not move in lockstep with expanding markets for high-skill labor. Rather, tertiary qualifications become attached to a growing proportion of jobs across the occupational structure and down the scale of rewards. The inexorable growth in participation is primarily driven by middle-class demand for social position through education. As Adam Smith stated in *The Wealth of Nations*, first published in 1776, "The desire of bettering our condition ... comes with us from the womb, and never leaves us till we go into the grave" (Smith, 1979/1776, p. 441).

TABLE 4.1: GROSS TERTIARY ENROLLMENT RATIO BY WORLD REGION, 1995 AND 2011

Region	1995 %	2011 %
North America and Western Europe	60	77
Central and Eastern Europe	33	68
Latin America and the Caribbean	17	42
East Asia and Pacific	10	30
Central Asia	23	24
Arab States	14	23
South and West Asia	6	18
Sub-Saharan Africa	4	8
WORLD	15	30

Source: UNESCO (2014)

Once participation reaches the mass level, tertiary qualifications, principally degrees, become a normal requirement for families aspiring to a modern middle-class life. The state becomes the facilitator rather than creator of the social demand for degrees, as was noted by Trow (1974) in his famous essay on the transition from elite to mass to universal higher education. The demand for advanced education is no longer determined by supply and becomes self-reinforcing. When participation takes in the majority of the age group, the rate Trow (1974) tagged as "universal," those without tertiary education incur substantial penalties. Advanced education is no longer a choice; rather, it has become a "defensive necessity" (Hirsch, 1976). For the urban middle class, higher education degrees no longer guarantee personal career success. But, without a degree, prospects of entering professional work are weak. Even opportunities in business are affected by levels of education. Thus the social demand for advanced levels of education moves in correlation not with labor markets or state labor-power planning but with the growth of the urban middle classes, defined by Kharas (2010) for the Organisation for Economic Co-operation and Development (OECD) as those living on $10 to $100 per day.[2] From 1995 to 2011, in less than one generation, the worldwide gross tertiary enrollment rate (GTER) doubled from 15 to 30 percent (Table 4.1). It rose sharply in every major region except Central Asia. It passed 50 percent across all of Europe. In East Asia and the Pacific, the GTER rose from 10 to 30 percent, exceeding 50 percent in all systems other than China and Vietnam (UNESCO, 2014).

By 2030 the Asian middle classes are expected to grow to several times their present size, to more than 3 billion people, primarily because of mobility in India and China from rural life to the modern urban-based economy (Vasconcelos, 2012). There will be an immense expansion of tertiary education to meet the growing demand. The known unknowns are the forms of supply and the quality of production.

Nation-Building States and Higher Education

In nearly all countries, governments continue to regulate the number of tertiary students. Policies on infrastructure affect supply. In most countries, governments subsidize some or all enrollments, and in many, they focus on extending participation to underrepresented social groups. States maintain the fiction that higher education expands to fulfill economic needs for human capital. The reality is more prosaic and political. All states, whatever the regime, depend on popular consent. They also find it cheaper to provide education than to provide jobs to soak up unemployment—and through education, state responsibility for economic outcomes is transferred into the self-responsibility of individuals, reducing pressures on government. In all countries, except the very poorest, it is inevitable that sooner or later government must facilitate the growing middle class demand for more places in tertiary education.

The state retains a more determining role in relation to research and science. Advanced science was once limited to a small proportion of countries in North America, Europe, and Japan. Building research capacity has now become part of the core responsibility of all states, though not all can afford it. To access worldwide innovations in science and technology, national economies need their own capability in science, their own trained people, and their own capacity to train people in government laboratories and universities. Because research is largely a public good subject to market failure (Stiglitz, 1999), it depends on state investment. Though it is irreducibly expensive, which rules out the poorest nations, middle-income countries are now building science. Between 1997 and 2011 the number of nations publishing more than 1,000 science papers a year increased from 38 to 51 (National Science Foundation [NSF], 2014). The growing emphasis on research has been joined with widely distributed national policies designed to achieve "world-class universities," that is, higher education institutions (HEIs) listed in the world top 100, 200, or 500 in the research rankings (Salmi, 2009).

Whether the state is creator or facilitator of higher education, the prevailing political culture always matters. Neither economic growth, labor markets, nor middle-class demand can alone launch a higher education system. Across all three Asian regions, higher education is closely influenced by the development and character of the state. In emerging systems, the capability and focus of the state are crucial to building infrastructure, teaching programs, student participation, and, later, research. In general, where the state is fragmented, weak, corrupt, or lacking coherent policies, the potential of higher education is limited, and research cannot begin. The role of the state is maximized at the foundation stages. Once higher education and indigenous science are established on an institutional basis, the imperatives change. It is especially important for research universities to nurture the operational autonomous strategic capacity of university leaders and the independent agency of faculty. Research universities also need to encourage direct relations between, on one hand, HEIs, and on the other hand, cities and localities, professions, employers, and higher education and science beyond the national border. However, state dependence never evaporates altogether. Government remains crucial to the funding of research even in the strongest systems.

At the same time, political cultures and state traditions vary within Asia, as they do across the world. University autonomy is not a wholly universal quality. It is also nested in differing histories and cultures. In East Asia and Singapore, even in high-participation higher education systems with established research, the state retains closer supervision than occurs in India and in some non-Asian systems including those of Western Europe and the English-speaking world. There is more than one way to sustain a high-performing higher education system. The U.S. and UK model—still the template of global rankings and World Bank development programs—is not the only possible idea of a university. By the same token, it would be misleading to argue that the comprehensive Sinic state is essential to maintaining advanced science universities and achieving high rates of tertiary participation, in Asia or anywhere else. Nevertheless, it is clear that this kind of state is effective in the accelerated development of higher education, under the right economic and cultural conditions.

South Asia

South Asia, historically dominated by India, also includes Pakistan, Bangladesh, Sri Lanka, Nepal, Bhutan, and the Maldives. Urbanization is proceeding, but is not as advanced as in East Asia. Gross domestic product (GDP) per capita and government spending levels are lower than in East Asia. From 1995 to 2011 the GTER in India rose from 6 to 23 percent. In 2011 the GTER was 15 percent in Sri Lanka, 14 percent in Nepal, 13 percent in Bangladesh, and only 8 percent in Pakistan (UNESCO, 2014).

Like all middle classes, the South Asian middle classes want higher education and social mobility for their children, but commitment to education does not permeate the population from top to bottom as in East Asia. The extension of participation depends crucially on state intervention and subsidization, as does research. However, in India and Pakistan, subregional languages, cultures, and administrations are often dominant. There is much variation by state and district. In India small and antiquated private colleges sit alongside unreformed public universities, joined to an incoherent mix of foreign initiatives. Individual states do not have sufficient tax revenue to lift higher education and research to a new level. National leadership is imagined. Higher education and research and development (R&D) are discussed in Delhi. There are research concentration schemes and legislation on foreign and private ventures. But there is no common national policy framework and reform dynamic. This is a major constraint (Agarwal, 2009). The Indian Institutes of Technology appear to be a successful model of elite education primarily because they remain small and select only high-achieving students. After a long period of slow growth, Indian research is increasing rapidly—between the year 2000 and 2011 the number of science papers rose from 10,276 to 22,481 (NSF, 2014)—but this growth is localized and the country still lacks a coherent strategy for developing its science system. In Pakistan, elite higher education and research are more scattered and localized than in India. Pakistan produces only one research paper for every 100,000 people, compared to 15,000 in China and 1,500 in the United States (NSF, 2014). In Bangladesh and Nepal, where per-capita GDP is less than half that of India, lack of resources blocks capacity building in science. Sri Lanka is better resourced, and the failure to develop an indigenous research system can only be attributed to lack of political will.

South Asia is a region of immense intellectual potential and the source of much of the world's mobile skilled labor. It is also a problematic case of higher education development. It would be pointless to argue that the region needs comprehensive states along East Asian lines, because the history is very different. It may be possible to develop national coordination without relying on extensive top-down intervention, thus avoiding the negatives of top-down models. If national policy can gain a more effective purchase in building capacity and resources, without constraining local and regional evolution, many things become possible. There is no sign of it happening yet.

Southeast Asia

Southeast Asia is less readily defined. It is a patchwork of distinct cultures and systems with unequal economic and educational resources. The region comprises nations that in geographical and historical-cultural terms lie between India and China. Further back in history it was more influenced by Hindu-Buddhism from India. More recently, Chinese immigration and commercial activity have played a dominant role.

Southeast Asia has been variously shaped also by Islam, European colonization, and global modernization (Joseph & Matthews, 2014). At present, China's growing power, and to a lesser extent investment and aid from Korea and Japan, are important factors. These nations constitute the intergovernmental Association of Southeast Asian Nations (ASEAN): Indonesia, Malaysia, the oil sultanate Brunei, Vietnam, Cambodia, Lao PDR (People's Democratic Republic), Myanmar (Burma), Thailand, the Philippines. Wealthy Singapore is also in ASEAN.

In most of Southeast Asia the drivers of education in the family are weaker than in East Asia. As in South Asia, the extension of participation is closely affected by both economic growth and state policies. Economic and governmental capacity varies. Thailand and Malaysia are middle-income countries with GTERs of 53 and 36 percent, respectively (UNESCO, 2014). Not all the ingredients for an East Asian style take-off are in place. In Malaysian public universities, research science is finally lifting after two decades of policy talk about the knowledge economy, and in the parallel private sector, the best colleges sustain student-friendly business models. However, tertiary participation is uneven by region, and the public universities are overly dependent on state funding. Much investment is squandered on benefits for affluent middle-class families who could be sharing costs. Most seriously, performance cultures are stymied by ethnic preference in favor of Bumiputra (predominantly ethnic Malay) vis-à-vis the Chinese and Indian populations. Ethnic preference corrupts meritocratic decision making in the selection of students, appointment of faculty, performance management and promotion of faculty, and competitive allocation of research grants. There are persistent anecdotes concerning students and high-quality researchers from Indian and Chinese backgrounds unable to secure funding support (Mukherjee & Wong, 2011). A further problem in Malaysia, as in many Asian systems, is that universities are tied closely to the ministry via state-appointed vice chancellors. The combination of arbitrary political intervention and nonmeritocratic values blocks world-class university development. In Thailand, recent policy has been lackadaisical within an unstable political system, but the growing middle class and an expanding private sector continue to sustain the growth of participation, and science paper output is growing fast, suggesting the presence of strong indigenous intellectual cultures. Thailand might to be an exception to the rule that an effective state is key to the evolution of higher education, though research universities in the top 200 have yet to appear.

Emerging Indonesia has 17,508 islands, 300 language groups, and profound problems of national coordination. The GTER reached 27 percent in 2011, but tertiary education is grossly underfunded, and there is uneven quality in the private sector, which has the majority of students. There is also little research activity. The Philippines achieved a GTER of 27 percent as early as 1995, but there has been little change since. National economic development is slow, and the state struggles to gain purchase amid chronic neo-colonialism, regional fragmentation, and crony politics. The leading state universities have been allowed to decline. Research is at the same level as Indonesia. In poorer Cambodia and Myanmar, national resources and state machinery are not yet sufficient for system building. There are signs of progress in Myanmar, where the GTER increased from 5 to 14 percent between 1995 and 2011. Authoritarian controls have been reduced, and international aid is now welcome. Cambodia has experienced sharper growth in the GTER, from 1 to 16 percent, but the Royal University of Phnom Penh is poorly resourced and lacks an authentic national mission, while in the private sector, where most of the growth is concentrated, quality is weak. There is no evidence of authentic state planning. However in Lao PDR, with the same per-capita income as Cambodia, a modernizing and focused state is making progress in both participation and the beginnings of research. Again, it is apparent that the capacity of the state to formulate a medium-term agenda for the development of higher education and to implement that agenda coherently in transparent fashion is as important as resources per se in moving forward in this sector. With the partial exception of Thailand, those Southeast Asian systems that have made significant progress toward high-participation and research-intensive universities owe their success to effective state interventions. This is even clearer in East Asia.

East Asia: The Post-Confucian Systems

The East Asian countries and education systems lie within the historical boundaries of Chinese (Sinic) civilization: mainland China, Hong Kong and Macau SARs, Taiwan, South Korea, and Japan. Arguably, Vietnam shares this geocultural region, as does the nonadjacent island state of Singapore in Southeast Asia, whose political, economic, and educational cultures are primarily Sinic. Though there are differences in language and political system, and tensions within the group, all sustain the comprehensive form of state that developed 2,200 years ago in Qin and Han China. East Asian countries do not exhibit the state/society and state/market tensions typical of the English-speaking world with its limited liberal states. Nor was East Asia closely affected by the egalitarian upheavals of the French revolution and 19th-century social democracy. Whether in single-party or multiparty polities, national states in East Asia exhibit strong continuity and a characteristically long-term view. Government posts enjoy high social status, attracting many of the best graduates. The Sinic state is not a welfare state—the Sinic family has a larger role than in Europe and North America—but it exercises overall responsibility for social order and prosperity. Though the Sinic state does not administer society in detail, it is supreme vis-à-vis economies and cities and intervenes at will (Gernet, 1996). The present East Asian state intervenes in education and science, which are seen as strategically significant.

The Sinic systems also share a common heritage of Confucian learning practices in the family (Zhao & Biesta, 2011). From infancy, self-cultivation through education is part of the mutual responsibilities of parent and child, even in poor families. It is believed that success in education derives primarily from effort, not talent. There is a broader and deeper commitment to learning than is found in other societies.

In addition to these elements from tradition, all Sinic countries have undergone an accelerated modernization stimulated first by imperial intervention and later by global competition. The central state goal to "catch up to the West," in education and elsewhere, has been made feasible by sustained high economic growth. One feature of the Sinic state is its capacity to mobilize the population on the basis of deep common commitment. While East Asian states play an essential role in developing educational infrastructure and in funding the leading universities and the science system, they do so in tandem with strong drivers in the household (Marginson, 2011). Intense family investment in tuition beyond the formal classroom combines with societywide pride in "rising China," "rising Korea," and so forth. The term *post-Confucian* captures something of the way that inner tradition has become hybridized with modernization pressures—external pressures that have been absorbed into personal and national identity.

In the last two decades the evolution of higher education and research in the East Asian nations has been very dynamic—except in Japan, which underwent accelerated modernization earlier, during the 1960s to 1980s. East Asia and Singapore now constitute one of the world's three leading regions in science and innovation, along with North America and Western Europe . In 2011 East Asia and Singapore invested $448 billion in R&D, already a third of the global total and just below the $453 billion spent in the United States and Canada. Europe, including the United Kingdom, allocated $320 billion (NSF, 2014). In the future, East Asia and Singapore will produce much of the world's scientific discoveries and applications.

The ambiguous exception is Vietnam. It is part of ASEAN, but despite recurring border tensions with China, it is also shaped by Sinic state traditions and Confucian educational cultivation at home. It is sometimes said that Vietnam uses China to beat China and thus sustains its independence. But, at present, higher education in Vietnam is the one Sinic system yet to share the common dynamism (Tran et al., 2014). The country has 40 percent of China's per-capita income (World Bank, 2014), the disciplined and meritocratic East Asian state is absent, corruption undermines performance, and higher education policy is inauthentic. Vietnam's present political culture derives not only from Sinic and local heritage but also from the alliance with the Soviet Union in its final period (1960–1990). Many current Vietnamese officials received training in the Eastern bloc countries and absorbed the habits of the decaying Soviet machine.

Participation

The GTERs in South Korea and Taiwan are exceptional. As Figure 4.1 shows, the GTER of South Korea was at 101 percent in 2011, the highest in the world, and Taiwan's GTER was 84 percent in 2010, not far below North America.[3]

FIGURE 4.1: GROSS TERTIARY ENROLLMENT RATES, EAST ASIA AND SINGAPORE, 2011

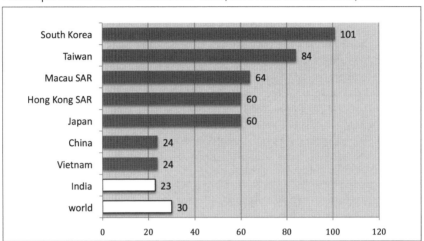

Source: UNESCO (2014) and the World Factbook (CIA, 2014). Data for Singapore not available. Red bars indicate post-Confucian education systems. For a discussion of gross enrollment ratios that explains why South Korea exceeds 100 percent, see text.

In Japan and Hong Kong, the GTER was 60 percent. In Hong Kong SAR and Singapore, participation has been expanded primarily by the increasing numbers of students in subdegree programs and/or the fee-paying private sector, with little change in the cohort proportion in high-quality, research-intensive universities. Likewise in Japan and Korea, most of the leading research universities are state institutions (exceptions are Keio and Waseda in Japan, and Yonsei, Korea University, and Postech in Korea), while at lower levels of status, the majority of students are enrolled in private universities and colleges. These private sectors are the low-unit-cost, demand-responsive sectors, which are growing as participation rates increase and contracting with demographic downturns. Korea and Taiwan also have relatively strong vocational sectors alongside their academic institutions. As the example of Germany also shows, countries with high-quality manufacturing sectors are best placed to support strong vocational HEIs.

In China the GTER increased from 4 percent in 1990 to 24 percent in 2011 and 30 percent by 2014. There is pronounced variation by region, reflecting inequalities in income per capita, patterns of industrialization and urbanization, and infrastructure development. In Beijing and Shanghai in 2010, the GTER had reached 60 percent, but it was 15 percent in Tibet and 18 percent in the Yunnan region (P. Yang, 2014). China's official national target is 40 percent in 2020. Figure 4.2 shows that the growth of the GTER was proportional to growth in per-capita income until the late 1990s, when the central government stepped up investment in leading universities and sanctioned the expansion of infrastructure and student numbers at the provincial level. Participation was normalized, social demand began to feed on itself, and subsequent growth in the GTER far outstripped the growth of economic wealth. Growing mass education has been accompanied by high early graduate unemployment, as graduates search for first jobs while adjusting their expectations downwards. This in itself is not a problem for the state (though it is a problem for displaced workers without qualifications), unless graduates continue to retain higher expectations about jobs than their qualifications can deliver. In 2014 China announced that 600 HEIs would be remade as vocational institutes, establishing a dual-track sector parallel to the German and Korean systems. The first vocational *gaokao* (end-of-school examination) was conducted in June 2014 (Postiglione, 2014). This development is consistent with high-skill manufacturing. Perhaps, also, the state is more comfortable about managing unemployed technically trained graduates than unemployed generic graduates in humanities or business.

FIGURE 4.2: TRENDS IN PER-CAPITA GDP (PPP, CONSTANT PRICES) AND GROSS TERTIARY ENROLLMENT RATIO (%), CHINA, 1980–2012

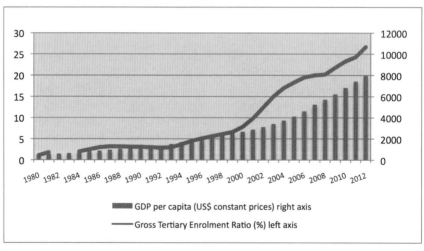

Notes: Constant 2005 U.S. dollars. PPP = purchasing power parity.
Sources: World Bank (2014) and UNESCO (2014).

In East Asia secondary education is intensely competitive, culminating in end-of-school examinations that determine who enters the high-prestige universities that are the fast track to stellar careers. Confucian self-formation in the home, a teaching profession in good standing, extra classes after school, and private tutoring all contribute to exceptional levels of learning. East Asia and Singapore dominate the OECD's comparison of student learning achievement at age 15, the Program for International Student Assessment (PISA). In the 2012 PISA statistics, the seven systems leading in mathematics were all post-Confucian. They did almost as well in PISA science and reading. Even Vietnam, with a per-capita income of only 10 percent of the United States in 2013, does better than both the United States and the United Kingdom in all three PISA disciplines.

TABLE 4.2: EAST ASIA, SINGAPORE, AND SELECTED OTHERS IN THE OECD'S PROGRAM FOR INTERNATIONAL STUDENT ASSESSMENT (PISA), 15-YEAR OLDS, MATHEMATICS, 2012

School System	Position in PISA Table for Learning Achievement of 15-Year-Olds in Mathematics(n = 65)	Mean Score in PISA Mathematics	Proportion of All Students in The Top PISA Group (Levels 5–6) %	Proportion of All Students in The Bottom PISA Group (Level 1) %
OECD Average	—	494	12.6	23.1
Shanghai, China	1	613	55.4	3.8
Singapore	2	573	40.0	8.3
Hong Kong China SAR	3	561	33.7	8.5
Taiwan	4	560	37.2	12.8
South Korea	5	554	30.9	9.1
Macao China SAR	6	538	24.3	10.8
Japan	7	536	23.7	11.1
Switzerland	9	531	21.4	12.4
Germany	16	514	17.5	17.7
Vietnam	17	511	13.3	14.2
United Kingdom	26	494	11.8	21.8
Russia	34	482	7.8	24.0
United States	36	481	8.8	25.8

Source: OECD (2014)

As Table 4.2 shows, not only are the average PISA scores very high, the size of the highest-achieving group is large, and there are few students in the lowest achieving group. In Singapore, 40.0 percent of students are in Levels 5–6 in PISA compared to 8.8 percent in the United States. Only 8.3 percent of Singapore students are in the bottom group in PISA compared to 25.8 percent in the United States (OECD, 2014). Post-Confucian societies are not egalitarian, but student learning achievement is distributed on a relatively egalitarian basis without a trade-off between equity and excellence. It is impressive.

The massive social effort to maximize teenage performance has downstream costs, however. Once selected by high-demand HEIs, most students coast through first degrees that nearly everyone passes. Such is the potency of end-of-school selection and its de facto credentials that first-degree performance and graduate education are unimportant. A chronic problem in East Asia is the weak interest in graduate studies and difficulty in establishing systems of lifelong learning, beyond informal and tacit learning at work. This is one of the limitations of the post-Confucian model.

Research and World-Class Universities

The drive toward comparative excellence also animates university research. In the last two decades all countries in the region have increased R&D at a rapid rate, except Japan, where the research take-off occurred two decades before, and Hong Kong SAR, whose allocation to research is modest. In 2011 South Korea invested 4.03 percent of GDP in R&D, the second highest such proportion in the world after Israel. China's R&D investment rose by more than 18 percent a year from 2000 to 2011. By 2011 it was 1.84 percent of GDP, higher than the United Kingdom. Total R&D funding was second only to the United States (NSF, 2014). While only 8 percent of R&D money reaches universities, half the U.S. proportion, university science has grown rapidly. Research is closely tailored to centrally determined disciplinary priorities and joined to strategies for building capacity and continually improved outputs. Singapore and China especially, and to a lesser extent other systems, pursue internationalization strategies designed to force early and rapid improvement, such as benchmarking with leading American universities and providing incentives to publish in English in leading journals (Wang, Wang, & Liu, 2011). Taiwan, Korea, and China have pursued successful policies designed to attract back overseas-trained nationals at postdoctoral and mid-career stages. Singapore, Hong Kong, and selected institutions and research fields in China offer internationally competitive salaries.

Published scientific research is increasing almost as quickly as funding. Between 1995 and 2011, the number of journal articles authored or co-authored by Chinese scholars rose by 16.5 percent a year. The number of published papers grew by 13.6 percent a year in Korea, 9.6 percent in Singapore, and 7.9 percent in Taiwan.

FIGURE 4.3: GROWTH IN THE NUMBER OF JOURNAL PAPERS PUBLISHED PER YEAR IN CHINA, SOUTH KOREA, TAIWAN, SINGAPORE, AND THE UNITED KINGDOM, 1997–2011

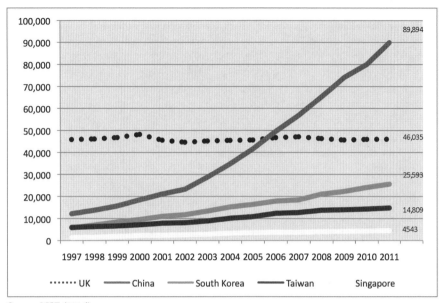

Source: NSF (2014)

Figure 4.3 compares these patterns to the constant output of the UK research system. It is often argued that East Asian scientific research has yet to prove itself, because the quality is lower than in the United States and Western Europe, as measured by citation rates. Average citation rates are much lower than in the leading English-language countries, Germany, and the smaller Northwest European systems: Switzerland, Sweden, Denmark, Finland, and the Netherlands. But relative quality is changing. Average citations are high in Singapore—the National University of Singapore has a research profile similar to a strong UK university—and fairly strong in Hong Kong SAR, which, like Singapore, is fluent in English. Citations in China, Korea, and Taiwan are improving rapidly. Take chemistry. In the year 2000, China published 3.7 percent of all papers in chemistry. In 2012 that proportion had reached 16.9 percent, and China's quantity of chemistry papers exceeded that of the United States. More strikingly, in 2000 Chinese researchers authored or co-authored just 0.6 percent of chemistry papers ranked in the top 1 percent on citation rate. Only 12 years later, in 2012, China published 16.3 percent of the leading 1 percent of papers, half as many as the United States—an astonishing improvement. There were similar patterns in engineering, physics, computing science—China publishes more top 1 percent papers in computing than the United States—and mathematics (NSF, 2014).

China, Taiwan, Korea, Japan, and, to some degree, Singapore have concentrated research development in the physical sciences and related applied fields like engineering, computing science, and materials science. In Korea and Japan this research focus supports advanced manufacturing. China emphasizes research related to accelerated modernization: energy, urbanization, construction, transport, and communications. In 2010 the government allocated 88.4 billion yuan to research in engineering and technology, 18.8 billion yuan to the natural sciences, 8.5 billion to agriculture, and only 5.0 billion yuan to medicine (Gao, 2014). The most recent development is a surge in papers in bioscience, but from a low base (Nature Publishing Index, 2014). Given aging populations in Japan and Korea, and China with its one-child policy, not to mention developments in biomedicine, the neglect of health-related science might become a constraint. The larger issue is the low status of humanities and social sciences, where there is no clearcut economic rationale for investment and the disciplines contribute little to global ranking performance. Social science research is underfunded across East Asia; and despite universities that emphasize liberal studies, such as Peking and Fudan Universities in China, the humanities struggle for status (R. Yang, 2014). Yet it is social science and the humanities that nurture nationally distinctive values and practices. As East Asian higher education becomes stronger, it may be freed to focus on nonscience disciplines. Jacques (2012) argued that as China rises, its cultural specificity will become more obvious. If so, the indigenizing tendency will need to overcome the homogenizing effects of internationalization strategies and global rankings, which mold all systems in the image of the dominant science universities in the United States and the United Kingdom.

In the short term, the dangers of homogenization have been enhanced by the success of all East Asian systems except Vietnam in creating world-class universities. Between 2005 and 2013 the number of Chinese universities in the Academic Ranking of World Universities (ARWU) top 500 rose from 8 to 28. Taiwan's top 500 universities grew from five to nine (ARWU, 2014). The ARWU understates the position of Asian universities, because 30 percent of the ranking position is determined by Nobel Prizes, and there have been few Nobel Prizes in Asia. The Leiden University Centre for Science and Technology Studies (CWTS) ranking, which provides several single indicators of research quantity, and quality as measured by citation rates, is useful. One Leiden indicator lists universities by the number of science papers in the top 10 percent of the research field by citation rate. There were 28 Asian universities in the world top 200 on the basis of 2009–2012 research papers, compared to 19 universities in the 2013 ARWU top 200. Table 4.3 shows that the highest placed Asian HEIs are the University of Tokyo (1,389 top 10 percent papers, 29th in the world), National University of Singapore (30th), and Tsinghua in China (49th) (CWTS, 2014). These are not remarkable figures. However, current research rankings reflect the R&D investments only up to about 2005. When the last decade of investment is realized in the rankings, there will be many East Asian universities in the top 200 and a larger number pushing up in the top 50.

TABLE 4.3: ASIAN UNIVERSITIES IN THE WORLD TOP 200 ON THE BASIS OF THE NUMBER OF HIGH CITATION (TOP 10% IN FIELD) PAPERS PRODUCED IN 2009–2012

World Rank	University	System	Papers 2009–12
29	University of Tokyo	Japan	1389
30	National University of Singapore	Singap.	1361
49	Tsinghua University	China	1025
53	Zhejiang University	China	1018
55	Nanyang University of Technology	Singap.	986
57	University of Kyoto	Japan	982
67	Peking University	China	906
70	Seoul National University	Korea	901
72	Shanghai Jiao Tong University	China	887
87	Fudan University	China	784
95	Osaka University	Japan	724
100	National Taiwan University	Taiwan	695
103	University of Hong Kong	HK SAR	669
117	University of Science and Technology of China	China	621
120	Tohoku University	Japan	606
123	Nanjing University	China	595
130	Sun Yat-Sen University	China	563
135	Chinese University of Hong Kong	HK SAR	548
145	Sichuan University	China	529
152	Harbin Institute of Technology	China	522
157	Yonsei University	Korea	517
169	Korea Advanced Institute for Science and Technology	Korea	493
180	Jilin University	China	466
182	Huazhong University of Science and Technology	China	463
183	Shandong University	China	457
185	Nankai University	China	456
199	Dalian University of Technology	China	428
200	Nagoya University	Japan	427

Source: CWTS (2014)

If the number of world-class universities is growing, what is happening to lower-tier HEIs? With the partial exception of Hong Kong SAR, all East Asian systems are steeply hierarchical, like the U.S. system but unlike the Scandinavian and German models. The peak universities—Tsinghua and Peking in China, Seoul National in Korea, Tokyo in Japan, National Taiwan University in Taiwan, and the top two in Singapore—enjoy overwhelming prestige. The distinction between national research HEIs and others is likewise steep. Hong Kong maintains a rough parity between its leading research universities, each kept at a modest size, but sharply demarcates them from the nonresearch HEIs below. When research universities are internationalized, and are the focus of public and private attention, other institutions tend to languish unless specific efforts are made to sustain their quality and prestige. A strength of the California model is the second-tier state university sector, which provides an avenue to graduate study in University of California institutions. The quality and resourcing of the provincial and local universities in East Asia are yet to receive comparable attention. This tends to devalue the credentials of mass institutions and exacerbate social inequalities, given that entry to elite sectors is dominated by socially advantaged families. These problems will be enhanced if and when state enthusiasm for expansion levels off and the funding is constrained, as is already the case in Japan.

In Japan fiscal restrictions, demographic downturn, state regulation of quality, and conservative academic cultures have together contributed to a loss of dynamism in higher education. Is this tendency specific to Japan, or is it the future of the post-Confucian model? Are the political and educational cultures of Sinic states as friendly to free disciplinary creativity as their equivalents in Europe and North America? The first question is impossible to answer. The second is the subject of many claims but little evidence. It would be unwise to judge East Asian practice with Western norms. Chinese notions of academic freedom are distinctive, with more emphasis on positive responsibility and less on freedom from constraint, compared to Anglo-American notions (Hayhoe, Li, Lin, & Zha, 2011). No one in any university likes to be told what to do, and devolution is normal to comprehensive Sinic states. However, there have been regular criticisms from within China of state interference in decisions about science funding. It may be more difficult for the Sinic state to step back—though it must be said that political interference is an issue in many systems across the world.

Time will tell if the central state imposes a fundamental limit on the model. The problem is greatest in the humanities and social sciences. Sinic tradition has no equivalent to the American critical public intellectual. Policy debate is important, but it takes place within the state rather than the public space. Humanities scholars in China freely express themselves within the university, which is seen as part of the state. Public criticism is much more fraught. Unlike the mostly powerless criticisms voiced by humanities intellectuals in the United States, public criticism by Chinese humanists is seen both as weighty in itself and carrying the potential for open challenge to the regime. Sinic scholars uphold public order, unless they believe state leaders have lost the mandate of heaven, the right to govern. This tradition is much older than the Chinese Communist Party (CCP). After all, the CCP regime in China is the latest in a longer succession of one-party dynasties at the helm of comprehensive states. There are informal constraints on public criticism by university professors also in multiparty Taiwan, Japan, and Korea. Sinic societies are less inclined to celebrate mavericks and more focused on issues of individual conduct and public conformity. The tradition does not prevent new ideas from emerging in any discipline, but it inhibits their free-wheeling discussion. In a robust civil society, the problem vanishes. Civil societies are emerging in East Asia, hastened by the Internet, but they have a long way to go. Nevertheless, given the brilliance of modern Sinic strategies in higher education, it would be unwise to assume that the post-Confucian model cannot transform itself to overcome this limitation.

REFERENCES

Agarwal, P. (2009). *Indian higher education: Envisioning the future.* New Delhi, India: Sage.

Academic Ranking of World Universities (ARWU). (2014). *Academic Ranking of World Universities 2013.* Retrieved from http://www.shanghairanking.com/ARWU2013.html

Central Intelligence Agency (CIA). (2014). *The world factbook: Taiwan.* Retrieved from https://www.cia.gov/library/publications/the-world-factbook/geos/tw.html

Gao, Y. (2014). An emerging giant of science: Achievements and challenges of STEM education in China. In B. Freeman, S. Marginson, & R. Tytler (Eds.), *The age of STEM: Educational policy and practice across the world in science, technology, engineering and mathematics* (pp. 47-66). New York, NY: Routledge.

Gernet, J. (1996). *A history of Chinese civilization* (2nd ed.). Cambridge, UK: Cambridge University Press.

Hayhoe, R., Li, J., Lin, J., & Zha, Q. (Eds.). (2011). *Portraits of 21st century Chinese universities: In the move to mass higher education.* Hong Kong SAR: Springer/Comparative Education Research Centre, University of Hong Kong.

Hirsch, F. (1976). *Social limits to growth.* Cambridge, MA: Harvard University Press.

Jacques, M. (2012). *When China rules the world: The end of the western world and the birth of a new global order* (2nd ed.). Harmondsworth, UK: Penguin.

Joseph, C., & Matthews, J. (Eds.). (2014). *Equity, opportunity and education in postcolonial Southeast Asia.* London, UK: Routledge.

Kharas, H. (2010). *The emerging middle class in developing countries.* OECD Development Centre, Working Paper No. 285. Paris, France: OECD.

Centre for Science and Technology Studies (CWTS). (2014). *CWTS Leiden Ranking 2014.* Retrieved from http://www.leidenranking.com/ranking/2014

Marginson, S. (2011). Higher education in East Asia and Singapore: Rise of the Confucian model. *Higher Education, 61*(5), 587–611.

Mukherjee, H., Wong, P. (2011). The National University of Singapore and the University of Malaya: Common roots and different paths. In P. Altbach & J. Salmi (Eds.), *The road to academic excellence: The making of world-class research universities* (pp. 129-166). Washington, DC: World Bank.

National Science Foundation (NSF). (2014). *Science and engineering indicators 2014.* Retrieved from http://www.nsf.gov/statistics/seind14/

Nature Publishing Index. (2014). Retrieved from http://www.natureasia.com/en/publishing-index/

Organisation for Economic Co-operation and Development (OECD). (2013). *Education at a glance 2013.* Paris, France: Author.

Organisation for Economic Co-operation and Development (OECD). (2014). *PISA 2012 results in focus: What 15 year olds know and what they can do with what they know.* Paris, France: Author.

Postiglione, G. (2014, 20 June). Reforming the gaokao. *University World News*, 325.

Salmi, J. (2009). *The challenge of establishing world-class universities*. Washington, DC: World Bank.

Smith, A. (1979). *The wealth of nations*. Harmondsworth, UK: Penguin. (Original work published in 1776)

Stiglitz, J. (1999). Knowledge as a global public good. In I. Kaul, I. Grunberg, & M. Stern (eds.), *Global public goods: International cooperation in the 21ˢᵗ century*, pp. 308–325. New York, NY: Oxford University Press.

Tran, L., Marginson, S., Do, H., Do, Q., Truc, L., Nguyen, N., Vu, T., Pham, T., & Nguyen, H. (2014). *Higher education in Vietnam*. New York, NY: Palgrave Macmillan.

Trow, M. (1974). Problems in the transition from elite to mass higher education. In Organization for Economic Cooperation and Development, *The general report on the Conference on the Future Structures of Post-secondary Education* (pp. 55–101). Paris, France: OECD.

United Nations Educational, Scientific and Cultural Organization (UNESCO). (2014). *Educational statistics*. UNESCO Institute for Statistics. Retrieved from http://www.uis.unesco.org/Pages/default.aspx

Vasconcelos, A. (Ed.). (2012). *Global trends 2030: Citizens in an interconnected and polycentric world*. European Union Institute for Security Studies. Retrieved from http://www.iss.europa.eu/publications/detail/article/espas-report-global-trends-2030–citizens-in-an-interconnected-and-polycentric-world/

Wang, Q., Wang, Q., & Liu, N. (2011). Building world-class universities in China: Shanghai Jiao Tong University. In P. Altbach & J. Salmi (Eds.), *The road to academic excellence: The making of world-class research universities* (pp. 33–62). Washington DC: World Bank.

World Bank. (2014). *Data and statistics*. Retrieved from http://data.worldbank.org/indicator

Yang, P. (2014, June). *Chinese higher education expansion*. Paper presented at the Summer School on Higher Education Research, National Research University–Higher School of Economics, Institute of Education, Pushkin, St. Petersburg, Russia.

Yang, R. (2014). China's strategy for internationalization of higher education: An overview. *Frontiers of Education in China, 9*(2), 151–162.

Zhao, K., & Biesta, G. (2011). Lifelong learning between "east" and "west": Confucianism and the reflexive project of the self. *Interchange, 42*(1), 1–20.

NOTES

[1] "Tertiary education" includes both degree-length programs of three years' equivalent full-time or more in duration (OECD Type 5A) and subdegree programs of two years' equivalent full-time (OECD Type 5B), many of them vocationally specific in nature. The data used here sometimes refer to "higher education" and sometimes "tertiary education." While at the world level, the majority of tertiary enrollments are in degree-level or graduate-diploma-level programs, the ratio between degree and subdegree program enrollments varies significantly by country, and international comparisons must be handled with caution. For more discussion, see OECD (2013).

[2] Currency is in U.S. dollars unless otherwise specified.

[3] The numerator of the GTER takes in enrollments of students of all ages, while the denominator refers to the school-leaver age cohort, so mature age enrollments can push the ratio above 100 percent.

Chapter Five

Internationalization in Asian Higher Education in the Era of Globalization

Futao Huang, Hiroshima University, Japan

Introduction

Internationalization in higher education is hardly new in Asia. As early as the late 19th century, most Asian countries, especially countries in East Asia and Southeast Asia, including China, Japan, and Thailand, established modern universities or higher education systems by introducing Western academic standards or modeling them on Western ideas. From an historical perspective, though it differs greatly by country, the changes in internationalization in higher education in Asia in terms of the circulation of models can be described by four phases. During the first phase, in the late 19th and early 20th centuries, higher education systems introduced Western academic standards and sent local faculty and students on exchanges to Western countries. During the second phase, from the 1930s to 1945, Japan began exporting academic conventions and values to other Asian countries, coupled with continued learning and adoption by these countries of Western patterns. The third phase occurred throughout the 1980s, in which some Asian countries adopted Soviet patterns from communist countries while also introducing American models to market-driven systems. The final, post-1980s phase is characterized by internationalization in higher education, driven by globalization. Although many studies have been conducted on internationalization in higher education in individual Asian countries, little is known about these changes at a regional level, especially in the context of globalization, which has influenced higher education worldwide. The purpose of this chapter is to identify the distinctive characteristics of internationalization in higher education in Asia in the era of globalization, in particular, how select countries like China, Japan, South Korea, and Malaysia have responded to new challenges posed by globalization by internationalizing their higher education systems. First, the chapter explores how internationalization in higher education and globalization are understood in Asia based on a review of literature. Second, it introduces some national strategies and action plans on internationalization in higher education in selected countries. Third, it deals with various practices and reality of internationalization in higher education in select Asian countries. Fourth, it explores issues and challenges facing internationalization in higher education in Asia. The chapter concludes by arguing that some Asian countries have attempted not only to reverse the historic "brain drain," but also to compete with Western universities in attracting international students and excellent academics and to create "world-class universities" of their own. Although Asia has not become a center of learning, and many issues need to be addressed, its higher education capacity, especially research and learning activities, will surely be strengthened and improved through internationalization.

Terminology

Before examining the nature and features of the internationalization of Asian higher education in an era of globalization, it is important to briefly review the literature of "internationalization in higher education" and "globalization" and the relationships between them, and to define how these concepts are used in this chapter.

Although over the past decades there has been abundant and multifaceted literature interpreting the phrase "internationalization in higher education," perhaps Jane Knight's concept is the most widely cited. According to Knight, "internationalization at the national, sector, and institutional levels is defined as the process of integrating an international, intercultural, or global dimension into the purpose, functions or delivery of postsecondary education" (Knight, 2008, p. 21). Robertson, who was the first sociologist to define the term "globalization," suggested that globalization "refers both to the compression of the world and the intensification of consciousness of the world as a whole"; in other words, it covers the acceleration in concrete global interdependence and in consciousness of the global whole (Robertson, 1992, p. 8). Grunzweig & Rinehart (2002, p. 7) also provided a similar definition of globalization as "the process and consequences of instantaneous world-wide communication made possible by new technology. The consequences include an explosive growth in the quantity and accessibility of knowledge and continually increasing integration and interdependence or world financial and economic systems."

With regard to the link between internationalization in higher education and globalization, Knight pointed out that "globalization is a phenomenon or a process which is affecting many sectors and disciplines and education is no exception. Internationalization of higher education is both a response to globalization as well as an agent of globalization. Internationalization is changing the world of higher education and globalization is changing the process of internationalization" (Knight, 2003, p. 2). According to Maringe and Foskett (2010), these two concepts are two sides of the same coin, though they are not synonymous. They argued that globalization entails the opening up and coming together of business, trade, and economic activities between nations, necessitating the need for greater homogenization of fundamental political, ideological, cultural, and social aspects of life across different countries of the world. The key strategic responses to globalization have come to be known as internationalization. Therefore, these two concepts can be viewed as mutually reinforcing ideas. Globalization largely provides the external impetus for accelerated institutional internationalization. On the other hand, the intensification of university internationalization activity reinforces accelerated globalization.

This chapter proposes that the phrase "internationalization in higher education" is basically the process of carrying out exchange activities, ideas, and values in education and research of various kinds among universities and higher education institutions in different countries and cultures. Fully fledged international exchange in higher education is typically regarded as an activity in the higher education sector, developed on the premise of the existence of a nation after modern states were established in Europe. The form, content, and pattern of the exchange vary across time and by country, as well as by social context. With respect to the relationships between internationalization and globalization, this study differentiates between the two concepts in three ways. First, internationalization has been widely discussed since at least the 19th century, whereas the globalization came into consideration mainly during the later part the 1980s. Second, internationalization emphasizes an exchange or communication among different nations and cultures, whereas the principal aim of globalization is to establish a single or universally acknowledged model, beyond nations and cultures. Third, internationalization occurs with the precondition that different nations and cultures exist, whereas globalization proceeds on the assumption that nations and cultures are of decreasing significance. There is, however, a close relationship between the two terms. With the rapid progress of globalization, advancement of new technology, and increasingly frequent exchanges between nations and cultures, some activities that were once conducted between nations or cultures (i.e., at an international level) are likely to reach a global level, possibly resulting in universally accepted standards or values. What is more important, because of increasing cooperative higher education activities occurring at regional and especially at global levels, is that it is becoming more difficult to differentiate between the meaning and practice of internationalization and globalization in higher education.

In some countries and regions, such as the United States and within the European Union, some practices concerning internationalization in higher education are now proceeding toward a phase of globalization (Huang, 2007).

Policies and Strategies

Brief Context

Since the early 1990s, internationalization in higher education has encountered unprecedented challenges. In general, the strategy and practice of internationalization in higher education in individual countries in Asia are not only affected by national policy, character, and identity (as other continents are), but are also influenced by calls and pressures from regional or even global organizations like the World Trade Organization (WTO), the advancement of information technology, and the introduction of market-oriented mechanisms. In a major sense, the ongoing internationalization in higher education is much more strongly driven by economic, political, and academic factors in a more competitive environment at a global level compared to previous phases. The situation in mature systems differs from that in developing or emerging countries. Relative to countries such as the United Kingdom, Australia, and the United States, in which internationalization in higher education is basically linked to commercial activities that are driven by an entrepreneurial spirit, in the majority of countries in Asia, internationalization is more affected by academic factors (as discussed in the next section). Especially in these emerging countries, internationalization in higher education is essentially viewed as an important tool to build their capacity of higher education, enhance the quality of their teaching and research, and expand the influence of their higher education worldwide.

Trends of Regionalization

When the Association of Southeast Asian Nations (ASEAN) and the Southeast Asian Ministers of Education Organization (SEAMEO) were established in Southeast Asia in the 1960s, their primary objectives were to achieve political confidence and facilitate subregional collaboration. With the rapid expansion of trade and economic activities in the region, which are increasingly motivated by globalization, accompanied by the influence of the Bologna process, collaboration in a wide range of activities has grown between Southeast Asian countries and East Asian countries. In 1989 the Asia-Pacific Economic Cooperation (APEC) was created with 12 Asia-Pacific economies, with three more—China, Hong Kong, and Chinese Taipei—joining in 1991. Since 1997, ASEAN has undertaken various collaborative activities with three East Asian countries—China, Japan, and South Korea—to foster educational collaboration. This has led to the emergence of a new regional organization, ASEAN Plus Three (APT or

ASEAN+3). In recent years, various collaborative activities in higher education have been undertaken by Southeast Asian countries and East Asian countries, and since the early 1990s, East Asian countries have placed more emphasis on a closer linkage and collaboration with their partners in the region. This is especially true of the three major countries in East Asia: China, Japan, and South Korea. In 2010, the three countries jointly launched the Campus Asia Project, a regional responses to globalization and worldwide competition in higher education (Ministry of Education, Culture, Sports, Science and Technology–Japan [MEXT], 2014c). Through this project, it is expected that universities in Japan, China, and South Korea will become places where students and professors from diverse cultural and regional backgrounds can come together and realize the merits of each university. Particularly, the Campus Asia Project aims at stimulating the regional mobility of students, faculty, and researchers and developing further collaboration in higher education. In the framework of this program, the three countries have formulated national policies and strategies to further integrate their higher education systems. These initiatives include the provision of financial support to build intraregional university networks, design joint curricula and joint degree programs that combine the three countries' cultural and academic strengths, and provide more English-taught degree programs. Currently, major universities in China, Japan, and South Korea are expanding their English language lectures and degree programs for undergraduate and graduate studies in order to of attract more students from the other Northeast Asian countries (Huang, 2013).

In reality, the region has also seen a growth in personal movement. With respect to student mobility, according to UNESCO statistics for 2013, approximately half of the students from Asia and the Pacific studying abroad actually do so within the region, compared to 36 percent in 1999. In some countries and territories, such as Indonesia, Japan, South Korea, Vietnam, Hong Kong, and Macao, students from Asia and Pacific had accounted for more than 90 percent of their foreign students. In China, Japan, and South Korea, the lists of the top five countries of origin of foreign students comprise, in addition to the United States, countries of the region, including Vietnam, Thailand, Malaysia, Mongolia, and Taipei, China (UNESCO Institute for Statistics, 2013). Parallel to the rapidly increasing numbers in student mobility, there has been corresponding growth in regional mobility of academics. In addition, there has been a gradual increase in the number of full-time foreign faculty members from neighboring countries who are recorded as being employed in higher education institutions in China, Japan, and South Korea (Huang, 2011). For example, the number of full-time faculty members from Asia, especially from China and South Korea, at Japanese universities had grown considerably by 2013 (Ministry of Education, Culture, Sports, Science and Technology [MEXT] 2013). Also, by 2009, of 345 full-time foreign faculty members in the University of Tokyo, 212 were from Asian countries (University of Tokyo, 2009). This means that the percent of the full-time foreign faculty members from Asia accounted for the largest share of the total

(Figure 5.1). Similarly, the number of full-time faculty members from China and Japan at Korean higher education institutions had tripled between 2003 and 2012 (MEXT & Korean Education and Development Institute [KEDI], 2012).

FIGURE 5.1: THE PERCENTAGE OF FULL-TIME FOREIGN FACULTY MEMBERS IN THE UNIVERSITY OF TOKYO BY REGION, 2009

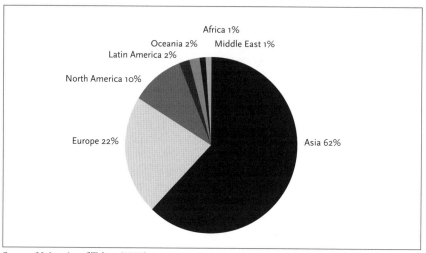

Source: University of Tokyo (2009).

National Initiatives

In parallel with the regionalization of higher education in Asia, many countries have developed strategies of internationalization in higher education in order to respond to the challenges posed by globalization. Although some differences exist between countries, new trends in the internationalization in higher education are seen widely among Asia, especially in mature and emerging countries in East and Southeast Asia. In general, the main objectives of these policies and strategies are not only concerned with a further expansion of personal mobility across borders and incorporating international perspectives and content into teaching and research activities. They also include the provision of joint- or double-degree programs, establishment of branch campuses in partnership with foreign institutions, delivery of English-taught programs, building of a regional hub, and support of several selected universities or disciplines with enlarged budgets with the aim of becoming world-class universities or world-renowned centers of excellence. In East Asia alone, prior to the mid-1990s, the internationalization of Chinese higher education was mainly concerned with dispatching students abroad and attracting international students to Chinese campus, as well as the implementation of English-taught degree programs. Since the mid-1990s, however, the Chinese government has implemented new national policies. They include the first document resulting from these policies issued in 1995 (Huang, 2003), "Contemporary Regulation on Operation of Higher Education Institutions in Cooperation with Foreign Partners," and the launch of Project 211 and Project 985. The two projects have been carried out with the purpose of building up several world-class universities in China in the near future.

In comparison with other Asian countries, the Japanese government devoted more efforts to the acceptance of international students from the 1980s to 1990s. One clear example is that the Japanese government developed the national policy, which was implemented in 1983, to host 100,000 overseas students by the year 2000. More recently, internationalization in higher education in Japan has entered a new phase with new characteristics. They include the following two aspects. First, the Japanese government has begun to revise the legislation concerning the approval of foreign institutions in Japan and to adopt new strategies for recognizing cross-border or transnational branches and programs. This approval makes it possible for foreign educational activities or services to be recognized by Japanese universities and allows Japanese students to apply to foreign educational programs or institutions in Japan. Meanwhile, more and more Japanese institutions have attempted to export their educational activities by providing transnational programs in other countries. Second, in June 2001, the Japanese government set the goal of fostering its "Top 30" universities toward the attainment of top global standards. Later, the program was changed into a scheme of cultivating Centers of Excellence in the 21st Century (COE21). By focusing on nine key disciplines, exemplified as life sciences, medical sciences, chemistry, material sciences, mathematics, physics, earth sciences, information, and electrical and electronic engineering, the central government expanded the budget for units in these nine disciplines. The government hopes that the quality of research activity in Japanese higher education can be enhanced and increased international dimensions can be integrated into campus research activities.

In 2009 the Japanese government launched a new Global 30 program. Its primary aim is to attract 300,000 foreign students by 2020, tripling the current number. In order to achieve that goal, 13 universities, including 7 national and 6 private, were selected to play a central role in implementing the program. For example, they were required to accept many more international students and to provide at least two English-taught degree programs. In 2012, the Japanese government issued another strategy to develop global human resources. In Japan "global human resources" was initiatively described and demanded by big enterprises in the context of increased global economic competition. Although there is still some debate about the meaning of the phrase "global human resources," and the interpretation of the term varies among individual universities, industry, and stakeholders in Japan, according to the government report (Ministry of Economy, Trade and Industry, 2010), this policy aims at developing people's abilities to

- Think independently;
- Make themselves easily understood by their colleagues, business acquaintances, and customers of various backgrounds;
- Overcome differences in values and characteristics arising from different cultural and historical backgrounds;
- Understand others and consider their standpoints;
- Use their differences to build synergy; and
- Create new values.

Shortly after China and Japan announced their plans, the Korean government announced its first national plan on internationalization in higher education in 1996, namely the Initial Plan for Opening the Higher Education Market to Foreign Countries, in response to upcoming WTO negotiations. This plan was based on the idea that importing higher education services, in close collaboration with overseas partners, would be an efficient and practical way to meet the challenges of internationalization. In 1999 the Korean government started the Brain Korea 21 project for the purpose of building world-class graduate schools and nurturing the development of research personnel. Based on the *choice and concentration* principle, the Korean government has allocated part of its budget to the project. A second stage, called BK 21, began in 2006. Although the Korean higher education has already moved into the stage of a near universal access to higher education and achieved a higher percentage of higher education enrollment at the age 18 population, it has very few research-intensive universities. Many Korean academics believe that only two or three universities are really research-intensive, and a huge majority of their universities are teaching-oriented. Therefore, the objective of the Brain Korea 21 is to establish the research-focused university system and attract expert personnel, including academics who are internationally recognized in their disciplines and researchers with an international reputation (Kim, 2008). In 2008, another national strategy called the World Class University Project was implemented. According to the project, several strategies are developed in order to build Korean world class universities. One of the most important strategies is to attract not only top scholars from foreign countries, but also Korean scholars abroad to Korean campuses and research institutes. It is expected that these inbound top scholars will be able to undertake joint research and co-author with local professors and researchers and therefore raise the ranking of Korean universities in major global university ranking systems, to help Korean universities improve the quality of their teaching and learning, as well as research activities, and to provide both Korean faculty members and students with more international learning and research environment (Byun and Kim, 2011).

Similar policies can also be found in other Southeast Asian countries. For example, in 1991, the Malaysia announced Vision 2020, which was conceived as a Malaysian ideal. In terms of internationalization, Vision 2020 calls for developing Malaysia as a regional hub for higher education. According to Vision 2020, the Ninth Malaysia Plan (2006–2010) aims at attracting 100,000 international students. The importance of the Private Higher Education Act, enacted in 1996, cannot be overestimated, for it has encouraged private higher education institutions to accept more international students, provide transnational higher education programs with foreign partners, and open branch campuses with foreign universities. Since the early 2000s, the Ministry of Higher Education launched several strategies and projects in order to widen Malaysia's global engagement through soft power and facilitate the internationalization of Malaysian higher education. In 2007, the government implemented the National Education Strategic Plan. This plan puts forth four strategies to achieve international hub status: (a) enhancing global networks of higher education and collaborative international academic activities at all levels; (b) expanding suitable programs of study for international students; (c) increasing the number of international students, especially in the private higher education institutions through promotion and marketing Malaysia as an excellent international hub for higher education; and (d) promoting higher education in Malaysia through gradual rebranding these institutions to attain international status (Yean, 2013). In 2011, the second National Higher Education Strategic Plan was launched by the Malaysian government. It focuses on the improvement and expansion of Malaysian higher education. Internationalization is regarded as an important means to achieve the objectives of the plan. They include (a) enhancing global outreach through sharing of knowledge, (b) establishing a hub for knowledge and skills via internationalization, (c) widening international networks via student alumni, and (d) increasing the visibility of Malaysia through contributions and reputation. Similar to countries like China, Japan, South Korea, and Singapore, Malaysia is no longer a "publish or perish" culture but a "publish in ISI Web of Knowledge or perish" culture. The focus is on quality, impact factor, citations, research, development, and commercialization outputs, including patents, copyrights, and commercialization. Exerting pressure may sometimes be appropriate to nudge universities to expedite their progression in becoming world-class institutions (Yunus and Pang, 2013).

With increased challenges from globalization and worldwide competition in the academic world, university performance and accountability have drawn much attention from various stakeholders. The impact of emerging global university ranking systems on internationalization in Asian higher education cannot be overestimated. Like other regions, in the last few decades, Asian countries have started to evaluate their universities and make efforts to enhance their rankings according to global university ranking systems such as Quacquarelli Symonds (QS), The Times Higher Education, and Academic Ranking of World Universities (ARWU, which is created by Shanghai

Jiao Tong University, China). This has greatly facilitated the internationalization in higher education in individual countries and universities. While not every country in the region has adopted the same policies of internationalization in higher education, it is worth mentioning that many Asian countries and systems, especially China, Japan, South Korea, Singapore, Malaysia, Thailand, Taiwan, and Hong Kong, have created clear national and institutional strategic plans to build their world-class universities by strengthening and improving their research capacity. National strategies include the following aspects:

- Allocating national funding and budget from local authorities for selected research universities

- Creating research-focused universities through mergers, as has been done, in China or by founding new institutions, as has been done in Hong Kong and South Korea

- Improving institutional governance and management arrangements, as well as evaluation systems

- Expanding inbound international students from more diversified origins of countries and backgrounds

- Attracting world-renowned scholars, as well as promoting joint research in collaboration with internationally renowned universities, labs, and professors

Practices and Reality

With the implementation of the policies and strategies already mentioned here, internationalization in higher education has advanced tremendously in individual countries at national, institutional, and individual levels.

Attraction of Inbound International Students and Faculty Members

There has been steady and rapid growth in the numbers of incoming international students in China, Japan, South Korea, and Malaysia. The total number of international students coming to Chinese universities reached approximately 140,000 by 2012, an increase of 10.7 percent over the previous year (Ministry of Education [MOE], 2014). In Japan, the number of international students studying in Japanese universities increased from 53,608 in 2000 to 110,518 in 2012 (MEXT, 2014d). In South Korea, the total number of foreign students increased from 49,270 in 2007 to 86,878 in 2012, including the number of foreign students enrolled in degree programs, which increased from 32,056 to 60,589 over the period (MEXT & KEDI, 2012, p. 49). Meanwhile, there has been a gradual rise in the number of foreign faculty in universities in some Asian countries. For example, between 2004 and 2008, in the Chinese universities that were founded and are administered by the Ministry of Education, the number of foreign experts and faculty members with long-term and short-term contracts nearly doubled. In Japan, over the period 1995–2012, the total number of full-time faculty members in Japanese universities and colleges increased from 4,563 to 6,835 (MEXT, 2012), although the number of full-time foreign faculty members in junior colleges decreased due to a drop in the number of these colleges. In South Korea, the overall number of full-time foreign faculty is smaller than in China or Japan; however, the number of full-time foreign faulty members working in all higher education institutions increased from 1,373 in 2000 to 5,964 by 2012 (MEXT & KEDI, 2012).

Since the mid-1990s, the National University of Singapore (NUS) has made huge efforts to pursue excellence in both teaching and research activities in order to become a globally oriented university. One of the obvious measures that it has taken is to attract top faculty members worldwide. Its annual reports show that the proportion of foreign faculty members increased from 39.0 percent in 1997–1998 academic year to 51.9 percent in 2007–2008 academic year (NUS, 2014).

Growth in the Provision of English-Taught Programs

Recently, there has been a rapid increase in numbers of English-taught programs and courses at both undergraduate and graduate levels in non-English-speaking countries in Asia such as China, Japan, and South Korea. For example, in 2001, a document issued by the Ministry of Education of China indicates that in the coming three years, 5 to 10 percent of all the courses in the leading universities must be taught in English, especially in such areas as biology, information science, new materials, international trade, and law, at undergraduate level in particular. While no national data have been issued about the total number of English-taught programs or courses in Chinese universities, currently it is estimated that 5 percent of all undergraduate courses in China's leading universities are taught entirely in English. These universities also offer a number of English-taught degree programs, mostly at the graduate level in the hard sciences. For example, in Shanghai Jiao Tong University, one of leading universities in China, the total number of programs that were taught in English was 110 by 2011, representing 5 percent of the total programs (Huang, 2012).

Although English-taught programs and courses were offered in some private, religious institutions at the end of World War II, by the early 1980s no significant effort had been made, especially by the national sector, to encourage Japanese universities to provide English-taught programs or courses. With the implementation of the Global 30 program in 2008 and as part of the policy to triple the number of international students by 2020, the Japanese government required each university that receives an additional budget from the Global 30 program to offer at least two independent English-taught degree programs for both local and international students. A national survey by MEXT indicates that by 2009 the total number of English-taught courses had reached 194 at the undergraduate level, mostly as a result of a steady growth of these courses in national and public sectors (national universities and local public universities) in particular; in the private sector, however, the number of these programs declined from 2007 to 2009. The number of graduate-level programs increased to 169, with a similar increase in the national and public sectors and decrease in the private sector (Ministry of Education, Culture, Sports, Science and Technology (MEXT), 2009a).

Similar to China, the Korean government has, since the early 2000s, allocated additional budget for colleges and universities to promote English-medium teaching through various national programs or projects (e.g., the BK 21 project). According to the previous research, in 2006, the proportion of English-taught courses had accounted for 2.2 percent of all courses (about 410,000 courses)(Byun et al., 2011; MEXT, 2014b). Another survey, which was done by the KEDI in 2007, revealed that 94 institutions (49 percent) of 190 responding universities had English-taught courses at the undergraduate level, and 58 institutions (30 percent) had offered English-taught courses at the graduate level. The proportion of English-taught courses experienced remarkable growth at leading universities such as KAIST (Korea Advanced Institute of Science and Technology), POSTECH (Pohang University of Science and Technology), Seoul National University, Yonsei University, and Korea University. However, it should be noted that in Japan and Korea, in recent years, English-taught programs and courses are provided not only to attract international students but also as an effective means to produce local graduates with global competiveness.

Development of Transnational Higher Education

Since the mid-1990s, as an integral part of the internationalization in higher education in the era of globalization, campuses in several Asian countries have developed transnational education institutions and programs. As of October 2013, Chinese universities provided 702 undergraduate programs and 169 programs at the graduate level in partnership with foreign universities, including Hong Kong and Macao (MOE, 2013). Forty Chinese universities provided undergraduate transnational education programs, and 16 provided graduate programs. A huge majority of foreign partners are English-speaking countries, with many of the institutions and programs being from the United Kingdom, the United States, and Australia. In Japan, the transnational higher education is mainly expanded in the form of both dual-degree programs and double- or joint-degree programs. According to the national data, the number of universities in which double-degree programs in partnership with foreign universities were taught had increased from 85 in 2008 to 143 (19 percent) in 2011 (MEXT, 2014a).

Additionally, starting in the 1990s foreign universities have set up branch campuses in some Asian countries. This is a mutually beneficial arrangement: The Asian countries can absorb demand that cannot be met by local higher education institutions and also attract international staff and students to these branch campuses (British Council, 2012). The foreign universities can recruit new entrants and generate more resources and also export their educational ideas and patterns of governance and management. This is of particular interest for Malaysia and Singapore, because both have ambitious targets on international student and hub status. Currently, among all the Asian countries, Singapore has the largest number of international branch campuses (Table 5.1).

TABLE 5.1: NUMBERS OF BRANCH CAMPUSES OF FOREIGN UNIVERSITIES IN SELECTED ASIAN COUNTRIES

Country	Branch campus
Cambodia	1
China (2011)	13
Malaysia	9
Singapore	16
South Korea	2
Thailand	2
Viet Nam (2011)	1

Source: Adapted from UNESCO Institute for Statistics (2014).

Another big change in the internationalization in higher education in several Asian countries is the increasing emphasis placed on the importance of the quality of academic research. Since the latter part of the 1990s, with the intent of building up world-class universities, the governments in China, Japan, and Korea selected a few universities for intensive funding. In all three countries, these designated national institutions have a long history and enjoy high prestige and social position. More importantly, the faculties in these universities are essentially research oriented. The publications included in the Science Citation Index and Social Science Citation Index are a good representation of a country's strength in research. Thus, in addition to the provision of lectures, the faculty members at these universities are particularly encouraged to publish scientific papers in major international journals. Table 5.2 shows that, although there has been a steady increase in total number of articles among Asian countries, China has had the most rapid growth among the three countries, followed by Korea. By 1998, the number of the articles published by Japanese scholars surpassed that of all other countries, except for the United States, but dropped to fifth place in 2008. In contrast, within 20 years, the rankings of China and Korea rose from 15 and below 25 to 2 and 12, respectively.

TABLE 5.2: NUMBERS OF ARTICLES PUBLISHED BY SCHOLARS BY COUNTRY

	USA		China		Japan		Korea	
Year	No. of Articles	Rank	No. of Articles	Rank	No. of Articles	Rank	No. of Articles	Rank
1988	192,730	1	6742	15	40,990	4		Below 25
1998	210,357	1	21,098	9	60,347	2	9,105	16
2008	275,625	1	104,157	2	69,300	5	30,016	12

Source: MEXT (2009, 2010, p. 9).

With a rapid rise in the number of articles published by university academics, several Asian universities have raised their placement in the global university ranking systems. This is especially true in China. As Figure 5.2 reveals, since the early 2000s, there has been not only a growth in the number of Chinese universities listed in the top 500 in ARWU, but also an increase in their rankings in the top 151–200, 201–300, and 301–400. This is an indication that the Chinese strategic plans to build world-class universities are effective.

FIGURE 5.2: MAINLAND CHINESE UNIVERSITIES AMONG TOP 500

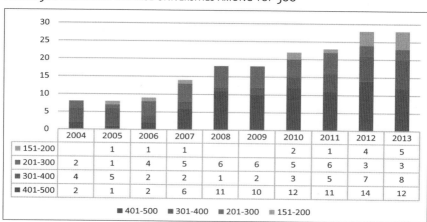

	2004	2005	2006	2007	2008	2009	2010	2011	2012	2013
151-200		1	1	1			2	1	4	5
201-300	2	1	4	5	6	6	5	6	3	3
301-400	4	5	2	2	1	2	3	5	7	8
401-500	2	1	2	6	11	10	12	11	14	12

■ 401-500 ■ 301-400 ■ 201-300 ■ 151-200

Source: ARWU (2013).

Figure 5.3 suggests that the academic ranking of Korean universities has also increased over the last decade. For example, the number of Korean universities which were ranked among top 200 grew from only one in 2004 to seven in 2013. The total number of Korean universities ranked among top 500 increased from eight in 2004 to eleven in 2013. This shows that a great deal of achievement has been accomplished in South Korea after the implementation of its national strategy of building world-class universities through various national-level projects.

	Top 200	Top 300	Top 400	Top 500
■ 2004	1	2	5	8
■ 2013	7	4	7	11

■ 2004 ■ 2013

Source: ARWU (2013).

As noted earlier, since the mid-1990s when the policy of cultivating globally oriented universities was beginning to be carried out, both NUS and Nanyang Technological University have implemented a wide range of initiatives, such as expanding the percentage of both international students and faculty members and encouraging their faculty members to publish more publications in internationally reviewed journals, to co-author with more foreign researchers or colleagues in foreign countries, and to improve the quality of their research productivity. As a result of these actions, the two universities have experienced considerable advancement in their quest for academic excellence. For example, from 1996 to 2006, the total number of journal articles published by NUS faculty members increased by nearly three times. The average citations per article over the period grew from 2.4 to 3.5 (Thomson ISI Web of Science, 2014). Further, in the case of Nanyang Technological University, its ranking in the ARWU had been raised from among top 400 in 2004 to top 300 in 2013 (ARWU, 2014).

Issues and Challenges

One issue concerning internationalization in higher education in Asia is the remarkable imbalance between mature systems and emerging or developing countries. The level of international involvement in the higher education systems in Cambodia, Indonesia, and Vietnam is very low compared to that of Japan, South Korea, Singapore, Malaysia, China, Taiwan, and Hong Kong. The developing countries attract much fewer international students to their campuses, they rely heavily on postgraduate education in other countries, and very few of their universities are listed in top 500 among the global ranking systems. Other regional issues include the quality assurance of incoming foreign educational services, the regulation of joint degree programs at an institutional level, and especially the influence of English-taught programs and English products on nationally based undergraduate education and teaching. In relation to the quality assurance of international students, given intensified competition for inbound international students in the region, some local and small private universities of Japan and South Korea tend to recruit international students to generate revenue without giving a full consideration to their quality. Further, although some countries, including China, Japan, Malaysia, and South Korea, have implemented various standards for transnational higher education programs, in most cases, their criteria are not as stringent as those for evaluating teaching activities in local universities. Hence, it is still difficult for these countries to ensure the quality of programs that are imported from foreign universities, and more difficult to ensure the quality of faculty members who come from foreign partners and provide these programs. More importantly, internationalization in higher education in most Asian countries is still largely being undertaken as a one-way process, overwhelmingly dominated by major English-speaking countries with respect to personal mobility, provision of educational programs, and utilization of academic norms and conventions.

Concluding Remarks

This chapter has discussed major changes and trends of internationalization in higher education in Asia mainly based on the experiences of China, Japan, South Korea, Malaysia, and Singapore, especially since the early 1990s when globalization started to exert a profound influence on almost every aspect of higher education worldwide. This study shows that both governments and institutions in Asia have made huge efforts to stimulate internationalization in their higher education systems. In practice, these strategies and policies appear to be quite effective in attracting inbound international students and faculty members, incoming transnational higher education programs, and branch campuses in terms of quantity. More importantly, some Asian countries have been seeking not only to reverse the historic brain drain, but also to compete with Western universities in attracting international students and excellent academics, to increase their academic productivity, develop regional hubs, and to create their own world-class universities. However, Asia has not yet become a center of learning. A huge majority of Asian universities are still receptive to new ideas from Western countries, and more achievements are still to be accomplished by individual countries based on their national strategies and plans. Thus Asia's capacity for higher education, especially its research, teaching, and learning activities will need to be further strengthened and improved through internationalization in higher education.

REFERENCES

Academic Ranking of World Universities (ARWU). (2013). *ARWU 2013 Press Release*. Retrieved from http://www.shanghairanking.com/index.html

Academic Ranking of World Universities (ARWU). (2014). *ARWU 2014 Press Release*. Retrieved from http://www.shanghairanking.cn/

British Council. (2012). *The shape of things to come: Higher education global trends and emerging opportunities to 2020*. Bradford, UK: Emerald Group.

Byun, K., & Kim, M. (2011). Shifting patterns of the government's policies for the internationalization of Korean higher education. *Journal of Studies in International Education, 15*(3), 467–486.

Byun, K., Chu, H., Kim, M., Park, I., Kim, S., & Jung, J. (2011). English medium teaching in Korean higher education: Policy debates and reality. *Higher Education, 62*(4), 431–449. Retrieved from http://dx.doi.org/10.1007/s10734-010-9397-4

Grunzweig, W., & Rinehart, N. (Eds.). (2002). *Rockin' in Red Square: Critical approaches to international education in the age of cyber culture*. Berlin, Germany: Lit Verlag.

Huang, F. (2003). "Transnational Higher Education: A Perspective from China", *Higher Education Research and Development*, 22(2). Higher Education and Development Society of Australia, 193-203.

Huang, F. (2007). Internationalization of higher education in the era of globalization: What have been its implications in China and Japan? *Higher Education Management & Policy,* 19(1), 47–61.

Huang, F. (2011). The Academic Profession in East Asia: Changes and Realities, in *The Changing Academic Profession in Asia: Contexts, Realities and Trends*. In (RIHE International Seminar Reports, No.17), 113-131. Hiroshima: RIHE Hiroshima University.

Huang, F. (2012). Information obtained from an interview with administrative staff in Shanghai Jiaotong University on December 3, 2013.

Huang, F. (2013). Chapter 1 The Internationalization of the Academic Profession. In F. Huang, M. Finkelstein, & M. Rostan (Eds.), *The internationalization of the academy: Changes, realities and prospects: Vol. 10, The changing academy—The changing academic profession in international comparative perspective* (pp. 1–21). Dordrecht, The Netherlands: Springer.

Kim, Y. (2008). *Universalization of tertiary education: Understanding Korean educational policy II*. Seoul, South Korea: KEDI.

Knight, J. (2003). Interview with Jane Knight. *IMHE OECD, 1,* 2.

Knight, J. (2008). *Higher education in turmoil: The changing world of internationalization*. Rotterdam, The Netherlands: Sense. London; pp. 1–2). Continuum International.

Ministry of Education, Culture, Sports, Science and Technology (MEXT). (2009). *2009 White Paper on Education, Culture, Sports, Science and Technology*. Retrieved from http://www.mext.go.jp/b_menu/hakusho/html/

Ministry of Education, Culture, Sports, Science and Technology (MEXT). (2009a). *Daigaku niokeru kyouiku naiyoudo no kaikaku jyoukyou ni tsuite* (Current situation of reforms on university teaching activities). Retrieved from http://www.mext.go.jp/a_menu/koutou/daigaku/04052801/__icsFiles/afieldfile/2011/08/25/1310269_1.pdf

Ministry of Education, Culture, Sports, Science and Technology (MEXT). (2010). *Secrets of an education powerhouse: 60 years of education in Korea: Challenges, achievements and the future*. Seoul: Korea: Author.

Ministry of Education, Culture, Sports, Science and Technology (MEXT). (2012). *Statistical Abstract, 2010 edition*. Retrieved from http://www.mext.go.jp (Retrieved on May 26, 2014).

Ministry of Education, Culture, Sports, Science and Technology (MEXT). (2013). *Statistical Abstract 2013 edition.* Retrieved from http://www.mext.go.jp (Retrieved on May 29, 2014).

Ministry of Education, Culture, Sports, Science and Technology. (MEXT). (2014a). *Daigaku ni okeru kyouikunaiyou no kaikaku jyoukyou do nit suite* [The ongoing reform on university education]. Retrieved from http://www.mext.go.jp/a_menu/koutou/daigaku/04052801/__icsFiles/afieldfile/2013/11/27/1341433_04_1.pdf (in Japanese)

Ministry of Education, Culture, Sports, Science and Technology. (MEXT). (2014b). *Daigaku no gurobaruka ni kansuru kakugi kette teigenn* [Decision and proposal of the Cabinet about globalization of university]. Retrieved from http://www.mext.go.jp/b_menu/shingi/chukyo/chukyo4/036/siryo/attach/1344786.htm (in Japanese)

Ministry of Education, Culture, Sports, Science and Technology. (MEXT). (2014c). *An outline of the Campus Asia project.* Retrieved from http://www.mext.go.jp/english/highered/1303550.htm(Retrieved on 17 May 2014)

Ministry of Education, Culture, Sports, Science and Technology (MEXT). (2014d). *Statistical abstract 2014 edition.* Retrieved from http://www.mext.go.jp

Ministry of Education, Culture, Sports, Science and Technology (MEXT) & Korean Education and Development Institute (KEDI). (2012). *Brief statistics on Korean Education*, Korea. p. 50.

Ministry of Economy, Trade and Industry. (2010). *Developing global human resource development through industry–academia–government collaboration.* Retrieved from http://www.meti.go.jp/english/press/data/20100423_02.html

Ministry of Education (MOE). (2013). *Zhongwai Hezuo banxue* (Chinese-foreign cooperation in running schools). Retrieved from http://www.crs.jsj.edu.cn/index.php/default/index

Ministry of Education (MOE). (2014).*Laihua liuxue* (Foreign students coming to Chinese universities for study) Retrieved from http://j.people.com.cn/94475/206577/8544061.html

National University of Singapore (NUS). (2014). *NUS annual report (various years).* Retrieved from http://www.nus.edu.sg/global/global_strategy.html

Robertson, R. (1992). *Globalization: Social theory and global culture.* London, UK: Sage.

Thomson ISI Web of Science. (2014). Retrieved from http://thomsonreuters.com/thomson-reuters-web-of-science/

UNESCO Institute for Statistics. (2013).*Dateset: Education.* Retrieved from http://www.uis.unesco.org/DataCentre/Pages/BrowseEducation.aspx

UNESCO Institute for Statistics. (2014). *Higher education in Asia: Expanding out, expanding up.* Retrieved from http://www.uis.unesco.org/Library/Documents/higher-education-asia-graduate-university-research-2014-en.pdf

University of Tokyo. (2009). *White paper of internationalization in the University of Tokyo.* Tokyo: University of Tokyo. (In Japanese).

Yean, T. (2013). From the movement of itinerant scholars to a strategic process. In T. Yean (Ed.), *Internationalizing higher education in Malaysia: Understanding, practices and challenges* (pp. 1–17). Singapore: Institute of Southeast Asian Studies.

Yunus, A., & Pang, V. (2013). Teaching and research concentration of academics in Malaysian public universities. In *RIHE International Seminar Reports No. 20: The changing academic profession in Asia: Teaching, research, governance and management* (pp. 131–152). Hiroshima, Japan: Hiroshima University, Research Institute for Higher Education.

Chapter Six

Education Hubs in Asia: A Common Facade for Uncommon Visions

Jack T. Lee, University of Toronto, Canada

Introduction

One of the most conspicuous developments in contemporary higher education is the proliferation of cross-border education. Discussions on cross-border or transnational education often highlight the growing numbers of mobile students and branch campuses worldwide. Asia figures prominently in these discussions as the largest supplier of mobile students and a major host of branch campuses. Less visible in these discussions is the recognition that Asia is actively adapting and innovating cross-border higher education to fit local and regional needs. Rather than merely supply students for the universities of the West, several Asian countries are now recruiting mobile students and integrating cross-border provisions into their existing higher education systems. Twinning programs, joint doctoral programs, branch campuses, and satellite research centers are evident in countries as varied as Singapore, Vietnam, and China. While some of these ventures are unique in their respective host countries, others are commonplace in a higher education system characterized by intense internationalization.

In the vibrant landscape of cross-border education, education hubs stand out as large-scale initiatives to transform a country, city, or zone into an eminent higher education destination. Over the last two decades, several education hubs have emerged in Asia and the Middle East. Rather than treat cross-border education as a supplementary sector, an education hub relies on cross-border engagements for its growth (Knight & Lee, 2014). Education hubs encourage multiple forms of mobility in higher education: student, faculty, researcher, program, and provider. These hubs actively recruit foreign students, researchers, universities, training providers, and multinational companies. While the rhetoric of globalization and internationalization permeates the policies of education hubs, the underlying rationales and objectives driving their growth vary widely. Many observers assume that revenue generation through student fees is the common imperative behind education hubs given the commercial nature of many cross-border education initiatives today. However, discussions with key policymakers and analyses of implementation strategies reveal a complex set of rationales and objectives extending well beyond economic interests. Rationales such as talent development, educational capacity, and soft power have emerged as salient rationales for many policymakers. Although the economic motives of an education hub are germane, these motives do not dominate or exclude other rationales. Rationales are also not stagnant, as the literature on education hubs may suggest. Rather, policy rationales fluctuate to reflect ongoing developments in local, regional, and global political economy. Education hubs often position cross-border education as a critical plank of their development. These hubs involve substantial participation from multiple individuals and institutions, both local and foreign. Therefore, for the purpose of this chapter, a single center of excellence at the national or institutional level is not equivalent to an education hub; however, such a center may be a constituent of an education hub.

The emergence of education hubs in Asia over the last two decades attests to the region's cumulative expertise in cross-border higher education. This chapter focuses on the development of Singapore, Malaysia, and Hong Kong as education hubs. The chapter draws from empirical research in the three locales in order to illuminate the phenomenon of education hubs in Asia and beyond. Specifically, the chapter compares the key rationales and objectives underpinning the development of education hubs by analyzing policy documents and interviews with senior-level policymakers. This comparison generates a framework for assessing other education hubs in the world. The first section of the chapter, "Background," provides a brief synopsis of the policy trajectory in the three case studies. The second section, "Rationales and Objectives," identifies the key rationales and objectives. The third section, "Comparative Analysis," reflects on the similarities and differences among the case studies in the Asian context.

Background

The idea of an education hub emerged in the late 1990s in different parts of Asia and the Middle East. Among its earliest advocates were policymakers in Qatar, Singapore, and Malaysia. Unsurprisingly, these countries were also early pioneers in cross-border education (e.g., twinning programs, franchised programs, and branch campuses). While early discussions took place in the 1990s, education hubs did not appear in formal national development plans and education plans until the first decade of 2000s. This section provides a synopsis of the emergence of education hubs in the context of Singapore, Malaysia, and Hong Kong.

Singapore

As early as the 1980s, Singapore came to the realization that its manufacturing sector had severe limitations given its small size and competition from cheaper production centers emerging in Asia. Therefore, the mantra at the time was to develop both manufacturing and services as "the twin engines of growth" (Economic Committee, 1986). This mantra guided Singapore's development for the next two decades. Following the 1985–1986 economic recession, Singapore identified 11 promising service industries that could diversify the country's economic portfolio. Education was one of the industries. However, the government could not make serious progress in commercializing education due to sociopolitical sensitivities (Contact Singapore, 2011). When the Asian financial crisis struck in 1997, policymakers at the Economic Development Board revitalized the idea of commercializing education once again. This early effort to transform Singapore into the "Boston of the East" faced resistance and skepticism at home and abroad, but it laid the foundation for the education hub (Tan, 2002). In 1998, Singapore formally launched its World-Class University program with the aim of attracting at least 10 world-class universities to set up operations in the country within 10 years. In 2003, a seminal economic review report concluded that the services sector in the country "helped cushion the sharp plunge in manufacturing output" during the recessions of 1981–1985, 1996–1998, and 2001 (Economic Review Committee, 2003, p. 4). This review justified the development of education services as "an engine of economic growth, capability development and talent attraction for Singapore" (Economic Review Committee, 2003, p. 3). The review also proposed a detailed market segmentation of education services: elite world-class universities, local universities, applied research, corporate training, primary education, and testing services. While capability development and talent attraction were mentioned as additional reasons for developing the education hub, revenue generation clearly dominated the review committee's recommendations. Over the next 10 years, Singapore would continually fortify its education hub by adding other related initiatives (e.g., Biomedical Sciences Initiative in 2000, Nepal Hill corporate training center in 2009, and the intellectual property hub in 2013). These initiatives reveal a shift in priorities as Singapore matures as an education hub. Interestingly, the key actor in developing Singapore as an education hub is its Economic Development Board and, more recently, the Agency for Science, Technology and Research. The Ministry of Education is only peripherally involved as a supporter.

Malaysia

Malaysia first approached the idea of an education hub with the determination to resolve a chronic economic problem: a trade deficit in the service sector. While Malaysia has historically netted a surplus in the trade of goods, its overall balance of trade suffered from a weak service sector, whereby dependency on foreign providers drained the country of funds. The quinquennial Malaysia Plans from the 1980s and 1990s repeatedly underscored this trade deficit as a factor that could trap the country at the middle-income level. Malaysia's aspirations to become a high-income country dates back to at least 1991, when Prime Minister Mahathir launched his seminal blueprint, Vision 2020, which continues to spur new policy initiatives. One factor that contributed to the service deficit was the large number of students leaving Malaysia to study overseas (5th Malaysia Plan, 1986). Understanding this phenomenon requires a brief introduction of the social and historical context of Malaysian higher education. Since the times of British colonialism, the country's Malay majority has been economically disadvantaged compared to other ethnic groups (i.e., Chinese and Indian). Therefore, affirmative action policies have been in place since the 1970s to provide greater life opportunities for the Malays. In higher education, ethnic quotas in student admissions have resulted in an overrepresentation of Malays in public universities. Although these quotas were abolished in 2002, enrollment data continue to show skewed ethnic composition (Sharma & Tan, 2013). Throughout the 1980s and 1990s, private higher education expanded rapidly in Malaysia to accommodate students who could not enter public universities. Many private institutions rely on cross-border provisions because they are not legally authorized to grant degrees. Therefore, private institutions partner with foreign universities to deliver twinning and franchised programs. In the 1990s, these programs were prevalent in Malaysia, especially the 2+2 and 2+1 twinning programs (i.e., a student studies in Malaysia for two years and then completes the program in one or two years overseas at a partner institution). However, the 1997 Asian financial crisis caused the Malaysian ringgit to depreciate sharply and reduced the number of Malaysian students who could afford the overseas sojourn (Tham, 2010). As a result of this crisis, many private institutions in Malaysia negotiated with their foreign partners to deliver the entire degree in Malaysia—essentially converting a twinning program to a franchised program (e.g., 3+0). Students can now pursue a full degree issued by a foreign institution without ever leaving Malaysia. Ultimately, the Asian financial crisis fueled the idea that Malaysia could become an education hub by opening its private education sector to international students and marketing the country's low cost of living. Currently, the education hub plan is prominent in the National Higher Education Strategic Plan 2020 (2007), the New Economic Model (2010), and the Economic Transformation Plan (2010). The Ministry of Higher Education is the key actor behind the education hub initiative.

Hong Kong

Hong Kong became serious about its education hub plan later than Singapore and Malaysia. References to becoming a "regional education center" appeared sporadically in the late 1990s in some policy documents by the University Grants Committee (UGC), which is the non-statutory body that advises the government on the development and funding of public universities. Hong Kong's desire to recruit Chinese students and forge closer relations with mainland China was apparent at this early stage (UGC, 1996).[1] In 2004, the Chief Executive of Hong Kong named education as one of the potential industries that could contribute to the city's economic growth as "Asia's World City" (Tung, 2004). Soon thereafter, pronouncements of an education hub appeared in other policy documents by the Education Bureau and the UGC (Li, 2004; UGC, 2004a, 2004b). However, visible strategies to attract more non-local students did not appear until 2007 (e.g., creating a scholarship fund and removing some employment restrictions). The worldwide recession in 2008 motivated the Hong Kong SAR government to conduct an economic review, which proposed that Hong Kong broaden its expertise beyond financial services and cultivate six key industries: medical services, education services, environmental industries, innovation and technology, testing and certification, and cultural and creative industries (Task Force on Economic Challenges, 2009). Again, mainland China figures prominently in this proposal. Large numbers of mainland Chinese students enroll in Hong Kong higher education institutions each year, motivated by the city's high-quality universities as well as its civic freedom and cosmopolitan ethos. Since 2000, the quota for non-local undergraduate students at public institutions has been raised successively from 4 percent to the current 20 percent limit. The key actor leading the education hub initiative is the Education Bureau.

Rationales and Objectives

Through policy document analysis and interviews with senior policymakers in Malaysia, Hong Kong, and Singapore, four key rationales are apparent in the development of education hubs: economic benefits, talent development, educational capacity, and soft power. While these rationales are not mutually exclusive, they are distinctive enough to generate disparate objectives and implementation strategies. In essence, these rationales orient an education hub toward a particular development trajectory. This section elaborates on each rationale using relevant examples from the three education hubs. Rather than reduce each education hub to a single rationale or pathway, this section presents the complex reality of higher education development with overlapping interests and pressures. Table 7.1 summarizes the key rationales and objectives in education hub development.

Economic Benefits

Deriving economic benefits is a key rationale behind the development of education hubs. Specifically, policymakers view education as an industry that can generate direct and indirect revenues. While this desire is evident in the early policy documents of the three education hubs, only Malaysia continues to pursue this goal fervently today. The explosion of the private education industry in Malaysia and the widespread use of market segmentation and recruitment fairs attest to the commercial orientation of its education hub. On the other hand, Singapore and Hong Kong are less interested in the revenue generated through student fees. In fact, both jurisdictions subsidize international students—sometimes to the chagrin of locals, who demand greater access to higher education and accountability in public spending.

In addition to earning tuition fees, Malaysia is also leveraging higher education as an economic multiplier. By cultivating higher education as an industry, other sectors of the economy are expected to expand to accommodate the large numbers of students (e.g., housing, food services, tourism, and transportation). An interesting example is the real estate sector in southern Malaysia. Currently, there are a few education hubs being established within the Iskandar economic zone located in southern Malaysia. Rather than education experts leading these efforts, entrepreneurs and real estate developers are the key actors. The logic is that universities and schools project an appealing image of a neighborhood that can ultimately command higher prices for residential properties. Some suburbs near Kuala Lumpur have already set a precedent by hosting many higher education institutions (e.g., Subang Jaya and Damansara).

For Singapore, deriving economic benefits is more about commercializing research innovations rather than generating revenue from tuition fees. Over the last 10 years, Singapore has invested heavily in research infrastructure and recruited eminent foreign scientists to lead its laboratories and research councils (e.g., Nobel laureate Sydney Brenner). In 2000, the Singapore Biomedical Sciences initiative started with several state-of-the-art laboratories (e.g., the Biopolis complex). Singapore also recently launched its plan to become an intellectual property hub by providing legal services for multinational companies and innovators. These efforts focus on applied research particularly in science, technology, engineering, and mathematics (STEM) areas and affirm Singapore's determination to profit from the knowledge economy. In this approach, Singapore expects that the research industry will become an economic multiplier that increases foreign direct investment, patent registration, and the marketing of new products.

Finally, Hong Kong may identify revenue generation in some of its education hub policy documents, but the reality is that the vast majority of its policymakers are vehemently against such commercialization. In interviews with senior members of the Education Bureau (equivalent to a Ministry of Education), Central Policy Unit (advisory council to the Chief Executive of Hong Kong), and UGC, the consensus was against revenue generation through differential fees. Earlier policy statements on developing higher education as an industry elicit skepticism from policymakers today. This discrepancy between policy documents and the views of policymakers in interviews was the greatest in Hong Kong in comparison to Malaysia and Singapore. In summary, the rationale of economic benefits contains three objectives: (1) to generate revenue through student fees, (2) to leverage education as an economic multiplier, and (3) to commercialize research innovations.

Talent Development

Another important impetus in creating an education hub is talent development. This rationale is broader than developing human capital to alleviate labor shortages. Rather, many policymakers recognize the importance of holistic development to cultivate human potential. Even in a place like Singapore that has historically aligned higher education to economic imperatives, there is emerging evidence that higher education is becoming more holistic (e.g., the new liberal arts Yale–National University of Singapore College). Hong Kong's sole foreign branch campus is the Savannah College of Art and Design from the United States. Therefore, talent development is distinct from economic benefits as a rationale. Evident in all three cases is the desire to develop local talent through an education hub. The use of public resources in building an education hub demands that it recognizes the needs of local students. Resources may be in the form of start-up capital, loans, land, and the considerable time spent planning and monitoring implementation. In addition to local talent, some education hubs also actively seek out foreign talent in the form of international students, scholars, and researchers. Singapore is a remarkable example of a state leveraging its education hub to attract foreign talent. The narrative of Singapore's miraculous rise as an economic powerhouse is peppered with the use of foreign talent (Chan, 2002; Ho & Ge, 2011). An international student in Singapore could qualify for reduced tuition fees if she or he agreed to work in Singapore or for a Singaporean firm for four to six years after graduation. Similarly, as a cosmopolitan city, Hong Kong has also utilized large numbers of foreign talent since the early days of British colonialism. The education hub initiative only magnifies Hong Kong's ability to attract talent from outside. Universities in Hong Kong can be very selective in admitting students from mainland China because the demand for an education in Hong Kong far outstrips the supply.

Hong Kong also recently relaxed its immigration restrictions to allow non-local students to work and settle in the city. On the contrary, while Malaysian policymakers recognize the shortage of talent in the country and talk frequently about the need to attract foreign talent (World Bank, 2011), its recruitment efforts falter due to political sensitivities. In a society where ethnic relations are highly politicized and unemployment among graduates is a concern, policymakers are wary about importing foreign talent (Lee, 2014). However, Malaysia is eager to use its education hub to repatriate its diaspora from around the world. Repatriating overseas Malaysians is politically more palatable than importing foreign talent outright. In summary, the rationale of talent development has three objectives: (1) to develop local talent, (2) to attract foreign talent, and (3) to repatriate the diaspora.

Educational Capacity

A less common rationale behind the development of education hubs is educational capacity. In both policy documents and interviews with policymakers, building an education hub to improve the higher education system was largely a secondary issue. Hong Kong policymakers expressed the need to expose local students to global perspectives through cross-border education (e.g., diversifying local campuses with non-local students). Planners are concerned that local students may develop insular views and lack the skills to work globally upon graduation (UGC, 2010). On a different note, Malaysian policymakers view foreign students and education providers as agents who can spark greater competition within its higher education system and thereby raise the overall quality of learning and research. The assumption that an education hub can generate positive academic outcomes in both Hong Kong and Malaysia pervades both societies. Whether or not these lofty expectations for an education hub can materialize remains highly questionable. On a more practical level, Singapore occasionally views its education hub as a means to diversify the programs and institutions in its higher education system. Having spent nearly two decades building itself as an education hub, Singapore can now afford to be highly selective about the types of foreign providers it works with. For example, the new Singapore University of Technology and Design was built in collaboration with the Massachusetts Institute of Technology (MIT) to fit a gap in Singapore's higher education landscape (i.e., design melded with technology). In summary, an education hub can improve educational capacity through the following objectives: (1) to expose local students to global perspectives, (2) to promote competition among institutions and students, and (3) to diversify programs and institutions.

Soft Power

As education hubs develop, their long-term vision extends beyond the realm of education to encompass broader geopolitical interests. In other words, a state leverages higher education to exert "soft power" influence in international relations. Soft power describes a state's ability to influence others through attraction rather than domination or coercion, as is typical with military and economic hard power (Nye, 2004). For example, the United States continues to attract and influence successive generations of international students and scholars despite widespread discontent toward its foreign policies. These individuals develop a personal understanding of American society that is difficult to attain through textbook and media consumption. Many of these bright minds later become influential leaders in their home countries and forge personal and professional ties with the United States in academia, arts, business, and politics. Similarly, policymakers in Malaysia, Singapore, and Hong Kong recognize the tremendous opportunity that an education hub presents in diplomacy. By becoming an international node known for higher learning and research, an education hub engages in public and cultural diplomacy. While this political dimension of an education hub is less evident in policy documents, policymakers unequivocally identify soft power interests during interviews when speaking about the long-term vision of an education hub. More importantly, soft power is not a state-centric narrative reduced to bilateral relations or multilateral pacts. An education hub exerts soft power by mobilizing both state and non-state actors to attract and influence outsiders.

Under the rationale of soft power, three policy objectives are evident among education hubs. First, at the most basic level, many policymakers seek to strengthen ties with outsiders based on cultural heritage. Malaysia and Hong Kong are particularly skilled in foregrounding their Islamic culture and Chinese culture, respectively, when promoting themselves as education hubs. Currently, large numbers of Islamic students study in Malaysia. Iranian and Indonesian students constitute the two largest groups of international students in the country (Ministry of Higher Education, 2012). Malaysia is also rapidly developing itself as an Islamic finance education hub, which educates scholars and trains professionals in an emerging niche market of banking that is guided by religious values. Hong Kong welcomes mainland Chinese students by touting its mixed heritage as a former British colony with Chinese cultural roots. Most universities in Hong Kong also have multiple ties and partnerships to counterparts in mainland China.

In contrast, Singapore rarely emphasizes its cultural roots despite its rich multicultural fabric. Instead, Singapore strategically seeks out external actors with the knowledge and skills that can benefit the city-state. This approach illustrates the second objective in the pursuit of soft power: to network with expert individuals and institutions worldwide. For example, Singapore touts partnerships with the likes of MIT, Yale, GlaxoSmithKline, the World Bank, and eminent scientists of Nobel pedigree.

Finally, the third objective under soft power is to become a regional leader and broker. Education hubs exhibit visible regional orientations whether they are physical regions (e.g., East Asia) or conceptual regions (e.g., the Third World). An education hub can lead by becoming the first or the best in one field (e.g., biomedical sciences). It can also broker relations between one region and its external partners (e.g., Asia and the West). Both strategies accrue influence for the education hub. For Malaysia, its education hub emphasizes ties with Third-World nations and the Islamic civilization. Malaysia actively recruits students from emerging economies such as the CLMV nations (Cambodia, Laos, Myanmar, and Vietnam), which have an unmet demand for higher education. An increasing number of African students are also studying in Malaysia.

Overall, Malaysia is positioning itself as a moderate Islamic country that can facilitate understanding between Islamic and non-Islamic civilizations. In a similar fashion, Hong Kong has historically functioned as the gateway to China given its Western and Asian sensibilities. In discussions with policymakers in Hong Kong, they emphasized that the education hub initiative must contribute to the city's legacy as an intermediary. Contributions may be in the form of hosting non-local students or drawing on Hong Kong's extensive international ties as a cosmopolitan city. In many public policies, Hong Kong's regional focus is the Pearl River Delta, a large swath of southern China that has witnessed rapid industrialization since the 1980s and become a national manufacturing hub. With nine major cities and two special administrative regions (Hong Kong and Macao), the Pearl River Delta is home to 56 million people. Hong Kong's esteemed higher education has a leadership role to play in the future of the Pearl River Delta (UGC, 2010).

Singapore's ambition has long outgrown the confines of Southeast Asia and extended to Asia and beyond. With the highest per-capita gross domestic product in Southeast Asia, a limited landmass, and a small population, Singapore continuously seeks out opportunities worldwide for economic and political engagement. Singapore's recent additions to its education hub initiative all exhibit an orientation toward Asia. The country's Agency for Science, Technology and Research (A*STAR) has launched a plan to turn the city-state into "Asia's innovation capital" (A*STAR, 2011). The Nepal Hill project targets human resource training for the Asian context (JTC, 2010). The intellectual property hub has a strategic plan that recognizes Asia's shortcomings in intellectual rights registration and protection (Intellectual Property Steering Committee, 2013). In addition, Singapore is also exporting its model of governance and management by helping other Asian countries to create technology parks, economic zones, and even small-scale education hubs (e.g., Sino Singapore Guangzhou Knowledge City in China). In summary, an education hub can exert soft power with the following three objectives: (1) to strengthen ties based on cultural heritage, (2) to network with expert individuals and institutions worldwide, and (3) to become a regional leader and broker.

Rationale	Objectives	Malaysia	Singapore	Hong Kong
Economic Benefits	To generate revenue through student fees	●	○	○
	To leverage education as an economic multiplier	●	●	
	To commercialize research innovations		●	
Talent Development	To develop local talent	●	●	●
	To attract foreign talent		●	●
	To repatriate the diaspora	○	●	
Educational Capacity	To expose local students to global perspectives			●
	To promote competition among institutions and students	●		
	To diversify programs and institutions		○	
Soft Power	To strengthen ties based on cultural heritage	●		●
	To network with expert individuals and institutions worldwide		●	
	To become a regional leader and broker	●	●	●

● Primary objectives   ○ Secondary objectives

Comparative Analysis

From the analysis of the three cases in this chapter, it is clear that diverse rationales and objectives underpin the development of education hubs. On the surface, these hubs may appear to be profit-driven initiatives in cross-border education. While this assessment may be accurate at the launch of these education hubs, the motives behind their development today are far more complex and sophisticated. Policy documents do not fully capture the realities of higher education development. Under the rationale of economic benefits, transforming education into an industry remains important to Malaysia and Singapore. Today, Malaysia continues to pursue the objective of revenue generation through student fees as vigorously as it did a decade ago. While this objective is still relevant to Singapore, the commercialization of research innovations has superseded the pursuit of student fees. Singapore's ambitious plan to become Asia's innovation capital relies on profits from the knowledge economy, particularly in STEM fields, rather than a holistic pursuit of knowledge. For Hong Kong, revenue generation through student fees is evident in policy documents from the government, especially former political leaders. However, policymakers today overwhelmingly reject this objective for practical and ethical reasons. Specifically, Hong Kong policymakers are concerned about the lack of student housing and the commercialization of education. For Malaysia and Singapore, the objective of leveraging education as an economic multiplier is also evident. While Malaysia eyes lucrative ancillary services and real estate development stemming from its education hub, Singapore is eager to attract foreign direct investment in the form of branch campuses, research institutes, and joint ventures.

For the rationale of talent development, supporting the needs of local students remains fundamental to the three education hubs. Given the deep public investments in both time and money, policymakers share a sense of responsibility to local needs in education, training, and research. The major point of contention is the objective of attracting foreign talent. For Malaysia, its political climate simply does not support the recruitment of foreign talent when affirmative action and graduate unemployment remain at the fore of policy thinking. Despite the recognition that foreign talent brings tremendous benefits, policy pronouncements remain rhetorical, with half-hearted attempts at attracting foreigners. In the case of Hong Kong and Singapore, foreign talent has been at the heart of their development for the last 50 years. An education hub is therefore a natural platform for recruiting foreign talent. Singapore pursues this objective much more aggressively than Hong Kong, most likely because the former must grapple with its small land mass and declining birth rate in all policy sectors, while the latter has mainland China to buffer its shortcomings. The objective of attracting the diaspora to return home is evident in Malaysia and Singapore, but for very different reasons. Bringing home the diaspora to Malaysia is a welcomed undertaking because these individuals are considered "locals" by kinship. However, the country's efforts at repatriating the diaspora have led to mixed results and remain removed from its education hub (Lee, 2014). On the contrary, repatriating the diaspora to Singapore is a highly orchestrated strategy that dovetails with its research and development agenda. Singapore's gleaming research laboratories aim to both attract foreign talent and provide jobs for elite Singaporeans training at top universities overseas. Without a robust research sector at home, public investment in emerging Singaporean scientists would be squandered.

The rationale of educational capacity manifests very differently across the three education hubs. Capacity may be in the form of teaching and learning, institutional performance, or systemic diversity. Hong Kong is eager to use an education hub to expose its students to a global perspective. Policymakers there express a strong interest in mixing local students with non-local students and scholars to enhance learning. In contrast, Malaysia expects the education hub to promote competition among institutions and students as foreign actors populate its education system. In the minds of Malaysian policymakers, competition will ultimately raise the quality of the entire higher education system—an optimistic assumption that ignores the protectionist measures erected for public universities over the last few decades. The objective of diversifying higher education provisions is evident to some degree in Singapore and Hong Kong. By importing foreign providers and programs, a higher education system can rapidly diversify its offerings and increase its cohort participation rate. Both Singapore and Hong Kong currently have low participation rates; therefore policymakers view the education hub as a useful initiative toward widening access. Yet, for both jurisdictions, diversification is of secondary importance in comparison to the other objectives under economic benefits and talent development.

Finally, a soft power rationale also drives the development of education hubs. Geopolitical interests and public diplomacy loom large in the long-term vision of education hubs. Malaysia and Hong Kong eagerly highlight their rich cultural heritage in an effort to attract students, scholars, and institutions. From Islamic finance education to research on China-related issues, cultural roots figure prominently in the higher education landscape of both countries. In contrast, Singapore does not dwell on its cultural heritage when engaging with international actors as an education hub. Instead, it pursues connections with experts and institutions worldwide in its eternal quest to remain competitive and relevant as a small state that lacks natural resources and human capital. In an effort to engage internationally, education hubs also aim to exert influence as regional leaders and brokers. The three case studies reveal divergent interpretations of *region*. Malaysia specifically engages with developing countries and Islamic states as a leader and broker in education and diplomacy. Hong Kong is positioning itself as a leader in higher education in the Pearl River Delta. An education hub can contribute to the future development of this vibrant region in China. In addition, Hong Kong views itself as a broker between China and the rest of the world to facilitate mutual understanding. For all its global ambitions, Singapore remains strategically oriented toward Asia at large. The unbridled economic opportunities in the region spur Singaporean higher education to contribute to teaching, research, training, and governance. Singapore also plans to broker ties between multinational companies and Asia (e.g., research collaborations, human resource management, and intellectual property rights).

These comparisons reveal fundamentally different contextual factors driving the development of education hubs, even though some may share the same objectives. Malaysia has remained true to its original intent of building an education hub, in that revenue generation is still the main objective. Singapore has rapidly expanded the scope of its education hub to include high-stakes research initiatives, which have eclipsed the objective of profiting from cross-border academic programs. As a relative newcomer to the education hub phenomenon, Hong Kong has made several pronouncements and conducted several studies to plan its education hub. However, it seems to lack the fortitude to carry forward the initiative. The central government's plan to develop education as a service industry received widespread criticism among the policymakers interviewed for this study. However, this discrepancy between policy rhetoric and the views of research participants is not a rejection of education hub as an initiative but rather a disagreement over rationales. Therefore, in terms of policy coherence, Malaysian and Singaporean policymakers are largely unified in their rationales for developing an education hub. Their views resonate with the rationales stated in policy documents. For Hong Kong, a deep schism exists between policy documents and contemporary policymakers. The official rhetoric views the education hub largely as a service industry to generate revenue, but policymakers unanimously reject this approach.

Implications

As one of the two regions in the world active in the development of education hubs, Asia continues to cultivate cross-border education to fit its needs. Despite sharp differences in economic development, higher education infrastructure, and research capacity, Asian states are launching various forms of education hubs. These hubs vary widely in scale: national, municipal, or zonal initiative (Knight, 2014). They also vary in their regional orientation. The policy rationales and objectives identified through empirical work in this chapter can provide a useful framework for evaluating other education hubs in the world. The framework is by no means definitive or prescriptive, given that higher education developments are dynamic and multifaceted. However, the experiences of Malaysia, Hong Kong, and Singapore raise questions about other education hubs. In addition to hubs in the Middle East, South Korea and Sri Lanka have also recently launched education hub initiatives. What are the fundamental motives and purposes for creating an education hub? What is beyond the growing body of policy documents and accumulation of foreign branch campuses? How closely do implementation strategies reflect policy rhetoric? Have education hubs changed their policy orientations over time? How can outputs and outcomes be compared across education hubs if their fundamental goals differ? These important questions about education hubs require further attention from both researchers and policymakers as cross-border education becomes more prevalent in many parts of the world. Asia's expertise in this area of higher education can provide many useful lessons for other countries and regions interested in adapting cross-border education for their needs.

REFERENCES

Agency for Science, Technology and Research (A*STAR). (2011). Science, Technology & Enterprise Plan 2015 (STEP2015). Singapore: A*STAR.

Chan, C. B. (Ed.). (2002). Heart work. Singapore: Economic Development Board.

Contact Singapore. (2011). Singapore the Global Schoolhouse. Synergy. September/October 2011, 12-15.

Economic Committee. (1986). The Singapore economy: New directions (Report of the Economic Committee). Singapore: Economic Committee.

Economic Review Committee (2003). Report of the Economic Review Committee: New challenges, fresh goals. Singapore: Ministry of Trade and Industry.

Ho, K. C., & Ge, Y. (2011). Education and human capital management in a world city: The case of Singapore. *Asia Pacific Journal of Education, 31*(3), 263–276.

Intellectual Property Steering Committee. (2013). *Intellectual property hub master plan: Developing Singapore as a global IP hub in Asia.* Singapore: Intellectual Property Office of Singapore.

JTC. (2010). Nepal Hill—Hub for leadership training and alternative investment. *Periscope, 3,* 13.

Knight, J. (Ed.). (2014). *International education hubs: Student, talent, knowledge-innovation models.* Dordrecht, The Netherlands: Springer.

Knight, J., & Lee, J. (2014). Three types of education hubs: Student, talent and knowledge. In J. Knight (Ed.), *International education hubs: Student, talent, knowledge-innovation models* (pp. 29–42). Dordrecht, The Netherlands: Springer.

Lee, J. T. (2014). Education hubs and talent development: Policymaking and implementation challenges. *Higher Education*, 68(6), 807-823.

Ministry of Higher Education. (2012). *Malaysia higher education statistics 2011.* Putrajaya, Malaysia: Ministry of Higher Education.

5th Malaysia Plan. (1986). *5th Malaysia Plan 1986–90.* Kuala Lumpur, Malaysia: Prime Minister's Department.

Nye, J. (2004). *Soft power: The means to success in world politics.* New York, NY: Public Affairs.

Sharma, Y., & Tan, E. (2013, September 5). "World-class" bid may have caused admissions fiasco. *University World News Global Edition*, 286.

Tan, C. M. (2002). Services: A road less travelled. In C. B. Chan (Ed.), *Heart work* (pp. 260–267). Singapore: Economic Development Board.

Task Force on Economic Challenges. (2009). *Recommendations from the Task Force on Economic Challenges.* Hong Kong: Task Force on Economic Challenges.

Tham, S. Y. (2010). Trade in higher education services in Malaysia: Key policy challenges. *Higher Education Policy*, 23(1), 99-122.

Tung, C. H. (2004). *2004–2005 Policy Address: Seizing opportunities for development, promoting people based governance.* Hong Kong: Hong Kong Government.

University Grants Committee (UGC). (1996). *Higher education in Hong Kong: A report by the University Grants Committee.* Hong Kong: University Grants Committee.

University Grants Committee (UGC). (2004a). *Hong Kong higher education: To make a difference, to move with the times.* Hong Kong: University Gants Committee.

University Grants Committee (UGC). (2004b). *Hong Kong higher education: Integration matters.* Hong Kong: University Gants Committee.

University Grants Committee (UGC). (2010). *Aspirations for the higher education system in Hong Kong.* Hong Kong: University Gants Committee.

World Bank. (2011). *Malaysia economic monitor: Brian drain.* Bangkok: World Bank.

NOTES

[1] In Hong Kong, the term "non-local student" refers to students from mainland China and the rest of the world.

Chapter Seven

Higher Education in India: Overcoming Mediocrity[1]

PHILIP G. ALTBACH, BOSTON COLLEGE CENTER FOR INTERNATIONAL HIGHER EDUCATION

Introduction

India, with the world's second largest higher education system and a rapidly growing economy as one of the BRIC nations, faces significant challenges in building both capacity and excellence in higher education. India's higher education system is characterized by "islands of excellence in a sea of mediocrity." The mainstream universities are recognized as lacking in quality. Only the Indian Institutes of Technology and related institutions garner international recognition. This article analyzes the challenges facing India's higher education system in the 21st century.

The saga of Indian higher education since the 1960s is complex, variegated, and reflects the country's development over time. India's education development has, for much of this period, lagged behind economic and social development. Like India itself, higher education realities are contradictory. India, in 2014, has the world's second-largest higher education system in terms of student numbers, having recently overtaken the United States in enrollments, with 20 million students enrolled in postsecondary education, attending more than 35,500 colleges and 574 universities. It is estimated that more than half of the world's postsecondary institutions are located in India; many of the colleges are uneconomically small. Approximately 20 percent of the 18-to-22-year-old age cohort is in postsecondary education—with a goal of enrolling 25 percent by 2017 and 32 percent by 2022—an extremely ambitious goal (Rashtriya Uchchartar Shiksha Abhiyan, 2013). Drop-out rates are high, with many of those who enter the system failing to complete a degree. Quality is generally poor—although there are significant islands of excellence—and the system overall is a sea of mediocrity; none of India's universities scores well on any of the international higher education rankings (Altbach 2006).

India, like many developing countries, has been swamped by massification—the rapid expansion of higher education enrollments that is the result of an unstoppable demand by growing segments of the population for access. India's challenges have been magnified by increased demand for access, combined with overall population growth. In no country has rapid expansion been accompanied by improvement in overall quality, and in this respect India is no different than many other countries (Carnoy et al. 2013).

India had several advantages at the time of independence in 1947, but was unable to capitalize on them. English was the near universal medium of higher education, giving India immediate links to the outside world, access to scientific information, and textbooks. Although fairly small, India had developed a fairly mature higher education system, with several reputable universities and specialized institutions at the top, and a respectable number of undergraduate colleges, a few of which were of international standards. While access was limited to a small urban elite and most higher education institutions were located in metropolitan areas, colleges and universities could be found throughout India.

Though the system grew fairly rapidly throughout most of the post-independence period, population growth and an expansion of primary and secondary education meant that higher education could not keep up with demand. In line with global thinking concerning education and development, emphasis was placed on primary education and not on higher education. In most developing countries, overall quality declined as enrollments increased.

Despite considerable rhetoric in the past few years about India's higher education "takeoff" and the link between higher education and recent economic growth, there is little evidence that economic success has had much effect on improvements in higher education. Indeed, it has argued that if higher education is not improved, India may lose the advantage of its "demographic dividend" of a large population of young people who could, if well educated, spearhead continuing economic growth (Altbach and Jayaram 2010).

It is worth examining some of the broad trends that characterize Indian higher education. These are presented in no special order of importance. They are, however, linked and constitute a pattern of development over time.

A Challenging History

Like much of the developing world, India experienced a long period of colonialism. British rule over much of the subcontinent lasted for several centuries—longer than the colonial experience of most other countries. British-style higher education dates back to 1823, when several colleges were founded. Universities were established at Bombay, Calcutta, and Madras in 1858—around the same time that higher education was expanded beyond Oxford and Cambridge in England (Kaur 2003). When compared to most developing countries, India has had a longer history of modern higher education. For example, higher education was largely absent from sub-Saharan Africa until the 1960s (Ashby 1966).

While the British were in general not avid supporters of higher education in India, they did not prevent its establishment. After a laissez-faire period, higher education was organized as part of colonial policy, ensuring that the language of instruction was English and that the organization and structure of academic institutions conformed to British patterns and policy. The British were more supportive of higher education in India than they were in their colonial possessions in Africa (Ashby 1966). The colonial authorities spent few resources on higher education, and the impetus for the modest expansion of higher education in India during colonial rule was from Indians. Indeed, there were efforts to keep enrollments small, in order to prevent the emergence of a subversive intelligentsia or unemployed graduates. Both of these goals were, at least in part, failures, since educated Indians spearheaded the independence movement. The British sought to ensure that the graduates of the colleges and universities were suited to serve the needs of the colonial administration, rather than emerging Indian society and industry.

At the time of independence, there were 19 universities and 695 colleges, with an overall enrollment of fewer than 270,000 students. By the standards of newly independent developing countries in the mid-20th century, India was well situated. It had a relatively comprehensive array of higher education institutions, although few were vocationally or scientifically oriented. The quality of this small system was relatively high. While serving only a tiny proportion of the age cohort—well under 1 percent—India had the basic structure of a higher education establishment on which to build.

The challenge of coping with the demands for expansion, combined with political and other pressures on higher education, meant that it was not possible to take advantage of existing strengths and to build for both quantity and quality.

Language: A Continuing Dilemma

At the time of independence, the language of instruction in higher education throughout India was almost exclusively English. While there are no accurate statistics for English literacy in India, it was quite unlikely that even 5 percent of India were literate in English in 1950. Thus, the huge majority of Indians did not have access to higher education. There were fundamental disagreements among the founders of modern India about language policy. Mahatma Gandhi argued strongly for the use of Hindi as the national language. India's first prime minister, Jawaharlal Nehru, was sympathetic to the continued use of English. Many political leaders in the south and in some other parts of the country were opposed to Hindi and, thus, favored English as a "link language" and emphasized the use of regional languages in education. India's federal constitution gave authority over education largely to the states, which had considerable power to decide on language issues. These post-independence realities resulted in a hodgepodge of policies in different parts of the country.

Some of the states in the "Hindi belt" in north India stressed the use of Hindi, and the central government made some efforts to produce and translate textbooks into Hindi, for use in undergraduate education. Almost all of the universities and specialized research institutions, sponsored by the central government, continued to use English as the language of instruction. The states varied considerably in language policy. Most southern states continued English as the main language for higher education. Some permitted the use of regional languages. States in other parts of India varied in their policies. Certain ones used a combination of English and the regional language. In some cases, specific universities preferred to retain instruction in English despite the state policy. Thus, language policy and practice in higher education was, and remains, varied throughout the country.

Without any reliable statistics, it is likely that the use of the English language has increased in Indian higher education, especially in the more prestigious universities and colleges and in the highly selective institutions—such as the Indian Institutes of Technology and the Indian Institutes of Management. Much of the private higher education sector functions in English as well. The research sector is entirely dominated by English, and most scholarly communication in journals and on the Internet takes place in English. While the language debate in Indian higher education has not entirely ended, English has emerged as the key language in Indian higher education. Its role, always strong, has increased in importance as globalization has affected the higher education sector in the 21st century.

The traditional role of English has given India significant advantages in global higher education. Professors and students can communicate easily with peers in other countries, and mobility is enhanced. Indian universities can more easily enroll international students. Indians may contribute directly to the global knowledge network (Altbach 2007b). Yet, there are some disadvantages, as well. English is not the mother tongue of Indians, and it remains to some extent a foreign language. The large majority of Indians do not speak and are not literate in English—thus putting them at a significant disadvantage in the higher education sector and unable to gain access to the social and economic mobility that English-medium conveys in India. While there seems to be no accurate estimate of the proportion of Indians who speak English, 10 percent seems to be a realistic number. This constitutes more than 100 million English speakers—more than the populations of the United Kingdom, Australia, and Canada combined—but still a modest percentage of Indians.

Indian Universities in a Globalized World

Indian higher education has interacted gingerly with the rest of the world. The higher education sector, as the economy in general until recently, has been largely protectionist. While many Indians have gone abroad for higher education—and many have contributed significantly to technological and economic development in, for example, the Silicon Valley in California as well as in India—Indian higher education has been largely closed to the rest of the world. Non-citizens cannot normally be hired as permanent members of the academic staff, and branch campuses and other foreign academic transplants have not been allowed.

In the past decade, there has been a lively debate in India concerning how Indian higher education should engage with the rest of the world. Kapil Sibal, the minister for human resource development from 2009 to 2012, proposed to open India's education market to the world and asked parliament to approve legislation for this purpose. However, the legislation was not passed, and thus India remains largely closed to foreign universities and other education providers. Even if the law had been passed, the conditions for establishing branch campuses and other initiatives were sufficiently unfavorable that few foreign institutions would have been attracted. However, many less-formal arrangements have been put into place—including a number of joint-degree programs, franchised arrangements, partnerships, and others. Thus, the door is perhaps half-open.

Some have argued that India is better off developing higher education on its own. Others favor an open door, and the idea that the rigors of the market would have a positive impact on Indian higher education. Clearly, India needs good ideas, and insulating the system from international concepts and practices is not helpful.

The Sea of Mediocrity

Indian higher education can be characterized by a sea of mediocrity, in which some islands of excellence can be found. A large majority of Indian students attend the 574 universities and the 35,500 colleges affiliated to them. While a few of the universities—most notably those without affiliated colleges, such as Jawaharlal Nehru University in New Delhi, several other universities sponsored directly by the central government, and some colleges offer high quality—most provide mediocre to poor quality of instruction. Most of the 286 public universities that are managed by state governments, 111 private universities, and 129 "deemed" universities provide poor to middling quality education. The vast majority of colleges, particularly newer private college that receive little or no government funding, are of quite low quality. A small number of well-established colleges managed by state authorities, some of those established by Christian and other religious organizations, and a small number of others are quite good—but these are a small percentage of the total. As with much in India, there are exceptions to these generalizations. For example, several new non-profit private universities established by wealthy philanthropists, such as Azam Premji University and Shiv Nadar University, show much promise.

Graduate unemployment in many fields, especially in arts and sciences subjects, is a perennial problem in India. This situation is due in part to producing too many graduates for available jobs in these fields and in part due to the low quality of many degree holders. Even in fields such as management and engineering, where there is demand from employers, graduates from many colleges and universities are considered deficient in quality and poorly trained for the positions available. Employers indicate that they must retrain many of those they do hire.

To some extent, a decline in quality at the bottom tier of Indian higher education is an inevitable result of massification and can be found worldwide. Students with poorer academic qualifications are able to gain access to higher education. In India, the complex system of reservations policy for disenfranchised groups has exacerbated this problem—while at the same time providing opportunities that did not exist before. The existing modest admissions standards are relaxed for these groups, while little extra help is provided for students without adequate secondary school achievement, thus contributing to high drop-out rates. The "reservation" system identifies specific historically disadvantaged groups, such as lower caste populations and tribal groups, and reserves a specific proportion of admissions place—and faculty slots—which can be filled only by these groups. The percentage that is reserved is often close to half the total.

Expansion has also brought many new types of institutions onto the postsecondary education landscape—mostly at the bottom of the system. Many of the "deemed universities" are institutions of modest quality—although some of the older ones are well established. New private universities present a similarly mixed picture, with most of lesser quality. Thousands of "unfunded" undergraduate colleges in engineering, information technology, and other fields have emerged in the past several decades and are affiliated with universities and thus able to offer degrees. Again, the overall quality of these colleges is often quite poor, and many are quasi-for-profit institutions.

The traditional universities and their affiliated colleges have proved resistant to reform. In terms of their structure, role, and governance these institutions have been virtually unchanged for a half-century, despite widespread recognition of their problems. Some reforms have been put into place, such as permitting some of the best colleges to become independent of the universities and offer their own degrees, but implementation has been limited. The entrenched bureaucracy of the affiliating system remains the core of higher education; and until it is significantly improved or modified, essential improvement in Indian higher education will not be possible.

Islands of Excellence

Despite the immense problems of the Indian higher education system, a small sector of globally competitive, high-quality postsecondary institutions exists. It is significant that all of them are outside the established university structure. Planners were unwilling to entrust new and innovative ideas to the traditional universities. The best known of these institutions are the Indian Institutes of Technology and Indian Institutes of Management. There are many others. These include the Indian Institute of Science, Bengaluru, the Tata Institute of Fundamental Research, and the Tata Institute of Social Sciences (both in Mumbai), the Indian Statistical Institute in Kolkata, and others. At least one of the national universities supported by the central government, Jawaharlal Nehru University in New Delhi is also held in high regard.

These institutions share several attributes. They are all public and funded by the central government. All are relatively small and are outside of the structure of the traditional universities. These institutions have a significant degree of autonomy that is somewhat unique in the Indian higher education system. They are all initiatives of the central government, with little or no involvement by the states. While none of these successful institutions are lavishly funded—indeed, by international standards they are all underfunded—they have achieved considerable success.

All of these successful institutions were able to attract professors committed to high standards of teaching and innovation—without paying exceptionally high salaries—showing that some Indian academics are attracted by new ideas and high standards. However, it is sometimes difficult to attract top talent, and some of the Indian Institutes of Technology have experienced difficulties in recruiting. These top institutions also attract the best students in India—and indeed they and some of the others may be the most selective institutions in the world, accepting only a tiny fraction of the students who take the national entrance examinations for these schools.

The Failure of Planning

Indian higher education has not failed to create a "world-class" system because of a lack of ideas. At least a half-dozen high-level commissions have issued intelligent reports over the past 40 years, starting perhaps with the University Education Commission (Radhakrishnan Report) in 1948, as recently with the National Knowledge Commission Report in 2007, and the Committee to Advise on Renovation and Rejuvenation of Higher Education (Yashpal Committee) in 2009. The most recent effort, the 2013 Rashtriya Uchchartar Shiksha Abhiyan (National Higher Education Mission), is the latest well-documented and thoughtful analysis of current realities and recommendations for the future. These reports have recommended many ideas for thoughtful reform, development, and improvement. Over time, elements of some of these reports have been partly implemented, but in no case at all have any been comprehensively applied. The Planning Commission's five-year plans generally paid little attention to higher education, although occasionally initiatives were outlined and funds provided. The current 12th Plan for the first time gives some comprehensive focus to higher education.

Although most of the funding and supervision of higher education is in the hands of the states, there is little evidence of planning or innovation at the state level. In general, the states have simply tried to keep up with the demand for expansion of higher education. A few have made some effort. Kerala has attempted to think systematically about higher education development, and Gujarat has recently focused on higher education as part of the state's development strategy in the "Vibrant Gujarat" project.

The University Grants Commission—responsible at the national level for funding, innovation and planning of higher education under the control of the central government—has developed some small-scale programs in curriculum, teaching, and other areas but by and large has not played an active role in large scale innovation. The current proposal to establish a National Commission of Higher Education and Research will bring together a number of central government initiatives and provide a central focus for planning, research, and innovation.

As a result of divided control—lack of coordination among the different agencies with responsibility for higher education at the central and state levels, inadequate authority for implementation of change, and inadequate funding—it is fair to say that higher education planning has not been successful, despite a range of good proposals over the years.

The Necessity of Systems

Massification requires a higher education establishment, with institutions serving different purposes and missions that are organized logically to cater to different clienteles and meet various demands. The best organized ones, such as the renowned California public higher education system, articulates the different kinds of institutions, so that students can move from one type of college to another. In the California case, the public system has community colleges, four-year and master's degree universities, and research universities—such as the University of California, Berkeley—that offer doctorates. Students may enter one type of school and, if the quality of their academic work permits, can transfer up to a different type of institution. Systems of this type hold costs at appropriate levels, provide access, and ensure that the various societal needs are met. Government authorities control the missions and budgets of the institutions at the various levels—preventing "mission creep" and ensuring that institutions will stay focused on their established mission.

India has never developed a clearly articulated academic system, at either the central or state levels, although informal systems have evolved over time. India is a federal system, with much of the responsibility for higher education in the hands of India's states but with the central government having some authority as well. India's 35 states have little in common and range from Uttar Pradesh, with a population of 200 million, to small states with just a few million. All of India's universities have a research mission; some are better able to engage in research than others. Few universities at the state level receive adequate budgets for research, and few have a research-oriented academic staff. The rapid expansion of undergraduate arts and sciences and also professional colleges has also taken place largely without planning. The specialized high-quality institutions such as the IIT's are treated separately from the mainstream colleges and universities.

The recent centrally supported initiative to establish state higher education councils is a move toward more rational higher policy and planning at the state level. However, only a small number of states, such as Kerala, have fully implemented councils and have appropriate coordinating bodies in place.

India requires, at both the state and central levels, higher education systems that are rationally organized and differentiated in order to ensure that the increasingly diverse needs of higher education can be rationally met.

Politics

Indian higher education, much to its detriment, is infused with politics at all levels. Colleges are often established by political leaders, as a patronage machine and a way of providing access and jobs for supporters. The location of universities is sometimes influenced by state or local politics. Even national universities have occasionally been enmeshed in politics.

University and college elections are frequently politicized. National, regional, and local political machines are frequently engaged in campus politics. Student unions are often politicized. Academic decisions are determined more by political than academic considerations. Political intrigue and infighting may infuse campus life. In extreme cases, campus politics can turn violent, and disruption of normal academic life is not uncommon. More often than not, the politics is not ideological but rather regional or caste-based.

Universities and colleges, which employ considerable numbers of staff and offer access to a highly sought after commodity—an educational credential—are valuable political engines. Academic institutions are often local power centers and clearly seen as valuable sources of patronage.

As long as political calculations enter into decisions about the location of universities, the appointment of vice chancellors and other academic leaders, approval for establishing new colleges and other institutions, and other aspects of higher education, India will be unable to fulfill its goals of quality, access, and the creation of a world-class higher education system.

A Pattern of Inadequate Investment

Higher education has never been adequately funded. In 2011-2012 India spent a modest 1.22 percent of its gross domestic product on postsecondary education—a more modest investment than some other rapidly expanding economies and below European levels of expenditure. From the beginning, emphasis was placed on meeting the demands of mass access and expansion rather than building up a meaningful high-quality university sector, and even financial support for mass access has been inadequate.

The divided responsibility for supporting higher education by the states and the central government was an additional detriment, since coordination was difficult. In any case, most of the responsibility fell to the states, many of which were unable to provide the needed support and in any case were more concerned with basic literacy and primary and secondary education rather than higher education. Indeed, for much of India's post-independence history, the concern of policymakers at all levels was for literacy and basic education rather than higher education.

In the 21ˢᵗ century, with the beginning of the Indian economic transformation, higher education has received greater priority. The National Knowledge Commission's (2007) reports stressed the significance of the universities and encouraged both expansion of access and improvement in quality. Little has been done to implement the recommendations. Without adequate funding, higher education can neither expand appropriately nor improve in quality.

The Fall and Rise of the Guru

At the heart of any academic institution is the professor. By international and particularly developing country standards, the Indian academic profession is relatively well off. While most Indian academics have full-time appointments, service conditions are poor in most private institutions, especially the private colleges. Academics typically have job security, although a formal tenure system does not exist. Salaries, when compared with other countries according to purchasing power parity measures, fall into the upper-middle ranks of a 2012 study of academic salaries in 28 countries (Altbach, et al. 2012). While Indian academics will not become rich with their salaries, they can generally live in a middle-class style, at least outside of the major metropolitan centers. This is in sharp contrast to many other countries, including China, where academic salaries must be supplemented by additional income.

Yet, the academic profession faces some serious problems (Jayaram 2003). The differences in status, working conditions, and salaries are significant between the large majority of the academic profession who teach in undergraduate colleges and the small minority who hold appointments in university departments and teach postgraduate students. Yet, even college teachers can in general live in a middle-class style, based on their academic salaries, due in large part to significant salary increases in the past few years.

The academic profession is characterized by high levels of bureaucracy and is bound by civil service regulations. Most colleges are hierarchical in structure and provide few opportunities for participation in college governance or decision-making. College teachers, particularly, possess little autonomy and only modest control over what they teach, and teaching loads tend to be fairly high. It has been observed that college teachers have little more autonomy than high school teachers (Altbach 1979). For the large majority of colleges that are affiliated to universities, control over many aspects of teaching, curriculum, and examinations is regulated by the university.

The small minority of academics with appointments in university departments is expected to produce research: they have modest teaching responsibilities and much greater autonomy. Indeed, almost all of the published research by Indian academics is produced by university-based academics and not by college teachers. Salaries are also more favorable. University staff also supervises postgraduate students and, thus, play a key role in educating the next generation of the academic profession. Many university departments work closely with the colleges to organize curriculum, set and administer examinations, and carry out the other responsibilities of the affiliating system.

Indian academics are seldom evaluated for their work. Their jobs depend mainly on longevity and rank. Few, if any, efforts evaluate productivity in teaching or research, and those whose performance is seen as marginal are allowed to continue. Salaries are also allocated by length of service and rank for the most part, and there is no way of rewarding good performance or punishing inadequate work. Where top quality is the norm, such as in the Indian Institutes of Technology, it is more the culture and tradition of the institution than any reward system that is responsible.

The Indian academic profession is in a somewhat paradoxical situation (Patel 2012). Compared to academics in other developing countries, Indian postsecondary teachers are not badly off—either in terms of salary or working conditions. Yet, for the most part, the organization of the higher education system does not encourage the academics to do their best work.

An Increasingly Dominant Private Sector

India's higher education system has always been a curious, and perhaps internationally unique, combination of public and private institutions. Almost from the beginning, most undergraduate colleges were established by private interests and managed by private agencies such as philanthropic societies, religious groups, or others. Most of these private colleges received government funds and thus were "aided" institutions. The universities were all public institutions, for the most part established by the states.

This situation has dramatically changed in recent years (Agarwal 2009). Most of the private colleges established in the past several decades are "unaided" and thus fully responsible for their own funding through tuition charges or other private sources of funds. Where tuition fees are capped, some institutions levy other capitation (a kind of required donation) fees and other charges. Similarly, many of the "deemed" (this term refers to an arrangement for government recognition of some institutions as universities outside of the normal pattern) universities are also private institutions— receiving no government funds. Some of the unaided colleges and universities seem to be "for profit," although management and governance is often not very transparent. Most, although not all, are in the lower ranks of the academic hierarchy. The unaided private colleges are affiliated to a university in their region; and it is increasingly difficult for the universities to effectively supervise the large numbers of colleges, particularly when the financial aspects of the institutions are not obvious.

As in many countries, massification has contributed to the rise of the private sector in higher education. The state has been unwilling or unable to provide funding for mass access, and the private sector has stepped into the void. Public control over the direction of the new private sector has often been lost, and quality has suffered as well. The Indian case is particularly complex, since the public sector universities that provide affiliation to the new unaided private colleges are directly involved in legitimizing and supervising this new sector.

A new trend in private higher education is emerging as well. In the past several decades, a small number of civic-minded philanthropists have begun to invest in higher education, several of them creating nonprofit universities with high standards and a social mission. The Azim Premji University, for example, focuses on the education system and is attempting to improve teacher education and research on education. These new institutions—if sustained, allowed sufficient autonomy, and endowed with innovative ideas as well as funds—may help to create world-class universities in India.

What Has India Done Right?

If one were searching for international "best practices" or "top ideas" in higher education, there is little if anything from India that would spring to mind. As this essay points out, India's contemporary higher education reality does not compare favorably with the most successful systems. When compared with the two other developing country BRICs, Brazil and China, India lags behind on most measures of higher education achievement.

At the same time, India has made significant progress in the context of post-independence challenges. India's policymakers stressed literacy and primary and secondary education in the first half century of independence and made significant progress in these areas, particularly taking into account continuing population growth. While postsecondary education did not receive the support it required, expansion was steady, and access has been steadily widened. Students from rural areas, disadvantaged groups, and especially young people from Dalit (formerly untouchable) communities have all gained greater access to higher education.

While the quality of Indian higher education has, overall, probably declined over the past half century, it has not collapsed. The rigidities of the affiliating system and the bureaucratic arrangements have no doubt prevented the segment of the system from improving, but at the same time these systems have ensured stability in the context of continuing stress.

India has produced remarkable talent in the past half century. The problem is that much of this talent left the country and is highly successful overseas. The statistics concerning graduates from the Indian Institutes of Technology are remarkable: a very high proportion of each graduating class leaves India and achieves remarkable accomplishments overseas. While a small number of graduates return to India, a somewhat larger group, based overseas, works with Indian colleagues and companies. Yet, it is fair to say that the "brain drain" is still alive in the 21st century, although it is now combined with "brain exchange" (Saxenian 2006).

A quite small but visible and impressive group of postsecondary institutions has flourished in the otherwise inhospitable soil of Indian higher education. Indian Institutes of Technology, Indian Institutes of Management, and a group of specialized teaching and research universities were built around the edges of the established academic system. Further, a small number among the thousands of colleges affiliated to India's universities have achieved high levels of excellence in undergraduate teaching. These examples clearly show that it is possible to build world-class higher education in India, if the conditions for development are right.

There is no shortage of ideas for improving higher education in India. Various reports and commissions have pointed to a variety of ways forward. Small-scale experiments and innovative institutions have also proved successful. If these ideas and experiences could be used as templates for improvement, India may be able to move forward.

The Challenges Ahead

Given the realities of contemporary Indian higher education, it is not possible to be optimistic about a breakthrough in quality. It seems quite unlikely that any of India's existing universities will soon become world-class. Even if the Indian government were, Chinese-style, identify a dozen or so existing institutions for massive investment and upgrading, significant reforms in management, governance to and in other areas would be required. It might be more successful to create entirely new institutions, without the constraints of existing universities. The establishment of the Indian Institutes of Technology shows that this can be successful, although in that case it was on a rather small scale. However, India does have the significant advantage of a diaspora that might be lured back for a worthy and realistic cause.

Due to the enormity of the challenges, the private sector will necessarily be a part of India's higher education future. But, so far, harnessing the private sector for the public good has been problematical. Yet, elements of solutions exist. Many of the traditional private nonprofit colleges provide excellent undergraduate education, as do some private postgraduate professional colleges. A few of the new nonprofit universities seem quite committed to their educational mission.

The greatest challenge is, of course, continued expansion of the system to provide access. India in 2012 enrolls approximately 20 percent of the relevant age cohort—well under China's 26 percent and below the other BRIC countries. Thus, India will need to devote resources and attention to continued expansion of postsecondary education. The National Knowledge Commission noted that 1,500 more universities will be needed. It has been estimated that China and India will account for more than half of the world's enrollment growth by 2050.

At the same time, India's increasingly sophisticated economy will need some colleges and universities of world-class standing—institutions that can compete with the best in the world, if manpower needs for the future are to be fulfilled. At the same time, if India is to take advantage of its "demographic dividend" and provide appropriate access and equity, the traditional universities and the thousands of colleges affiliated to them must be improved and reformed—this perhaps is the greatest challenge facing Indian higher education.

REFERENCES

Agarwal, Pawan. 2009. *Indian higher education: Envisioning the future.* New Delhi: Sage.

Altbach, Philip G. 1979. The distorted guru: The college teacher in Bombay. In, *The Indian academic profession,* ed. Suma Chitnis and Philip G. Altbach, 5–44. Delhi: Macmillan.

Altbach, Philip G. 2006. Tiny at the Top, *Wilson Quarterly* (Autumn, 2006): 49-51

Altbach, Philip G. 2007. The imperial tongue: English as the dominating academic language. *Economic and Political Weekly* (September 8): 3608–11.

Altbach, Philip G., Liz Reisberg, Maria Yudkevich, Gregory Androushchak, and Iván F. Pacheco, eds. 2012. *Paying the professoriate: A global comparison of compensation and contracts.* New York: Routlege.

Altbach, Philip G., and N. Jayaram. 2010. Can India garner the demographic dividend? *Hindu* (December 8): 10.

Ashby, Eric. 1966. *Universities: British, Indian, African: A study in the ecology of higher education.* Cambridge, MA: Harvard Univ. Press.

Carnoy, Martin, Prashant Loyalka, Maria Dobryakova, Rafiq Dossani, Isak Froumin, Katherine Kuhns, Jandhyala B. G. Tilak, and Rong Wang. *University expansion in a changing global economy: Triumph of the BRICS?* Stanford, CA: Stanford University Press.

Jayaram, N. 2003. The fall of the guru: The decline of the academic profssion in India. in *The decline of the guru: The academic profession in the Third World,* ed. P. G. Altbach, 199–230. New York: Palgrave.

Kaur, Kuldip. 2003. *Higher education in India: 1781–2003.* New Delhi: University Grants Commission.

National Knowledge Commission, 2007. *Report to the nation.* New Delhi: National Knowledge Commission.

Patel, Pravin J. 2012. Academic underperformance of Indian universities, incompatible academic culture, and the societal context. *Social Change* 42: 9–29.

Rashtriya Uchchartar Shiksha Abhiyan (National Higher Education Mission). 2013. New Delhi: Ministry of Human Resource Development.

Saxenian, AnnaLee. 2006. The new Argonauts: Regional advantage in a global economy. Cambridge, MA: Harvard University Press.

NOTES

[1] This chapter was originally published as, Altbach, P.G. (2012). Afterword: India's higher education challenges. In Agarwal, P. (Ed.), A Half-Century of Indian Higher Education: Essays by Philip G Altbach. Thousand Oaks, CA: Sage Publications. It is presented here with permission from Sage Publications.

Chapter Eight

Locating Malaysia's Place Within the ASEAN Higher Education Landscape: Current Status, Challenges, and Future Prospects

MOHD. ISMAIL ABD AZIZ, MINISTRY OF EDUCATION, MALAYSIA, AND UNIVERSITI TEKNOLOGI MALAYSIA

DORIA ABDULLAH, UNIVERSITY TEKNOLOGI MALAYSIA

Introduction

Malaysia is heading into interesting and challenging times. In 2015, the country took over the chair of the Association of Southeast Asian Nations (ASEAN), a sovereign region with 10 member countries[1] covering 4.43 million square kilometers and a population of more than 617 million. It will witness the realization of an integrated ASEAN Community by December 31, 2015, with a vision towards free regional movement of goods, services, investment, and skilled labor (ASEAN Secretariat, 2014b). In addition, the country will also need to step up efforts in fulfilling its high-income, developed nation aspirations by 2020, on top of its own target of becoming a hub of international higher education excellence (Knight &

Morshidi Sirat, 2011). The Malaysian higher education system as a whole and its higher education institutions (HEIs) will experience two significant acid tests in the next five years (2015-2020): (1) its relevance and contribution towards national development and (2) its position as a higher education provider capable of serving the region and beyond.

Of interest within the context of this chapter is the looming regional agenda on ASEAN 2015 Community integration (ASEAN Secretariat, 2014b). The region is rich in culture, social norms, religion, natural resources, and history. From its inception in 1967—with Thailand, Malaysia, Indonesia, Singapore, and the Philippines as founding members — to the current 10-country membership, ASEAN has weathered conflicts, territorial disputes, civil and economic crises within national boundaries and across the region. The member countries are in varying stages of development. In 2012, the lowest recorded gross domestic product (GDP) per capita was $978 (Cambodia) while the highest being $52,069 (Singapore) (ASEAN Secretariat, 2014a)[2]. More than 51 percent of the ASEAN population is between 20 and 54 years old, with Cambodia, Lao PDR, Myanmar, and Vietnam, the group of four also known as CLMV, having a bulging population between the ages of 5 and 19. Other than Cambodia (76.7 percent) and Lao PDR (75.3 percent), the remaining member countries have recorded an adult literacy rate of more than 90 percent. Myanmar has the lowest ratio of cellular or mobile phone density per 1,000 people (15.7), while countries such as Brunei Darussalam (1,125), Malaysia (1,192.2), Singapore (1,435.7), Thailand (1,066), and Vietnam (1,296.3) recording higher telecommunication accessibility. Even the percentage of population under national poverty line varied, with four countries i.e. Cambodia (21.1 percent), Lao PDR (24 percent), Myanmar (25.6 percent), and the Philippines (26.3 percent) recording more than 20 percent poor population.

Despite the growth disparity, the ASEAN region has immense economic opportunities. Projections place Indonesia as the seventh largest global economy by 2030 with a strong 135 million members of the consumer class, a significant increase from 45 million in 2010 (Oberman, Dobbs, Budiman, Thompson, & Rosse, 2012). There was a 9.9 percent increase in the growth of hotels and restaurants in Vietnam that was fueled by an 11 percent increase in tourist arrival (Asian Development Bank, 2014). As a result, the service sector became the greatest contributor to Vietnam's GDP in 2013. In terms of trade, intra-ASEAN trade stood at 24.3 percent while trade with China, Japan, EU-28, and the United States constituted 40 percent of its total trade in 2012 (ASEAN Secretariat, 2014a). Its proximity to China, specifically the Yunnan province and the Guangxi Zhuang Autonomous Region, has also stimulated the establishment of the Greater Mekong Subregion grouping together with Thailand and CLMV countries. These countries concentrate on projects relating to agriculture, energy, environment, human resource development, investment, telecommunications, tourism, trade, transport, and multi-sector economic corridors (Sanchita Basu Das,

2013). As such, the socio-economic potential within and across member countries will be a force to watch, given the looming 2015 integration deadline.

How might Malaysia contribute to and complement the ASEAN 2015 agenda? How would the integration process impact knowledge and innovation systems of the country? More importantly, where is the Malaysian higher education system in the grand scheme of things, and where will it be in the future? The objective of this chapter is twofold: (1) to provide a brief narration of the ASEAN Community integration and its current status and (2) to give an overview of the Malaysian higher education system and its place in the integration process. Scholars have researched and written about the ASEAN 2015 agenda and its impact on higher education; however, the discussion thus far is limited in scope. Existing literature concentrates on the feasibility of emulating the European Higher Education Area (EHEA) within the context of the Asian region in general and ASEAN in particular (Chao, 2014; Hawkins, 2012; Jones, 2004; Koh, 2007; Zeng, Adams & Gibbs, 2013), a general overview of the higher education systems within the region (Lee, 2006; Lek, 2014; Welch, 2007), and the role of regional organizations in stimulating regionalization of higher education in ASEAN (Nguyen, 2009). The most recent endeavor, which justly reflects the current status and shape of things to come, is a paper by Morshidi Sirat, Norzaini Azman, and Aishah Abu Bakar (2014) on harmonization of the ASEAN higher education. This paper became part of the materials for Week 4 of a seven-week MOOC (massive open online course) under Coursera entitled *Globalising Higher Education and Research for the Knowledge Economy.*

This chapter is structured as follows. First, the context and the key pillars underlining ASEAN 2015 are presented. This is followed by a description of the regional higher education landscape through the use of key indicators, current developments, and challenges observed concerning higher education within the ASEAN 2015 context. Next, an overview of the Malaysian higher education system and its current state of development is presented to illustrate how one ASEAN member country copes with the dynamics within the regional grouping. The chapter ends with a commentary on Malaysia's competitive edge and recommendations on how the country should play greater role with regard to the integration process.

The ASEAN Community Integration 2015

The ASEAN Community integration is a vision that was first developed in 1997 at the Second Informal ASEAN Summit in Kuala Lumpur, Malaysia. One of the directives was: "We envision the entire Southeast Asia to be, by 2020, an ASEAN community conscious of its ties of history, aware of its cultural heritage and bound by a common identity" (Jones, 2004, p. 141). Six years later, at the Ninth ASEAN Summit in Bali in 2003, the heads of states agreed that ASEAN's 2020 vision would encompass three key pillars: the ASEAN Economic Community (AEC), the ASEAN Socio-Cultural Community (ASCC), and the ASEAN Political-Security Community (APSC). The three pillars provided greater clarity for the envisioned regional integration, consequently strengthening the original objective of uniting the ASEAN population under a single identity. Table 8.1 illustrates the objective of each key pillar and its desired characteristics.

TABLE 8.1: THREE KEY PILLARS UNDER ASEAN COMMUNITY INTEGRATION 2015

ASEAN Economic Community (AEC)	Enhancing competitiveness for economic growth and development through closer economic integration, characterized by: 1. A single market and production base, 2. A highly competitive economic region, 3. A region of equitable economic development, and 4. A region fully integrated into the global economy.
ASEAN Socio-Cultural Community (ASCC)	Nurture human, cultural and natural resources for sustained development in a harmonious and people- centered ASEAN, characterized by: 1. Human development; 2. Social welfare and protection; 3. Social justice and rights; 4. Ensuring environmental sustainability; 5. Building the ASEAN Identity; and 6. Narrowing the development gap.
ASEAN Political-Security Community (APSC)	Enhancing peace, stability, democracy and prosperity in the region through comprehensive political and security cooperation, characterized by: 1. A rules-based community of shared values and norms; 2. A cohesive, peaceful, stable and resilient region with shared responsibility for comprehensive security; and 3. A dynamic and outward-looking region in an increasingly integrated and interdependent world.

Source: ASEAN Secretariat (2009)

At the Twelfth ASEAN Summit in 2007 in Cebu, Philippines, a consensus was reached to accelerate the implementation of the 2020 vision to 2015 (ASEAN Secretariat, 2007). By the Thirteenth ASEAN Summit in 2007 in Singapore, the member countries have agreed to prioritize the AEC pillar and its implementation in the integration process. A more solid plan of action on the ASEAN 2015 agenda came into being during the Fourteenth ASEAN Summit in 2009 in Cha-am, Thailand, with the launch of the *Roadmap for an ASEAN Community 2009–2015*.

Mittleman (2000, p. 112) remarked that the formation of ASEAN denoted a new form of regionalism with "concentrations of political and economic power competing in the global economy, with multiple interregional and intraregional flows." Koh (2007) argued that economic benefits are not the sole motivator in regionalization. This is true of ASEAN, where the cultural elements are embedded in the economic dimension, stimulating what has been termed "the cultural economy" or "the circuit of culture." ASEAN is also a product of politically motivated regional cooperation; it was the political tension between member countries that originally stimulated the formation of ASEAN (Narine, 2008).

A distinctive feature of the regionalization efforts in the Southeast Asian region is the ASEAN Way, which promotes a sense of belonging to the larger community through adherence of particular norms, values, and practices distinctive within the region. ASEAN Way has also shaped the interaction between the member countries and influenced the stance of any member country towards issues and conflicts occurring in other member countries. Narine remarked that the ASEAN Way

> stresses informality, organization minimalism, inclusiveness, intensive consultations leading to consensus and peaceful resolutions of disputes".... [It] encourages ASEAN to work around contentious issues rather than letting those problems derail cooperation in other areas.... If ASEAN members cannot agree on a common policy they agree to go their separate ways, while couching their disagreements in language that obscures differences.... [It] allows member states to opt out of multilateral agreements with the option of joining later, thereby preventing recalcitrant members from blocking institutional progress. (Narine, 2008, pp. 413–414)

Higher Education Within the ASEAN Region

As shown earlier, ASEAN is rich in diversity, with its member countries located in different stages of economic development. The same can be said of the higher education systems within the region. ASEAN experienced a rapid expansion of higher education over the past few decades (Lee, 2006). Even though ASEAN recognizes the importance of knowledge and knowledge industries to its future development, significantly different higher education profiles exist across the region. Practitioners remain skeptical of a common space for higher education due to the broad range of limitations such as incompatible degree systems; nontransferable credit systems; the lack of quality assurance mechanisms, political will, and commitment by the member countries; funding and resources in promoting the establishment of said common space; tensions between member countries; language barriers; and the lack of competitiveness of HEIs in the global arena; among other drawbacks (see, e.g., Hawkins, 2012; Nguyen, 2009; Welch, 2013; Zeng, Adams, & Gibbs, 2013). Figure 8.1 provides a comparative overview of the 10 higher education systems within the region based on enrollment figures, teaching staff, and public expenditure on higher education. As can be seen in

Figure 8.1, Indonesia, the Philippines, Thailand, and Vietnam recorded high enrollments in their higher education systems, with Indonesia and the Philippines having greater enrollments in the private higher education sectors. On the other hand, Singapore and Malaysia allocated the highest public expenditure for higher education among the 10 member countries.

FIGURE 8.1: COMPARATIVE OVERVIEW OF HIGHER EDUCATION SYSTEMS IN ASEAN

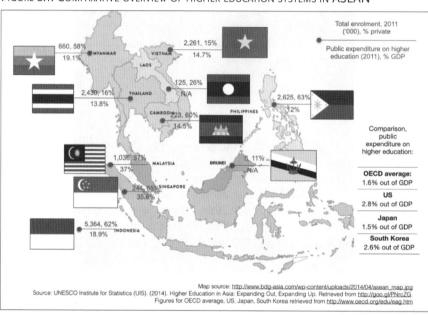

Source: UNESCO Institute for Statistics (UIS). (2014). Higher Education in Asia: Expanding Out, Expanding Up. Retrieved from http://goo.gl/PNrcZG. Figures for OECD average, US, Japan, South Korea retrieved from http://www.oecd.org/edu/eag.htm

Figure 8.2 showcases the patterns of outbound mobility of students across ASEAN. There is a huge outflow of students to conventional higher education markets, particularly Australia, the United States, the United Kingdom, and the greater European Union (EU) region, while Thailand and Malaysia are becoming notable intra-ASEAN destinations for cross-border education.

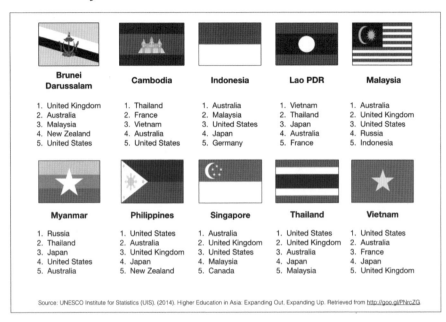

Source: UNESCO Institute for Statistics (UIS). (2014). Higher Education in Asia: Expanding Out, Expanding Up. Retrieved from http://goo.gl/PNrcZG.

In an analysis of ASEAN scientific publication output, Nguyen and Pham (2011) found that the region only contributed 0.5 percent, or 165,020, original articles in Institute of Scientific Information (ISI) publications globally over a 20-year period, with Singapore, Thailand, and Malaysia as top contributors. The countries were clustered into four groups based on the quantity and quality of publication: Singapore as the first group, with the highest publication output in the region; Thailand and Malaysia in the second group; Vietnam, Indonesia, and the Philippines in the third group; and Cambodia, Lao PDR, Myanmar, and Brunei in the fourth group, with the lowest scientific output (Nguyen & Pham, 2011). The first two clusters exhibited better research output in engineering, technology, and biotechnology, having the economic advantage and investment in research and development activities. On the other hand, it was found that scientific publications from Vietnam, Cambodia, Laos, Indonesia, and the Philippines were skewed towards low-tech fields (e.g., public health) and theoretical fields (e.g., theoretical physics and mathematics). Despite the increased volume of scientific publication, the region is rather isolated from international collaboration with the rest of the world, as noted in a recent publication of the UNESCO Institute for Statistics (UIS) on higher education expansion in Asia (UIS, 2014). Table 8.2 illustrates this observation.

TABLE 8.2: COUNTRY CLASSIFICATION BASED ON PATTERNS OF INTERNATIONAL COLLABORATION IN SCIENTIFIC PUBLICATIONS, 2003–2012

Trend	Country or territory by income level		
	High income	Middle income	Low or lower middle income
Positive	Singapore		Cambodia
Negative		Indonesia, Malaysia, Philippines, Thailand, Vietnam	Myanmar
No significant trend	Brunei Darussalam		Lao PDR

Adapted from UIS (2014)

The role of higher education is featured prominently in the integration process through the ASCC and is seen as complementing the efforts of the AEC and the APSC. In general, the higher education systems in ASEAN are expected to concentrate on the quality and adaptability of education within the region, which include providing technical and vocational education and training (TVET); establishing regional skills recognition framework; increasing literacy and integration of information and communication technology to promote lifelong learning; promoting university networking, student and staff exchanges, and research clusters; teaching common values and cultural heritage; developing and offering courses on ASEAN studies and ASEAN languages; enhancing English language proficiency for ASEAN citizens; and applying science and technology for sustainable development (Shaeffer, 2014). In a comparative review of three regional organizations—University Mobility in Asia and the Pacific (UMAP), ASEAN University Network (AUN), and the Regional Center for Higher Education and Development (RIHED) under the Southeast Asian Ministers of Education Organization (SEAMEO)—Nguyen (2009) conceded that the process of ASEAN higher education regionalization through these organizations is a stepwise process best taken gradually rather than as a massive Bologna Process-like undertaking. The stepwise approach is also seen as pertinent in the regional environment, where governments have greater say over the operations and direction of their higher education systems (Lee, 2006). Morshidi Sirat et al. (2014) referred to the regionalization process as "harmonization" rather than regionalization, as they believed that finding commonalities across higher education systems should be the basis of developing standards and practices for the region's higher education development, with student and staff mobility realizing the raison d'état of the ASEAN 2015 agenda.

The ASEAN Credit Transfer System (ACTS) is a credit transfer mechanism that was launched in 2011 to facilitate regional student mobility, harmonization of standards and quality assurance among ASEAN institutions. It is a notable achievement that reflects the potential for harmonization of higher education within Southeast Asia. It enables university students to apply for more than 12,000 courses offered across ASEAN universities. It also allows students to undergo academic evaluation that offers grading scales without conversion (ASEAN Secretariat, 2013). The establishment of ACTS has stimulated a pilot mobility program called the MIT (Malaysia-Indonesia-Thailand) Mobility Program, which involves HEIs from Malaysia, Indonesia, and Thailand, and its subsequent expansion to the ASEAN International Mobility for Students (AIMS) program. The AIMS program is a multilateral collaboration among HEIs in Malaysia, Indonesia, Thailand, and Vietnam, with South Korea and Japan set to become part of the mobility movement in the near future. AIMS is an undergraduate-focused, fully funded, semester-based mobility program in disciplines predetermined collectively by participating institutions. The end goal in 2015 is to have 500 students moving within 10 member states and 10 identified disciplines. The underlying principle of AIMS is to enhance students' higher education experience through academic and cultural immersion in another country, hence transforming short-term student mobility into a regular feature in the ASEAN higher education landscape (Morshidi Sirat et al., 2014).

An Overview of the Malaysian Higher Education System

The Malaysian higher education system has undergone different stages of development over the past five decades in response to the country's economic transformation (Abdul Rahman Haji Ismail & Mahani Musa, 2007). It currently aspires to achieve a high-income economy with a targeted GDP of $17,700 per capita by 2020 (Performance Management and Delivery Unit [PEMANDU], 2010). To move Malaysia forward, higher levels of knowledge and skills are required, in the form of capacity building and knowledge management (Welch, 2013). As such, the higher education system is responsible for knowledge workforce development and strengthening the country's core toward a knowledge-driven economy through research- and innovation-led activities (Nguyen & Pham, 2011). Malaysia's higher education development reflects the global trend of marketization, corporatization, and commercialization (see Conner & Rabovsky, 2011; SW Ng, 2012), in addition to the gradual decline in state funding for higher education (Mok, 2011) and the concentrated focus on positioning higher education excellence globally through global ranking leagues (see Marginson, 2007; Salmi, 2009). As such, Malaysia's higher education system could serve as a model for taking stock of higher education development within the region and a springboard for projecting possible scenarios of the ASEAN higher education development in the future.

There are five legal frameworks regulating the provision of higher education in the country: the Private Higher Educational Institution Act (PHEI Act), the National

Council on Higher Education Act, the University and University Colleges Act 1971 (amended in 1996), the National Accreditation Board Act, and the National Higher Education Funding Act (Marimuthu, 2008; Mok, 2011), which have since undergone reviews and amendments to fit current development needs. To help expend Malaysia's higher education system, the PHEI Act allows greater private higher education participation through the establishment of degree-granting private providers and joint ventures between local and foreign partners in setting up foreign branch campuses in the country (SY Tham, 2013; Mohd Ismail Abd Aziz & Doria Abdullah, 2014). The expansion started in the 1990s when the country experienced exponential demand for higher education due to limited number of HEIs within the country. The demand became critical as the Asian economic crisis in 1998 made higher education abroad an expensive affair for Malaysian families. As a result, a greater number of HEIs were established to meet the exponential demand and to enable domestic students to obtain affordable higher education within the country (Wilkinson & Yussof, 2005). The increased HEIs also fulfilled the industrial demand for the development of a skilled workforce (Marimuthu, 2008). As of June 2014, Malaysia has 20 public HEIs, 59 private universities, 32 university colleges, 8 foreign branch campuses, and 433 private colleges. Table 8.3 details the annual enrollment figures of the Malaysian higher education system over a 10-year period. The expansion of higher education within Malaysia has enabled greater domestic as well as foreign access to higher education.

TABLE 8.3: ANNUAL HIGHER EDUCATION ENROLLMENT IN MALAYSIAN HIGHER EDUCATION SYSTEM (2002–2012)

	Public HEI	Private HEI	International students
2003	294,359	314,344	30,397
2004	203,978	322,891	31,674
2005	307,121	258,825	40,525
2006	331,025	323,787	44,390
2007	382,997	365,800	47,928
2008	419,334	399,897	69,174
2009	437,420	484,377	80,750
2010	462,780	541,629	86,919
2011	508,256	428,973	71,101
2012	521,793	454,616	83,538

Source: Ministry of Education Malaysia (2013)

Malaysia is one of the countries within the ASEAN region, alongside Singapore and Thailand, which recruits international students in significantly larger numbers than the other member countries (Lek, 2014). Malaysia is able to recruit a greater number of international students because of the rapid expansion of its private higher education sector; approximately 70 percent of its annual international student recruitment comes from the private sector. In addition to conventional full-time degree programs, in which students are required to study for the full duration in the HEIs, some institutions have partnered with foreign institutions for twinning arrangements in the form of 1+2, 2+1, and 3+0 modes of delivery. The first number denotes the number of years a student undertakes his or her academic program within Malaysia, and the second number represents the number of years needed to complete the remaining duration of study in partner institutions. The attraction of this arrangement is the cost advantage of obtaining partner institutions' certification for a fraction of the cost required to complete the program abroad (Lee, 2004; Marimuthu, 2008; Wilkinson & Yussof, 2005). Because such degree programs require the foreign partner to consistently monitor the provision of academic programs from the Malaysian partner, the twinning arrangement establishes a dimension of quality control for academic programs at the private HEIs. Coupled with other factors, such as affordable cost of living, the use of English as a medium of communication and instruction, and cultural diversity, Malaysia not only managed to retain its domestic students within the country for higher education, but it also enhanced the system's appeal to the global international student market, strengthening expansion initiatives of the country with regard to international student recruitment.

Malaysia attracts a distinctive profile of international students into the country. Table 8.4 shows the breakdown by nationality of the international student body between 2008 and 2011.

TABLE 8.4: TOP 10 SENDING COUNTRIES TO MALAYSIA (2008–2011)

2008	2009	2010	2011
Indonesia (9,358)	Iran (10,932)	Iran (11,823)	Iran (9,888)
China (7,966)	Indonesia (9,812)	China (10,214)	Indonesia (8,569)
Iran (6,604)	China (9,177)	Indonesia (9,889)	China (7,394)
Nigeria (5,424)	Nigeria (5,969)	Yemen (5,866)	Nigeria (5,632)
Yemen (4,282)	Yemen (4,931)	Nigeria (5,817)	Yemen (3,552)
Saudi Arabia (2,752)	Libya (4,021)	Libya (3,930)	Bangladesh (2,323)
Botswana (2,350)	Sudan (2,433)	Sudan (2,837)	Sudan (2,091)
Sudan (2,307)	Bangladesh (1,957)	Saudi Arabia (2,252)	UK (1,530)
Bangladesh (2,021)	Botswana (1,939)	Bangladesh (2,041)	Pakistan (1,346)
Libya (1,788)	Iraq (1,712)	Botswana (1,911)	Iraq (1,329)
Total: 44,852	**Total:** 52,893	**Total:** 56,580	**Total:** 43,654
% of total international student population			
64.8	65.5%	65.1%	61.4%

Source: Education Malaysia Division, Department of Higher Education, Ministry of Education Malaysia

As can be seen from Table 8.4, international student enrollment from Asia, especially from Middle East and North Africa regions, constituted more than 60 percent of overall international student figures. This proportion has remained stable over the years, and the listed countries have been acknowledged as the major sending countries for international students to Malaysia. Students note on the country's ability to provide quality and affordable higher education. Existing promotional campaigns, scholarship offers, and good bilateral relations between Malaysia and the Arab world have also encouraged students from that area to study in Malaysia (Morshidi Sirat, 2008).

Malaysia is now classified as a "regional student hub" due to its growth in student numbers and the strategies in place to attract a greater number of students to the country for higher education (Knight & Morshidi Sirat, 2011). Regarding intra-ASEAN international student mobility, it was found that Malaysia is a choice destination for students from the ASEAN region for graduate education, with Indonesia becoming the major sending country, along with Singapore and Thailand. The inflow of students has also transformed education as one of the 12th National Key Economic Areas under the Economic Transformation Plan, with a total of RM 27 billion in gross national income generated in 2009 (PEMANDU, 2010). The country is currently en route to becoming an international hub of excellence for higher education, with a targeted enrollment of 150,000 international students by 2015 and 200,000 by 2020.

Malaysia and Thailand are reported as having one of the highest exponential growth rates for graduate education and scientific publication within Asia (UIS, 2014). Governments of both countries see the investment in higher education as a means of enhancing national economic growth through a virtuous cycle of developing and educated workforce, attracting international investment, and gaining international recognition through research and academic excellence. It is also driven by lessons learned from their Western counterparts that reputable HEIs make higher education systems more attractive globally, thus bringing in greater numbers of talent to respective HEIs (Selingo, 2013). Within the past decade, there was significant growth in the volume of scientific publication as well as greater graduate student enrollment in the two countries. The HEIs from both countries, in particular the research universities, also recorded the highest percentage increment for publication growth rate and in-region collaboration among ASEAN countries in 15 disciplines (UIS, 2014). Table 8.5 reports on this observation.

Discipline	Highest publication growth rate	Highest in-region collaboration
Agricultural and biological sciences	Universiti Teknologi Malaysia (MAL) Universiti Malaya (MAL) Universiti Sains Malaysia (MAL) Universiti Putra Malaysia (MAL)	Universiti Putra Malaysia (MAL) Kasetsart University (THAI) Universiti Sains Malaysia (MAL) Universiti Malaya (MAL) Chiang Mai University (THAI) Chulalongkorn University (THAI)
Biochemistry, genetics, and molecular biology	International Islamic University Malaysia (MAL) Universiti Sains Malaysia (MAL) Universiti Teknologi Malaysia (MAL) Universiti Malaya (MAL) Universiti Putra Malaysia (MAL)	
Chemistry	Universiti Putra Malaysia (MAL) Universiti Teknologi Malaysia (MAL) Universiti Kebangsaan Malaysia (MAL) Universiti Malaya (MAL)	Universiti Sains Malaysia (MAL) Universiti Malaya (MAL) Prince of Songkla University (THAI)
Computer sciences	Universiti Teknologi Malaysia (MAL) Universiti Putra Malaysia (MAL) Universiti Kebangsaan Malaysia (MAL)	
Earth and planetary sciences	Universiti Putra Malaysia (MAL) Nanyang Technological University (SIN)	
Economics and business science	Universiti Sains Malaysia (MAL) Universiti Kebangsaan Malaysia (MAL) Universiti Malaya (MAL) Universiti Putra Malaysia (MAL)	
Engineering	Universiti Malaysia Pahang (MAL) Universiti Malaya (MAL) Universiti Kebangsaan Malaysia (MAL) Universiti Putra Malaysia (MAL) Universiti Teknologi Malaysia (MAL)	
Environmental science	Universiti Malaya (MAL) Universiti Putra Malaysia (MAL) Universiti Teknologi Malaysia (MAL)	Universiti Putra Malaysia (MAL)
Health professions and nursing	Universiti Kebangsaan Malaysia (MAL) Universiti Malaya (MAL)	Mahidol University (THAI)
Materials science	Universiti Putra Malaysia (MAL) Universiti Kebangsaan Malaysia (UKM) Universiti Malaya (MAL) Universiti Teknologi Malaysia (MAL)	Universiti Sains Malaysia (MAL) Universiti Malaya (MAL)
Mathematics	Universiti Putra Malaysia (MAL) Universiti Malaya (MAL) Universiti Teknologi Malaysia (MAL) King Mongkut's University of Technology (THAI)	
Medicine	Universiti Putra Malaysia (MAL)	Universiti Malaya (MAL)

Discipline	Highest publication growth rate	Highest in-region collaboration
Multidisciplinary	International Islamic University Malaysia (MAL) Universiti Sains Malaysia (MAL) Universiti Putra Malaysia (MAL) Chiang Mai University (THAI) Universiti Teknologi Malaysia (MAL) Universiti Kebangsaan Malaysia (MAL) Universiti Malaya (MAL) Universiti Malaysia Pahang (MAL)	Universiti Putra Malaysia (MAL) Universiti Kebangsaan Malaysia (MAL) Universiti Teknologi Malaysia (MAL) Universiti Malaya (MAL) Universiti Sains Malaysia (MAL)
Other life and health sciences	Universiti Putra Malaysia (MAL)	Mahidol University (THAI) Universiti Putra Malaysia (MAL) Chulalongkorn University (THAI)
Physics and astronomy	Universiti Malaya (MAL) Universiti Putra Malaysia (MAL) Universiti Teknologi Malaysia (MAL) Universiti Sains Malaysia (MAL) Universiti Kebangsaan Malaysia (MAL)	Universiti Malaya (MAL) Universiti Sains Malaysia (MAL)
Notes: MAL = Malaysia; THAI = Thailand; SIN = Singapore		

Adapted from UIS (2014)

Moving Forward

This chapter has thus far presented an overview of ASEAN, current developments concerning higher education in ASEAN, and snapshots representative of the Malaysian higher education system and its place within the region. ASEAN is an engineered, elite diplomatic project, which has been translated into various political, social, economic, and cultural efforts across its 10 member countries (Thianthai & Thompson, 2007). Geographical and cultural connections bond communities within the region together through shared norms and practices, yet each community is able to maintain respective ideologies and belief systems within a common space. However, clear boundaries are drawn between countries in terms of the diverging paths charted in political stability and national development, which can be traced through the economic power and the investments made in critical sectors, such as that of higher education, which has formed the focal point for this chapter. Despite the differences observed, one commonality remains: The region's higher education system will grow significantly and will expand faster than the current observed rate. This growth will provide immense opportunities for member countries to innovate and experiment on different operational higher education models to enhance higher education within the region. This is even more crucial as the region is bracing itself to meet the vision of an integrated ASEAN Community by 2015.

What is Malaysia's competitive advantage within the integration process? Malaysia occupies a central location of the ASEAN region, which has a total population of more than 617 million. As noted by Nguyen and Pham (2011), the country is standing tall behind its neighbor Singapore with its internationally recognized higher education and cutting-edge technologies and research. The country is also in a good comparative position with its other neighbor Thailand, which has been consistent in embedding the ASEAN philosophy in its actions within and beyond national borders, including higher education. Lek (2014) observed that Malaysia's current efforts in higher education complements ASEAN's higher education development as a whole rather than competing with other higher education systems within the region, a unique feature despite the lack of deliberate plans on the creation of a common area similar to that of the EHEA.

Malaysia is one of the biggest recruiters of international students in the region. The country is accepted as a destination of choice for intra-ASEAN mobility especially in graduate education within public HEIs. In a quantitative research study involving a sample of 3,825 international students from both the public and private HEIs, it was found that the students' decision to come to Malaysia for their studies was largely dependent on recommendations of friends, family members, and word of mouth, especially for international graduate students who planned on undertaking PhDs in the country (Rohana Jani, Yong Zulina Zubairi, Siti Aishah Ali, Huam Hon Tat, & Abdul Hafaz Ngah, 2009). Online information, especially information on academic programs and hosting institutions also facilitated the students in their decision. Students chose Malaysia as a study destination for its internationally recognized and competitively priced academic programs, with the opportunity to establish international contacts and experience different cultures yet be able to live and practice their own culture. It was also found that students were attracted to the fact that English is widely spoken and used in academic and social settings in Malaysia, and the cost of study is comparable to conventional English-speaking host destinations such as the United States, Australia, and the United Kingdom. Even though the number of its private HEIs is considerably large, the private higher education sector in the country is still regulated. As an example, academic programs enrolling international students must receive accreditation from the Malaysian Qualifications Agency (MQA), with double accreditation processes in the case of programs offered by foreign branch campuses through the involvement of MQA and national accrediting bodies of parent institutions.

How might Malaysia play greater role in the ASEAN 2015 agenda? Three recommendations are provided for consideration. First, the country has yet to tap on regionalism as a strategy in internationalizing its higher education system. This was highlighted recently by a team of multidisciplinary scholars who was tasked to study on the country's higher education transformation. Lincicome (2005) defined regionalism as "the creation of transnational networks inclusive of nonofficial actors, whose identification with a particular state and set of national interests does not preclude the creation of a regional identity (or identities) and support for regional interests" (p. 181). Even though regionalism and regionalization shared fundamental definitions in terms of collaboration for mutual interests, the former emphasized the process of forming a common identity, shared values, and rights for each member of the community in regional development. Although individual HEIs have long pursued on international collaboration opportunities with HEIs within the ASEAN region, there is still room for greater involvement of the Malaysian higher education system as a collective. To be seen as a key role player in the ASEAN 2015 agenda, Malaysia needs to exert strong political will, commitment, and resource allocation in driving the initiatives and action plans agreed upon under the three pillars described earlier in this chapter.

Second, the mode of operation in which initiatives and action plans are implemented should also be reengineered. While the ASEAN Quality Assurance Framework is a work in progress at this time, the HEIs within the region should understand that the formation of such a framework and its ensuing implementation is a laborious process that requires a long time to coordinate. As such, each institution should work on intensifying greater bilateral relations before a common framework in academic accreditation is implemented in full force. Communities within the region, especially nongovernmental organizations, should also be empowered to take on initiatives under the integration process, rather than rely on a top-down approach that might not reach the masses in a timely and inclusive manner. The Malaysian public and private HEIs can champion this cause through community engagement programs and research projects involving communities within the region.

Third, Malaysia should look at establishing different structures that provide greater access and flexibility for higher education to the ASEAN communities. It is widely acknowledged that the great disparity in earning potential, higher education access, and provision of higher education within the region has made both regionalism and EHEA-like space for ASEAN higher education a particularly daunting goal. It is high time that the technical and vocational education and training (TVET) sector be at the forefront of the ASEAN higher education development. As the AEC is a key focus for the integration process, the expanding 5- to 19-year-old cohorts, who are agents in driving national economic agenda, should be empowered to take the lead, especially those coming from the CLMV cluster.

Conclusion

It is appropriate to end this chapter by citing Morshidi Sirat et al.'s observation concerning the ASEAN higher education:

> ASEAN countries are rich in culture, diverse in language and region but have one common goal, to be united as one…. The role of Southeast Asian Ministers of Education Organization (SEAMEO) is very critical to a successful implementation of this idea of harmonization of the [ASEAN] higher education systems. It is the nations and the individual higher education institutions who are the deciding actors who will determine the progress of the idea of harmonization in the region. Equally important, national prejudices and suspicions need to be put aside if we are to realize regional aspirations and goals. (Morshidi Sirat et al., 2014)

This chapter is developed with the aim of reporting on ASEAN, the imminent integration process in 2015, and snapshots of the region's higher education development in general and the Malaysian higher education system in particular. Presenting general snapshots of ASEAN 2015 and related discussion points through the use of Malaysian higher education as a case study enables greater adaptation of the corpus of information on the subject to a broader range of audience, hence complementing current scholarly contributions on the subject matter. Based on the above narration, it is clear that the space for ASEAN higher education is diverse, expanding, and gaining prominence within the global higher education landscape. Malaysia's case illustrates these observations well; as such, the lessons drawn out of Malaysia's higher education can serve as an example in projecting the growth of the higher education system within the region. While the intentions of having a common space for higher education are much lauded, it is the member countries—in the current discussion, Malaysia—that should play a significant role in the successful integration under the ASEAN 2015 agenda. Malaysia is in a good position to pave the way with its competitive edge among the member countries, provided that greater commitment and political will are exerted to achieve this objective.

Acknowledgments

The discussion points in this chapter originated from an ongoing research identified through research grant number 4B160 (Funding source: Department of Higher Education, Ministry of Education Malaysia) under the Research Management Centre, Universiti Teknologi Malaysia (UTM). The points raised were also presented during the UTM Seminar on Current Trends and Global Scenarios in Higher Education (Series 2/2014) at the Senate Hall, UTM Johor Bahru campus on July 7, 2014.

REFERENCES

Abdul Rahman Haji Ismail & Mahani Musa. (2007). History of the growth and development of higher education in Malaysia until 2007. In Zailan Moris (Ed.), *50 years of higher education development in Malaysia (1957-2007)*. Penang, Malaysia: National Higher Education Research Institute.

ASEAN Secretariat. (2007). Chairperson's statement of the 12th ASEAN Summit H.E. the President Gloria Macapagal-Arroyo. "One caring and sharing community." Retrieved from http://www.asean.org/news/item/chairperson-s-statement-of-the-12th-asean-summit-he-the-president-gloria-macapagal-arroyo-one-caring-and-sharing-community. Jakarta, Indonesia: ASEAN.

ASEAN Secretariat. (2009). Roadmap for an ASEAN community 2009-2015. Jakarta: ASEAN.

ASEAN Secretariat. (2013). Mid-term review of the ASEAN socio-cultural community blueprint (2009-2015). Jakarta, Indonesia: ASEAN.

ASEAN Secretariat. (2014a). ASEAN community in figures (ACIF) 2013. Jakarta, Indonesia: ASEAN.

ASEAN Secretariat. (2014b). Thinking globally, prospering regionally—ASEAN economic community 2015. Jakarta, Indonesia: ASEAN.

Asian Development Bank. (2014). Asian development outlook 2014: Fiscal policy for inclusive growth. Mandaluyong, Philippines: Author.

Chao, R. Y., Jr. (2014). Pathways to an East Asian higher education area: A comparative analysis of East Asian and European regionalization processes. *Higher Education*. Advanced publication. 1–17. doi 10.1007/s10734-014-9728-y.

Conner, T. W., & Rabovsky, T. M. (2011). Accountability, affordability, access: A review of the recent trends in higher education policy research. *Policy Studies Journal*, 39(1), 93–112.

Hawkins, J. N. (2012). Regionalization and harmonization of higher education in Asia: Easier said than done. Asian Education and Development Studies, 1(1), 96–108.

Jones, M. E. (2004). Forging an ASEAN identity: The challenge to construct a shared destiny. Contemporary Southeast Asia: *A Journal of International and Strategic Affairs*, 26(1), 140–154.

Knight, J., & Morshidi Sirat. (2011). The complexities and challenges of regional education hubs: Focus on Malaysia. *Higher Education*, 62(5), 593–606.

Koh, A. (2007). Deparochializing education: Globalization, regionalization, and the formation of an ASEAN education space. *Discourse: Studies in the Cultural Politics of Education*, 28(2), 179–195.

Lee, M. N. (2004). Global trends, national policies and institutional 790 responses: Restructuring higher education in Malaysia. *Educational Research for Policy and Practice*, 3(1), 31–46.

Lee, M. N. (2006). Higher education in Southeast Asia in the era of globalization. In J. J. F. Forest & P. G. Altbach (Eds.), *International handbook of higher education* (Vol. 18, pp. 539–555). Dordrecht, The Netherlands: Springer.

Lek, D. (2014). Cross border higher education in ASEAN: Structures, policies, development and integration. *ASEAN-Canada Research Partnership Working Paper Series #4*. S. Rajaratnam School of International Studies, Nanyang Technological University, Singapore.

Lincicome, M. (2005). Globalization, education, and the politics of identity in the Asia-Pacific: The ethical dilemma of "East Asian bioethics." *Critical Asian Studies*, 37(2), 179–208.

Marginson, S. (2007). Global university rankings: Implications in general and for Australia. *Journal of Higher Education Policy and Management*, 29(2), 131–142.

Marimuthu, T. (2008). The role of the private sector in higher education in Malaysia. In D. Johnson & R. Maclean (Eds.), *Teaching: Professionalisation, development and leadership* (pp. 271–282). Dordrecht, The Netherlands: Springer.

Mittleman, J. H. (2000). *The globalization syndrome transformation and resistance*. Princeton, NJ: Princeton University Press.

Mohd Ismail Abd Aziz & Doria Abdullah. (2014), Finding the next "wave" in internationalisation of higher education: Focus on Malaysia. *Asia Pacific Education Review* (Advance publication). doi 10.1007/s12564-014-9336-7

Mok, K. H. (2011). Liberalization of the privateness in higher education. In P. N. Teixeira & D. D. Dill (Eds.), *Public vices, private virtues? Assessing the effects of marketization in higher education* (Vol. 2, pp. 19–43). Dordrecht, The Netherlands: Sense.

Morshidi Sirat, Norzaini Azman, & Aishah Abu Bakar. (2014). Towards harmonisation of higher education in Southeast Asia. Retrieved from http://www.insidehighered.com/blogs/globalhighered/towards-harmonization-higher-education-southeast-asia

Morshidi Sirat. (2008). The impact of September 11 on international student flow into Malaysia: Lessons learned. *International Journal of Asia-Pacific Studies*, 4(1), 79–95.

Morshidi Sirat. (2009). Strategic planning directions of Malaysia's higher education: University autonomy in the midst of political uncertainties. *Higher Education*, 59(4), 461–473.

Narine, S. (2008). Forty years of ASEAN: A historical review. The Pacific Review, 21(4), 411–429.

Ng, S. W. (2012). Rethinking the mission of internationalization of higher education in the Asia-Pacific region. *Compare: A Journal of Comparative and International Education*, 42(3), 439–459.

Nguyen, A. T. (2009). The role of regional organisations in East Asian regional cooperation and integration in the field of higher education. In Kuroda, K. (Ed.), *Asian regional integration review* (Vol. 1, pp. 69–82). Tokyo, Japan: Waseda University.

Nguyen, T. V., & Pham, L. T. (2011). Scientific output and its relationship to knowledge economy: An analysis of ASEAN countries. *Scientometrics*, 89(1), 107–117.

Oberman, R., Dobbs, R., Budiman, A., Thompson, F., & Rosse, M. (2012). The archipelago economy: Unleashing Indonesia's potential. McKinsey Global Institute.

Performance Management and Delivery Unit (PEMANDU). (2010). Economic transformation programme. Putrajaya, Malaysia: Prime Minister's Department.

Rohana Jani, Yong Zulina Zubairi, Siti Aishah Ali, Huam Hon Tat, & Abdul Hafaz Ngah. (2009). The perception of international students on Malaysian education. Report prepared for Education Promotion Division, Ministry of Higher Education Malaysia. Putrajaya: Ministry of Higher Education Malaysia.

Salmi, J. (2009). The challenge of establishing world-class universities. Washington DC: World Bank.

Sanchita Basu Das. (2013). Enhancing regional and sub-regional co-operation and connectivity in ASEAN. ISEAS Working Paper #3. http://www.iseas.edu.sg/documents/publication/iseas_working_paper_sanchita_basu_das.pdf

Selingo, J. (2013). *College (un)bound: The future of higher education and what it means for students*. New York, NY: Houghton Mifflin Harcourt.

Shaeffer, S. (2014). Post-2015 education scenarios, ASEAN integration, and the post-EFA education agenda. Retrieved from http://seamolec.org/cnx/Background-Paper.pdf

SY Tham. (2013). Internationalizing higher education in Malaysia: Government policies and university's response. *Journal of Studies in International Education*, 17(5), 648–662.

Thianthai, C., & Thompson, E. C. (2007). Thai perceptions of the ASEAN region: Southeast Asia as "prathet phuean ban." *Asian Studies Review*, 31(1), 41–60.

UNESCO Institute for Statistics (UIS). (2014). Higher education in Asia: Expanding out, expanding up. Retrieved from http://www.uis.unesco.org/Library/Documents/higher-education-asia-graduate-university-research-2014-en.pdf

Welch, A. (2007). Governance issues in South East Asian higher education: Finance, devolution and transparency in the global era. *Asia Pacific Journal of Education*, 27(3), 237–253.

Welch, A. (2013). Different paths, one goal: Southeast Asia as knowledge society. Asia Pacific Journal of Education, 33(2), 197–211.

Wilkinson, R., & Yussof, I. (2005). Public and private provision 924 of higher education in Malaysia: A comparative analysis. *Higher Education*, 50(3), 361–386.

Zeng, Q., Adams, J., & Gibbs, A. (2013). Are China and the ASEAN ready for a Bologna Process? Factors affecting the establishment of the China-ASEAN higher education area. *Educational Review*, 65(3), 321–341.

NOTES

[1] The 10 member countries are Brunei Darussalam, Cambodia, Indonesia, Lao PDR, Malaysia, Myanmar, Philippines, Singapore, Thailand, and Vietnam.

[2] Currency is in U.S. dollars, unless otherwise specified.

Chapter Nine

Vietnam's Higher Education System in Transition: The Struggle to Achieve Potential

Pham Thi Ly, Vietnam National University and
Nguyen Tat Thang University, Vietnam

Martin Hayden, Southern Cross University, Australia

Introduction

Vietnam's higher education system is under pressure. The economy is steadily becoming more market oriented, but the higher education system retains many of the organizational and cultural characteristics of a past characterized by Soviet-style centralized state planning. In 1993, the first of a series of reforms intended to modernize the system was introduced. Since then, the system has undergone extensive change. Most noticeably, it has expanded dramatically. Its quality continues, however, to fall short of the standards required for global integration and regional significance. In this chapter, we review the struggle of the system to achieve its full potential. The chapter draws especially on insights documented in an unpublished master plan for Vietnam's higher education system that was prepared for the Ministry of Education and Training (MOET) in 2012. The authors, one of whom was the international team leader for the project, contributed significantly to that document.

Overview of the System

There are 2.2 million higher education students in Vietnam, representing about 25 percent of the relevant age group. Vietnam has more than 400 universities and colleges, some of which have enrollments of more than 30,000 students, but many of which are recently established and relatively small. The system is extremely diverse. It includes two universities that are designated as being "national" (one in Hanoi and one in Ho Chi Minh City), three universities that are designated as being "regional"(one in Da Nang, one in Hue, and one in Thai Nguyen), 11 other universities that are designated as being "key" universities (located mainly in Hanoi or Ho Chi Minh City), and a large number of other specialized universities, vocational and technical colleges, teacher training colleges, and community colleges. More than two-thirds of all higher education students attend a university. The system is predominantly a publicly owned and state-managed system, with only 14 percent of all students enrolled in private-sector universities and colleges. The private sector relies entirely on income from tuition fees, and its focus is more or less exclusively on the delivery of low-cost undergraduate programs in areas of high market demand (e.g., business studies, information technology, and foreign languages).

According to the Education Law of 2005, universities in Vietnam are permitted to deliver undergraduate degree and diploma programs and may be permitted to offer postgraduate programs. Colleges are responsible for delivering two- and three-year diploma programs. The law prescribes that universities and colleges should have a research role, but, in practice, most do not. Colleges are inclined to aspire to become universities, and institutional drift within the system is relatively widespread. Many public universities offer master's degree programs, but not all universities (only 44 in the year 2011) are permitted to offer PhD programs. Specialized research institutes also provide PhD programs. There are hundreds of these research institutes in Vietnam, many dating back to the Soviet period of influence from the 1960s up to the late 1980s. Under the Soviet model, universities and colleges were principally teaching-only institutions, and research institutes were responsible for research. Though they are not officially regarded as being part of the higher education system, many of the research institutes (70 in the year 2011) are permitted to offer PhD programs.

Members of academic staff in Vietnam typically hold at least a master's degree qualification, and only a small proportion of all academic staff members (about 11 percent in 2013) hold a PhD qualification. Those with PhDs tend to be concentrated in 16 universities—the two national, the three regional, and 11 other designated key universities. PhD graduates also obtain employment in research institutes. The salary levels of academic staff members are generally considered to be low by national standards, and many take on second jobs, including part-time teaching in the private sector, to supplement their income. Their working conditions are such that few have a dedicated office space in which to prepare for teaching or to consult with students, and laboratory facilities for teaching and research are mostly rudimentary.

One of the most striking aspects of the system in Vietnam is its continuing rapid expansion. In 1993, there were only 162,000 higher education students, accounting for less than 5 percent of the relevant age group. Currently, there are about 2.2 million students, accounting for about 25 percent of the relevant age group. The scale of the expansion of the system has been so dramatic that the annual average rate of enrollment growth during the decade from 2001 was 9 percent, resulting in more than 200 new universities and colleges having to be established to accommodate the growth. Demand for access to higher education continues, however, to outstrip the supply of higher education places, resulting in intense competition among young people to gain admission to a higher education institution.

The expansion in the size of the sector has been made possible by Vietnam's remarkable economic recovery since the mid-1980s. A national policy of *doi moi* (economic renovation) was proclaimed in 1986, resulting in the privatization of agriculture, the introduction of property rights, the reduction of reliance on state-owned enterprises, the easing of price controls and controls on foreign trade, and the encouragement of foreign investment and joint ventures with foreign-owned companies. As a consequence, an economy characterized by widespread poverty, rampant inflation, and serious food shortages has been transformed into an economy with a strong rate of economic growth, a controllable rate of inflation, and a capacity to export rice, the national food staple. Vietnam remains, however, a relatively poor country by international standards. It is heavily reliant on intensive agriculture to support its population of nearly 90 million, and its per-capita income level in 2012 was only $1,550, which is below that of most of the 10 Association of Southeast Asian Nations (ASEAN) member states, including Malaysia ($9,820), Thailand ($5,210), and Indonesia ($3,420) (World Bank, 2014). (All currency is in U.S. dollars unless otherwise specified.) Compared with these other countries, though, Vietnam invests heavily in its education system. About 20 percent of the state budget is spent on education, and in 2010, national expenditure on education accounted for 6.6 percent of the gross domestic product (GDP), which was the highest for any of the countries in the ASEAN region (ASEAN Secretariat, 2012).

Challenges and Prospects

There are many significant challenges being faced by the higher education system in Vietnam. Some of the more immediate of these are discussed here, together with relevant policy options available to the government. This account is by no means exhaustive and might be read in conjunction with other accounts of the higher education system in Vietnam (Harman, Hayden,& Pham Thanh Nghi, 2010; Hayden & Le Thi Ngoc Lan, 2013; London, 2011).

Coordination and Governance

A significant challenge for the higher education system in Vietnam remains the lack of overall national coordination of the system. Vietnam is relatively unique among Asian countries because it does not have a single entity responsible for the whole of its higher education and research system. Instead, it has a large number of individual ministries, state instrumentalities, and provincial governments that are responsible for the line management of different clusters of institutions. The two national universities (which themselves are comprised of multiple specialized universities) are directly managed by the cabinet; 54 other public universities and colleges are directly managed by MOET; another 260 or so public universities and colleges are directly managed by at least 10 other ministries and by more than 60 state instrumentalities and provincial governments; and, as with all public universities and colleges, the 80 or so privately owned universities and colleges are accountable to MOET for approving their curriculum structures and enrollment quotas, and they are also accountable to local governments for many other aspects of their performance.

MOET has system wide responsibility for regulating the establishment of new higher education institutions, setting guidelines for student admissions and the employment of lecturers, approving curriculum structures, and implementing a national quality assurance (QA) system. Its ability to enforce compliance with its regulations is, however, restricted because of the limited reach of its authority. Indeed, its main influence is confined to the universities and colleges that are under its direct management.

Research funding is an exclusive responsibility of the Ministry of Science and Technology (MOST), which is also responsible for directly managing the public research institutes. As noted earlier, these institutes function independently of the higher education system, and yet they compete with it for research funds.

The dispersal of authority, which is so strongly evident in Vietnam's higher education system, results in a great deal of fragmentation in terms of the policy implementation. The government routinely approves strategic plans and related policy directions for the system, but it falls on 12 ministries (MOET, MOST, and 10 others) and more than 60 state instrumentalities and provincial governments to implement them. Policy enforcement is a weak aspect of the system. Against this background, having a single point of authority for the coordination of the higher education and research system would appear to be a sensible arrangement for Vietnam. It would contribute greatly to achieving more consistency and increased effectiveness in the implementation of national strategic objectives. To date, however, there appears to be little or no movement in this direction. Individual ministries (other perhaps than MOET), state instrumentalities, and provincial governments appear to be comfortable with the present situation. There would almost certainly be strong resistance to giving MOET overall responsibility for the system. An alternative approach that may prove to be more acceptable is to establish a new ministry with exclusive responsibility for higher education and research. The need to integrate the management and funding of teaching and research is especially important to the future of Vietnam's universities, which need to become far more research-oriented if they are to achieve regional and global recognition.

Another challenge for the system concerns institutional governance. A university charter approved in 2010 required all public universities to establish their own governing councils of between 15 to 31 members, including various ex-officio members, elected members, and invited members. Important responsibilities given to university councils include the right to decide on institutional objectives and strategies; approve guidelines for organizational structures, staff recruitment, and staff training policies; approve policies regarding institutional finances, property, facilities, and equipment; conduct annual assessments of the performance of the rector and vice rectors; and approve matters related to tuition fee rates, the enrollment quota, and the membership of an institution's academic committee. The charter was consistent with a government policy of eventually enabling public higher education institutions in Vietnam to become self-managing, with public universities less dependent on line-management control by ministries, state instrumentalities, and provincial governments.

The process of establishing governing councils is, however, proceeding very slowly. There is a widespread view that these councils are unlikely to have much impact because they have not been given sufficient authority. One significant problem is that, because they have no authority in relation to the appointment or dismissal of rectors, they have no formal capacity to hold rectors accountable for the effectiveness of their institutional management. There are also other problems. Their constitutions permit the members of academic staff of a university to account for a majority of the membership of a governing council, which will inevitably mean that their focus will be institutional rather than on the needs of external stakeholders including employers, regional communities, and even the national government. Another problem is that there is a lack of clarity about the role of the chair of a governing council. The legislation stated that the chair position should be fulltime, but in that case, there is the risk of the chair becoming directly involved in issues of institutional management, thus compromising the role of the rector. Not surprisingly, rectors, who must already work under the guidance of their responsible line-management authority and who must also take account of the views of their institutional Communist Party Committee, will be understandably reluctant about being further controlled. To date, there is a general lack of energy being invested by public universities in the establishment of governing councils, and their potential is being constrained in various ways, including a requirement that they meet no more than once each year.

The need for institutional autonomy is, however, critical to the future development of Vietnam's public higher education institutions. Universities, in particular, need to be able to make their own decisions about a wide range of academic and nonacademic matters if they are to be successful in developing their international reputation and become a source of innovation for the economy. At present, public universities in Vietnam are not readily able to make their own decisions about matters of importance relating to their institutional priorities, finances, or senior personnel appointments. They have no ability, for example, to select, appoint, or dismiss the rector; to borrow funds or retain a financial surplus; to own their campus buildings; or to determine academic staff salaries and working conditions. Even more importantly, they cannot decide freely on academic issues concerning student admissions, academic content, quality assurance, and the introduction of new degree programs. Compared even with higher education systems in former Soviet-bloc countries, Vietnam's higher education system continues to be strongly influenced by a culture of state control.

Finance

In 2005, the government approved a significant reform plan for the higher education system. Popularly known as the Higher Education Reform Agenda (HERA), it proposed a wide range of reform initiatives, including some that were extremely ambitious (Hayden & Lam Quang Thiep, 2006, 2007). One of the important commitments made was that there should be a doubling of the higher education enrollment rate by 2020. Fulfilling this commitment would mean adding an additional 2 million students to the higher education system. The question of how this further expansion of the system can be financed is, therefore, an issue of concern. Though, as noted earlier, the government is a strong financial supporter of the public higher education system, its capacity to find the additional funds required to achieve continued rapid expansion of the system is considered by most informed observers to be extremely limited.

There seems little doubt that tuition fees will need to increase significantly over the coming years. The government has traditionally sought to keep the tuition fees for attendance at public higher education institutions as low as possible, but the World Bank (2012, p.102) has estimated that the average cost per student (the "unit cost") for participation in higher education in Vietnam will need to be three to four times higher in 2015 than it was in 2007, and five to six times higher by 2019, if Vietnam's aspirations for the growth of the system and for improvements in its quality are to be attained. The government has already come to the realization that tuition fees must increase. Since 2010, the tuition fees charged to students for attendance at public higher education institutions have been scheduled to increase annually, and different tuition fee rates have been introduced for different fields of study, according to their cost of delivery. More recently, the government has permitted four public universities to raise their tuition fees to levels charged by some private higher education institutions. The tuition fee increases approved to date will not be large enough, however, to meet the funding needs predicted by the World Bank. Inevitably, there will be additional financial strain on families to support the cost of higher education participation by their children. Private households in Vietnam already bear a significant cost burden for the education of their young people (Hayden & Le Thi Ngoc Lan, 2013, p. 334). A significant challenge for them will be the future affordability of higher education.

Not unrelated to this matter is the extent of public concern about how efficiently and effectively current levels of public expenditure on the higher education system are being applied. Restrictions on the financial autonomy of public higher education institutions have an important bearing on this question. On average, public universities receive about one-half of their income from the state. They are then obliged to conform to state norms for all forms of expenditure of these funds. They must also achieve certain enrollment targets and provide certain types of training programs. There are, therefore, no strong incentives for them to become more involved in long-term financial strategic planning or to engage seriously in attempts to improve their long-term cost efficiency. In 2009, the extent of their financial autonomy was widened in relation to their use of technology-transfer earnings to purchase equipment, invest in facilities and services, and bid for equipment. Public higher education institutions were also given more freedom in determining their personnel quotas and in conducting recruitment processes. In practice, however, their budgets from technology-transfer earnings are relatively small, and their freedom in making decisions about personnel remain heavily circumscribed by requirements for all civil service appointments. By comparison, private higher education institutions have significantly more expenditure autonomy. They can allocate funds in support of their own corporate objectives, and many are now engaged in large-scale capital expansions, funded with borrowed money that will be repaid from future income. Private higher education institutions are allowed to set their own tuition fees, provided they comply with specified quality assurance requirements, but their enrollment quotas continue to be controlled by MOET.

Equity

The government has maintained a long-standing commitment to the provision of tuition fee deductions and exemptions for students from poor and ethnic backgrounds and also for students in certain training programs, especially teacher education. The effect of this policy is that about one quarter of all students attending public higher education institutions pay no tuition fees or benefit from some form of tuition fee reduction. In 2006, the government introduced a student aid scheme that provided some financial support for students from ethnic minorities. In 2007, it increased the value of the scholarships it provides for disadvantaged students to cover the full cost of tuition fees. It also significantly increased the credit allowance available under the student loan scheme, from which a significant proportion of all higher education students in Vietnam now derive some benefit. The student loan scheme is also available to students attending private higher education institutions, and without the support it provides, many of the students attending these institutions could not continue their studies.

However, equity remains a major issue for the higher education system in Vietnam. In 2009, the poorest quintile of families in Vietnam was shown to be spending 70.1 percent of their household income to support participation by a young person in higher education, whereas the richest quintile of families was spending only 29.6 percent of their household income (World Bank, 2012, p.106). Young people from rural and low-income backgrounds continue to have less access to higher education than young people from urban and high-income families, and young people from ethnic minority backgrounds continue also to be underrepresented. Increasing tuition fees will, of course, add significantly to the extent of the inequities.

Research

It is widely agreed that the current settings for science and technology (S&T) research management in Vietnam are not satisfactory. The main issues are the mismatch of funding between the universities and the research institutes, the general level of underinvestment in S&T initiatives, and the lack of competitiveness and transparency in research funding allocation mechanisms. In addition, the importance of the research role of universities continues to be underappreciated.

In terms of research intensity, the evidence indicates that, while publication output is growing in Vietnam, it is not doing so at anywhere near the same rate as is evident in some neighboring countries, including Thailand, Malaysia, and Singapore. Figure 9.1 provides a graphic illustration of how the rate of growth of publication output in Vietnam during the past 20 years has been falling further behind the rate in these other countries.

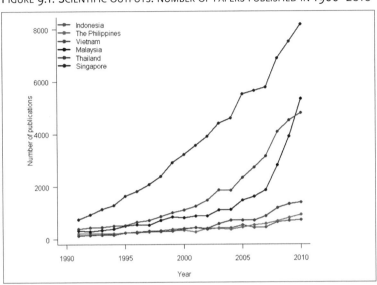

Source: Nguyen Van Tuan & Pham Thi Ly, 2011b

An important reason for the slow rate of growth in publication output in Vietnam is the privileged treatment given to the research institutes, regardless in many cases of their research productivity or their contribution to the training of future researchers. Universities have far more research capacity because of their larger size and the greater availability of PhD-qualified staff members, but they receive a smaller percentage of the overall S&T budget. MOST is mainly responsible for the allocation of the national research budget, but it has a specific responsibility for maintaining the system of research institutes, and so there is a significant flow of funds to these institutes. Universities receive their research funds indirectly through particular line-management ministries or other state instrumentalities, and these bodies do not generally attach as much importance to the research role of universities that attach to their teaching role. The research funds available to university researchers are also reduced by the need of line-management ministries and agencies, and of the universities themselves, to support their own research bureaucracies.

In terms of research funding, Vietnam lags behind other important regional neighbors. Nguyen Van Tuan & Pham Thi Ly (2011a, p. 611) have shown that by 2012 investment by Vietnam in S&T initiatives had increased to 0.27 percent of GDP, which was a significant improvement on the level recorded some five years earlier. Though higher than for Indonesia (0.05 percent) or the Philippines (0.12 percent), the rate was lower than for Thailand (0.3 percent), Malaysia (0.5 percent), and Singapore (2.2 percent).

Ideally, the rate should continue to increase, and the government is strongly encouraging of such a trend, but it is looking to the private sector to invest more in S&T initiatives. In September 23, 2012, the minister of Ministry of Science and Technology Nguyen Quan stated, for example, that "the most challenge is [that] the majority of research funding is from the state budget. In developed countries, nonstate budget accounts for a large number, usually three- to fivefold, or even 10-fold, but in Vietnam, 70 percent[is] from the state budget, whereas only 30 percent[is] from the private sector." Increasing the level of private investment for S&T in Vietnam is, however, likely to be quite difficult. As Fatseas (2010, p. 110) reported, universities in Vietnam lack an understanding of intellectual property issues, and they have a distrust of the private sector in relation to matters of intellectual property. Furthermore, the quality of their research infrastructure is well below the standards elsewhere in Southeast Asia, and the kind of research favored by universities and research institutes in Vietnam continues to be driven more by theoretical interests than by the explicit needs of industry.

Another problem is that the processes of research funding in Vietnam are bureaucratic and uncompetitive. There is unanimity of viewpoint, even up to the highest levels of government, that the research budget in Vietnam is poorly managed and is not being effectively utilized. The practices followed for evaluating research projects are not in line with international standards. There is a general lack of transparency, and the procedures for assessing outcomes focus more on compliance with expenditure norms and detailed line-item budget allocations than they do on the production of referred publications and the creation of patents. The recently established National Fund of Science and Technology Development is providing a new model for appraising research proposals against international standards and for assessing outcomes in terms of research publications, but it plays only a small part in the overall distribution of research funds across the higher education and research systems.

There are many other obstacles to research productivity in Vietnam (Pham Thi Ly, 2013). These include the relatively small proportion of PhD-qualified academic staff members, the absence of a system-wide coordinated approach to the production of research outcomes and to the provision of research training, and the general shortage of world-class scientists in Vietnam. In addition, peer-review processes for vetting scientific articles are weak; there is a general lack of appreciation of the importance of the role that might be played by applied research; and academic promotion within higher education institutions pays negligible attention to the relevance of scientific publications produced.

Quality

Vietnam has made significant progress during the past 10 years in terms of the implementation of a QA framework for its higher education system. In 2003, the General Directorate for Educational Testing and Accreditation was established within MOET, with responsibility for, among other things, establishing an accreditation process for the system. In 2004, the directorate published 10 quality standards for the accreditation of higher education institutions. These were subsequently pilot-tested by a sample of universities. In 2007, a revised set of standards was approved. Since 2008, many more higher education institutions had prepared self-evaluation reports and as many as 40 universities had reviews completed by external panels. Three leading universities had also participated in quality reviews by international panels. Most universities now have Quality Assurance Centers, and there is the National Accreditation Council that promotes the system-wide importance of QA. Vietnam does not, however, have an agency responsible for QA assessments or for program accreditation that is completely independent.

Institutional self-study is an important element in Vietnam's approach to QA. Institutions are required to address their own performance against performance standards. Some weaknesses, however, are that the standards are more strongly focused on inputs than outcomes, and that it may be difficult for institutional leaders to be entirely objective when implementing institutional self-studies. The approach has also been identified as having too much of an emphasis on meeting minimum standards set by the state, which limits its usefulness for research-oriented universities for which the QA focus might be better placed on fitness-for-purpose considerations.

External peer review is another important element. External review panels, composed often of university academics and retired MOET personnel, determine the extent to which higher education institutions have complied with the standards and criteria. This process is, however, being implemented more slowly than was anticipated, and the main problem appears to be institutional delays in completing self-studies.

In 2009, an important quality-related development was approval of a "three-disclosures" policy whereby all higher education institutions are required to publicly disclose information in relation to the nature of what they do (including details of their curriculum, research activities, and quality accreditation processes), the capital and human resources available to them (including details of teaching and student accommodation facilities and of the number and attainments of lecturing and management staff), and the income they receive (tuition fees and income from training contracts, scientific research, etc.) and expenses incurred (including salaries, training costs and expenditures on construction, repairs, and equipment purchases). Once fully implemented, the impact of this policy on the level of transparency of all higher education institutions will be significant.

Some particular quality-related concerns for Vietnam's higher education system need to be acknowledged. One relates to the fact that the lecturer-to-student ratio (1:29 in 2011) is well below the goal of a 1:20 ratio set by HERA. It has also not improved much since 2001, when it was 1:28.5. Another relates to the fact that, in order to achieve the enrollment growth proposed in HERA to be achieved by 2020, there will need to be a growth rate of almost 300 percent between 2011 and 2020 in the number of academic staff members. This growth rate is extremely ambitious, given that the growth rate in the number of academic staff members from 2001 and 2011 was already very high at 232 percent. The average levels of qualified academic staff members seem highly likely to decline.

The Private Sector

Under *doi moi*, Vietnam shifted toward the development of a socialist-oriented market economy, thereby making way for the introduction of a private sector of higher education. In 1993, the first nonpublic higher education institution was officially approved. Subsequently, a private higher education system of universities and colleges has developed. As noted earlier, the system now accounts for about 14 percent of all higher education enrollments. Its rate of growth has, however, been slower than might have been expected, and there have been periods at which its growth has been negligible. Given Vietnam's socialist tradition, the development of the sector has been marked by a level of suspicion and by the lack of a proper official appreciation of its distinctive needs. The sector itself has on occasions contributed to its own difficulties, mainly by engaging in irregular business practices and by entertaining excessively ambitious growth plans.

A point of major difficulty for the government and for shareholders has been the lack of clarity concerning the difference between for-profit and not-for-profit private higher education providers. The Education Law of 2005, together with related and subsequent regulations, clearly authorize private ownership and provide also for the existence of shareholders, who are permitted to retain that part of the net operating surplus of an institution that remains after the payment of taxes and the contribution of funds to a general reserve. A favorable rate of taxation has been set for those private higher education providers considered to be not-for-profit providers, meaning that they are not making a large profit. The problem is, though, that the level of profit permissible for a not-for-profit private higher education provider has not, until recently, been specified. The matter has been addressed in the Higher Education Law of 2012, which defines nonprofit private higher education providers as those for whom the "annual profit[s] are not divided but used for reinvestment; shareholders do not receive interest or receive it but not [at a rate that] exceed[s the] government bond [rate]." This provision leaves many questions unresolved, however.

The private higher education sector is officially predicted to expand to a point where it accounts for 40 percent of all higher education enrollments by 2020. On present trends, this goal seems unattainable. There were 83 private higher education institutions in 2013, accounting for only 14.3 percent of all higher education student enrollments. Many private universities and colleges appear to be having difficulty in attracting sufficient enrollments. To maintain their enrollments, they are forced to accept more students who are less academically capable, which then contributes to a poor public image for the sector. The fact that, in order to remain viable, they must charge higher tuition fees than is the case for public universities and colleges places a significant restriction on their attractiveness to students and their families.

There exists is a small number of private higher education institutions established as enterprises under Vietnam's Foreign Investment Law. RMIT University, a branch campus of the publicly owned Royal Melbourne Institute of Technology (RMIT) in Australia, is a well-established example. It functions autonomously within the higher education system, thereby enjoying immense advantages over public universities. The uneven conditions applying to the operation of local and international higher education providers present a significant policy problem for the future.

Regional Comparisons

Within the framework of ASEAN, there is an increasing inclination for higher education systems across the Southeast region to compare their performance and establish agreed-upon benchmarks. Progress in this regard is slow, however, and there are critical gaps in available data. The ASEAN member states are also at different stages of development, which makes some comparisons fruitless. Singapore, for example, is a high-income economy with several world-class higher education institutions. Myanmar, on the other hand, is desperately poor, and its higher education system is in the process of being rebuilt after nearly 50 years of neglect.

Thailand is more developed than Vietnam, but not to an extent that comparisons between the higher education systems in the two countries are implausible. Nguyen Van Tuan has assembled figures comparing the two higher education systems in terms of student enrollments, staffing profiles, and publication outputs.[1] The student enrollment and staffing figures relate to the 2007–08 period, and the publication output figures are for 2009. In 2007–08, Thailand had a population of about 64 million, compared with Vietnam's population of about 88 million. Thailand had fewer universities than Vietnam (112, compared with 163), more students in private universities than Vietnam (948,445, compared with 143,432), more graduate students (334,103, compared with 152,272), and many more lecturers holding PhD qualifications (14,099, compared with 5,643). Importantly, Thailand had 4,527 articles published in international journals in 2009, compared with only 956 articles published by Vietnam. Though crude, the comparison points to some areas of deficit in Vietnam's higher education system. Vietnam needs a much better qualified academic staff profile, and it possibly also needs fewer universities (many of those that currently exist are quite small in terms of student enrollments, and they are also narrowly specialized). Vietnam does not seem to be making progress with the establishment of a private higher education sector, and it appears also to be lagging, when compared with Thailand, in terms of the number of graduate students in its universities. The most important discrepancy between the two systems is, however, that there were five times more academic journal articles produced in 2009 by Thai researchers than there were by Vietnamese researchers. Vietnam's higher education system does, it seems, need to shift some of its focus from teaching to research.

Recent Policy Developments

The Higher Education Law of 2012 has provided some new directions for the higher education system. It has, for example, explicitly identified research-based universities as composing one of three tiers of higher education institution, thereby giving them more incentive to focus on the cultivation of their research capabilities. It provides for increased institutional autonomy and more investment funds to be provided to the two national and the three regional public universities. It gives increased definitional clarity to the nature of nonprofit private higher education; though, as noted earlier, there are questions that remain unresolved. Moreover, the law emphasizes the importance of internal and external accreditation of higher education institutions, but QA clearly remains under control by MOET.

In a subsequent regulatory document, providing guidance for the implementation of the law, more details are provided about the possible entitlements of private higher education institutions that are officially recognized as being nonprofit institutions. These institutions may in the future be entitled to tax benefits, priority in land acquisitions or leasing, exemption from land use fees, support with academic staff development, and priority in access to research funds. Their nonprofit status will be determined on the basis of their annual financial and audit reports. If not deemed to be for-profit, their access to benefits will be cease and all benefits provided to them up to that date will have to be returned to the state. How this process will work in practice has yet to be clarified.

Indeed, a great deal of detail relating to the Higher Education Law of 2012 remains to be clarified. The process of restructuring the higher education system into three tiers will, for example, require many difficult decisions in terms of the allocation of individual institutions, and the way forward for the for-profit private higher education institutions remains for the moment uncertain. Importantly, however, the law has recognized the need for more regulatory clarity regarding types of higher education institutions, the nature of private higher education institutions, the scope of QA responsibilities, and the importance of the research role of particular types of universities. It also creates more opportunities for the exercise of institutional autonomy by, for example, removing the cap on the tuition fees that may be charged by public higher education institutions (subject to meeting certain conditions) and allowing higher education institutions to issue their own degrees, exercise more freedom in the management of their academic affairs, and select their preferred education quality accreditation agency from a list approved by MOET.

Conclusion

This chapter has paid particular attention to the challenges faced by the higher education system in Vietnam as it seeks to achieve its full potential. In many respects, the system continues to be constrained by the organizational and cultural characteristics of the period of Soviet-style centralized state planning that existed from the 1960s (in the North) up to 1986. It is also constrained by the fact that Vietnam is a developing economy with a relatively low level of national income per capita. There is, however, a strong commitment in Vietnam to higher education, as is evidenced by the extent of public and private expenditure and the fact that the system has been expanding very rapidly, with further strong growth projected for the future.

In a relatively short chapter, it is not possible to comment on the full range of attributes of the higher education system in Vietnam. There has been little or no discussion, for example, about the extent of the influence on the system of the forces of globalization, internationalization, and commercialization. Neither has it been possible to expand fully on the impact of the higher education system's rapid transition from being an "elite" to being a "mass" higher education system (Trow, 1974). The implications of this transition in terms of attitudes to access, views about the function of education, preferences for different forms of academic administration, and perceptions of responsibilities for internal governance are likely to be immense (Trow, 2005) and well worth more detailed consideration. Neither has it been possible to focus on challenges that are unique to Vietnam when compared with other higher education systems in the ASEAN region.

To conclude on a positive note, though lacking resources and in need of fundamental reforms, the higher education sector in Vietnam has recorded many achievements since 1993 and is now providing an enormous range of opportunities for young people. The Vietnamese people are adaptable and determined. The Higher Education Law of 2012 presents hope that there may be more scope in future for the exercise of initiative.

REFERENCES

ASEAN Secretariat. (2012). *ASEAN community in figures 2012*. Jakarta, Indonesia: ASEAN.

Fatseas, M. (2010). Research-industry cooperation supporting development in Vietnam. In G. Harman, M. Hayden,& Pham Thanh Nghi (Eds.), *Reforming higher education in Vietnam: Challenges and priorities*(pp.103–115). Dordrecht, The Netherlands: Springer.

Dao Van Khanh, Pham Thi Ly, Nguyen Van Tuan (2012). Scientific Research in Vietnam: Contemporary Issues and Proposed Strategic Solutions. Paper presented at National Conference on Vietnamese Higher Education in Globalization Context held by Vietnam National University Ho Chi Minh City, Nov 9, 2012, Ho Chi Minh City, Vietnam. Published in Conference Proceedings, (pp. 164-198), 2012, Vietnam.

Harman, G., Hayden, M., & Pham Thanh Nghi. (Eds.). (2010). *Reforming higher education in Vietnam: Challenges and priorities*. Dordrecht, The Netherlands: Springer.

Hayden, M., & Lam Quang Thiep. (2006). A 2020 vision for Vietnam. *International Higher Education, 44,* 11–13.

Hayden, M.,& Lam Quang Thiep (2007). Institutional autonomy for higher education in Vietnam. *Higher Education Research and Development, 26*(1), 73–85.

Hayden, M., & Le Thi Ngoc Lan. (2013). The education system in Vietnam: A need to improve quality.In C. Brock & L. Symaco (Eds.), *Education in South-east Asia* (pp. 323–344). London, UK: Bloomsbury Academic.

London, J. (Ed.). (2011) *Education in Vietnam*. Singapore: Institute of Southeast Asian Studies.

Nguyen Van Tuan &Pham Thi Ly. (2011a). The role of university in knowledge-based economy in Viet Nam. In*200 years of Humboldt: International experiences and Viet Nam* (pp. 661–680). Hanoi, Vietnam: Knowledge.

Nguyen Van Tuan & Pham Thi Ly. (2011b). Scientific output and its relationship to knowledge economy: An analysis of ASEAN countries. *Scientometrics89*(1), 107–117.

Pham Thi Ly. (2013). Case study: The effectiveness of research and innovation management at policy and institutional levels in Vietnam. In A. Olson & L. Meek (Eds.), *Effectiveness of research and innovation management at policy and institutional levels: Cambodia, Malaysia, Thailand and Vietnam* (pp. 140–163). Paris, France: OECD.

Trow, M. (1974). Problems in the transition from elite to mass higher education. In *General Report on the Conference on Future Structures of Post-Secondary Education: Policies for higher education*(pp. 55–101). Paris, France: OECD.

Trow, M. (2005). Reflections on the transition from elite to mass to universal access: Forms and phases of higher education in modern societies since WWII (Working Paper of the Institute of Governmental Studies). Berkeley: University of California. Retrieved from http://escholarship.org/uc/item/96p3s213

World Bank. (2012). *Putting higher education to work*. Washington DC: Author.

World Bank. (2014). *Data bank*. Retrieved fromhttp://data.worldbank.org

NOTES

[1] Using figures derived from the Thai Commission of Higher Education, 2007–08 and comparable figures from the MOET website in Vietnam. Source: Khanh Dao, Ly Pham and Tuan Nguyen (2012).

Chapter Ten

Global Influences on the Internationalization of Higher Education in Japan: The Role of the Bologna Process and Other European Initiatives

TAKAO KAMIBEPPU, TOKYO JOGAKKAN COLLEGE, JAPAN

Introduction

In the last three decades, internationalization of higher education in Japan has long centered on internationalization at home rather than internationalization outside home. To internationalize at home, Japanese higher education institutions (HEIs) increased English-medium instruction classes and programs, hired international faculty members and researchers, and reformed their curricula to match international standards, with the strong support from the Japanese government. The Japanese government and Japanese HEIs have implemented strategies to increase the number of international students, which they consider to be the most important indicator of internationalization, and to enhance the attractiveness of Japanese higher education. For internationalization outside home, the Ministry of Education, Culture, Sports, Science and Technology (MEXT) made it possible for Japanese HEIs to offer Japanese degrees abroad by setting up an international branch campus in 2004, though none currently exist.

The government has long believed that the presence of international students would expose domestic students to various types of diversity, bring about innovations in teaching and learning, facilitate Japanese HEIs to improve the quality of their education and research, and help promote Japanese language and culture abroad. There are also many other reasons and factors that encourage Japanese HEIs to internationalize, including a reputation race through the world rankings tumult, demand and competition for global talent, a need to recruit more foreign students to augment the shrinking Japanese student population, and a need to maintain the Japan's share of the increasing number of globally mobile students (Central Council on Education, 2008). These factors are well studied and analyzed (Goodman, 2007; Horie, 2002; Pokarier, 2010; Yonezawa, Akiba, & Horiuchi, 2013). However, there are other understudied factors that inspire and influence the internationalization of Japan's higher education, including the progress of internationalization and harmonization of higher education in the world (e.g., the Bologna Process and Association of Southeast Asian Nations [ASEAN] mobility frameworks) and the emergence of Asian countries as competitors to Japan (Central Council on Education, 2008).

In this context, this chapter focuses on the influences of European systems, such as the Erasmus Program[1] and the Bologna Process, on the historical developments of internationalization of higher education in Japan. The data on this topic were collected primarily from policy documents and literature on higher education internationalization. Before examining European influences, though, the chapter will explore the internationalization of higher education in Japan in terms of its current landscape and historical developments.

Current State of Internationalization of Japanese Higher Education and its Historical Developments

Japan's first national policy to host international students sought to enroll 100,000 students by 2000. This goal was met in 2003 after making a variety of policy adjustments to deal with many contingencies. Five years later, in 2008, the government set another target to host 300,000 international students by 2020. At present, with some five years remaining, the number of international students has yet to reach the halfway mark. Also in 2008, the government began encouraging Japanese students to study overseas, thus promoting reciprocal mobility of students. This initiative was partially in response to a continual decline in the number of Japanese students studying abroad.

Current Landscape

As of May 2013, Japan hosted 135,519 international students,[2] which is 2,237 fewer students (1.6 percent) than the previous academic year of 2012–13. These numbers include both degree-seeking and short-term[3] (not for degree) international students, but exclude the 24,902 international students enrolled in Japanese language schools. Partly thanks to ever-increasing governmental funding for university internationalization programs, the total number of international students reached a record high of 141,774 in 2010. However, after the Great East Japan Earthquake on March 11, 2011, and subsequent meltdowns at the Fukushima Daiichi Nuclear Power Plant, the number has been on a gradual decline. The share of short-term students (included in the statistics) is only 8.6 percent (Japan Student Services Organization [JASSO], 2013).

If we look at the geographical breakdown of international students in Japan (Table 10.1), Asia is still overwhelmingly dominant with a 91.9 percent share, but the number of students from Asia has decreased.

TABLE 10.1: DISTRIBUTION OF INTERNATIONAL STUDENTS IN JAPAN BY REGION OF ORIGIN, 2013

Region	Number of All International Students (Including Short-Term Students)	Share (%)	Change from 2012	Short-Term Students	Share (%)	Change from 2012
Asia	124,542	91.9	–3,000	7,095	60.6	+219
Europe	4,753	3.5	+297	2,482	21.2	+243
North America	2,391	1.8	–44	1,634	13.9	+83
Middle & Near East	1,233	0.9	+121	55	0.5	+10
Africa	1,155	0.9	+49	55	0.7	–11
Central & South America	946	0.7	+20	135	1.2	+34
Oceania	499	0.4	–44	233	2.0	–34
Total	135,519	100.0	–2,237	11,717	100.0	+571

Source: JASSO (2013)

As for country or region of origin (Table 10.2), the top 10 countries are all in Asia except the United States. Out of the top 20 countries, only six are outside Asia. For European countries, France, Germany, and the United Kingdom send students at a meager 400s to 700s level. This landscape of international students in Japan thus illustrates the extent to which Japan attracts students exclusively within Asia. In recent trends, both China and South Korea show a big dip, while the students from Vietnam have increased significantly.

TABLE 10.2: TOP 20 COUNTRIES/REGIONS OF ORIGIN OF INTERNATIONAL STUDENTS IN JAPAN (INCLUDING SHORT-TERM PROGRAMS), 2013

Rank	Countries or Regions of Origin	Number	Share (%)	Change from 2012
1	China	81,884	59.6	−4,440
2	South Korea	15,304	14.8	−1,347
3	Vietnam	6,290	4.0	+1,919
4	Taiwan	4,719	2.4	+102
5	Nepal	3,188	2.4	+737
6	Indonesia	2,410	1.8	+134
7	Thailand	2,383	1.8	+216
8	Malaysia	2,293	1.7	−26
9	United States	2,083	1.5	−50
10	Myanmar	1,193	0.9	+42
11	Mongolia	1,138	0.8	+24
12	Bangladesh	875	0.6	−177
13	France	793	0.6	+53
14	Sri Lanka	794	0.6	+124
15	Germany	599	0.4	+33
16	India	560	0.4	+19
17	Philippines	507	0.4	+10
18	Saudi Arabia	472	0.3	+59
19	United Kingdom	452	0.3	+23
20	Russia	339	0.3	+6

Source: JASSO (2013)

If we separate the numbers for short-term students from overall numbers, the majority of the students from developed (Organisation for Economic Co-operation and Development [OECD]) countries are on short-term programs (Table 10.3). Approximately three out of four American students are in short-term programs. OECD countries such as The Netherlands, Finland, Italy, and Spain do not appear on the top 20 list of total number, but they do appear on the short-term top 20 list. On the contrary, Asian countries have smaller shares of students in short-term programs, which indicate a strong orientation of degree-seeking students from developing countries in Asia to Japan either under scholarships or self-funding.

TABLE 10.3: TOP 20 COUNTRIES OR REGIONS OF ORIGIN OF INTERNATIONAL STUDENTS IN JAPAN FOR SHORT-TERM PROGRAM, 2013

Rank	Countries or Regions of Origin	Number and Changes of All Short-Term International Students In Japan		Share Among All Short-Term International Students in Japan (%)	Share in the Total Number of International Students from the Country
		Number	Change from 2012		
1	China	3,719	+241	31.7	4.5
2	United States	1,480	+71	12.6	71.1
3	South Korea	1,473	−122	12.6	9.6
4	Taiwan	871	+48	7.4	18.5
5	France	521	+67	4.4	65.7
6	Germany	433	+18	3.7	72.3
7	Thailand	345	+44	2.9	14.5
8	UK	325	+27	2.8	71.9
9	Australia	203	−20	1.7	65.1
10	Vietnam	176	+18	1.5	2.8
11	Indonesia	158	−38	1.3	6.6
12	Canada	154	+12	1.3	50.0
13	Sweden	123	+1	1.0	48.4
14	Italy	120	+28	1.0	55.3
15	Russia	105	+3	0.9	31.0
16	Finland	104	+12	0.9	–
17	Netherlands	88	−11	–	–
18	Spain	82	+10	0.7	–
19	Norway	60	+6	0.5	–
20	Malaysia	57	+13	0.5	2.5

Source: JASSO (2013)

Thus, general and long-standing trends can be summarized as follows: (a) students from Asia, particularly Chinese students, continue to be highly dominant; and (b) many Asian students are enrolled in degree programs while many students from OECD countries (except South Korea) favor short-term programs.

100,000 in 1983

The current landscape is a result of the accumulated interplays between policy and practice, which went through an array of trial and error with many contingencies. In the 1980s, Japan was still enjoying high economic growth when the government initiated its first internationalization policy. When Prime Minister Nakasone set a numerical target in 1983 to host 100,000 international students by 2000, there were 10,428 international students in Japan. The Japanese government chose the number 100,000 as a goal because that is how many international students were in France in 1983. The target was designed under the assumption that 10 percent of the students would come to Japan with public funding, and the remaining 90 percent with private and other funding. As soon as the 100,000 plan was announced, the Ministry of Justice allowed international students to work part time in Japan. At that time Japan was experiencing acute shortage of labor during the so-called bubble economy, and many Japanese language schools were established at a very fast pace and rather chaotically in the absence of establishment standards and guidelines. As a consequence, international students flocked to Japanese language schools and moved on to Japanese HEIs after graduation. In 1989, the number of international students reached 30,000. However, a lack of regulations on entry to the market and governance of Japanese language schools led to problems such as overstays and illegal labor increased. The Ministry of Justice responded in the same year by revising immigration policy, distinguishing between a college student visa for four-year HEIs, junior colleges, and professional training colleges and a precollege visa for Japanese language school students, which have fewer benefits than college student visas (Shiraishi, 2006).

Under the tightened immigration policy, the number of international students went up and down, and finally the number reached 50,000 in 1999. In the same year, after recognizing the successful impact of the tightened immigration policy in the 1990s, the Ministry of Justice once again relaxed the policy, this time simplifying the application package (no requirement for the submission of financial statements and academic certificates). As a result, the number of international students reached 60,000 in 2000, 70,000 in 2001, and 90,000 in 2002. The target was finally met in 2003, slightly behind schedule, when the number reached 109,508.

In December 2003, when it was confirmed that the international students in Japan finally exceeded 100,000 in number, the Central Council on Education (2003)[4] of MEXT announced new proposals on study abroad students for 2004–2008. First, the council pointed out the following reasons for the dramatic increase of international students in Japan since 2000: (a) the increase of applicants from Asian countries[5] with high economic growth, represented by China; (b) the focus by Japanese universities on international students to augment the financial loss resulting from the decline of the university-age Japanese student population; and (c) the relaxation of immigration procedures for international students in 2000. Based on this analysis, the council announced a new policy proposal, which included (a) balanced student mobility (i.e., encouraging Japanese students to study abroad), (b) stronger support for Japanese students who study abroad, (c) recruiting top-ranked international students to Japan, and (d) improving support systems for international students in Japan (Central Council on Education, 2003). Indeed, it was the first time that MEXT's consultative bodies refereed to the study abroad of Japanese students who have been long overlooked in education policy.

However, despite MEXT's consistent push from the policy and program side to attract more international students to Japan, the immigration policy was tightened again by the Ministry of Justice in 2003. This policy change was in response to the increased overstays and illegal work of international students (as described earlier). This action once again resulted in slowing the rate of increase. Thus, the numerical changes of international students were largely determined by immigration policy, which changes on an ad hoc basis without a consistent and long-term immigration plan.

300,000 in 2008

Amid new stagnation in the growth of international students in early 2000s, MEXT shifted its international student policy from international understanding and foreign aid rationales to more strategic rationales with an emphasis on enhancing international competitiveness and recruiting highly skilled workers. MEXT was long concerned that Japan had been lagging behind in attracting international students compared to other popular destinations, and that Japan was losing its premier status in East Asia because of its own low-profile policy and competition from other countries.

As a way to give a powerful impetus to international student recruitment, Prime Minister Yasuo Fukuda announced an ambitious plan in January 2008 that the government would host 300,000 international students by 2020. This plan was a culmination of many policies of the previous years and officially started in July 2008. It described several strategies, such as (a) expanding Japanese language education overseas; (b) making entrance examinations, enrollment, and entry into Japan more student friendly; (c) "globalizing" Japanese HEIs; (d) improving hosting environments (i.e., housing and financial support); and (e) supporting postgraduation life and employment in Japan (MEXT, 2008). Thus, the government maintains a tendency to translate the rise of international student population in Japan into the internationalization of higher education.

In August 2009, the Democratic Party of Japan won the general election to become the ruling party after many years of Liberal Democratic Party rule. Cutting the budget was high on their agenda. In late 2009, the newly formed Administration Innovation Council (*Gyosei sasshin kaigi*) at the Prime Minister's Office organized public sessions for budget screening and reductions for the 2010 fiscal year. The council scrutinized and slashed the budget of MEXT's Global 30 initiative[6] (a major accelerator of the 300,000 plan), which led to its significant downsizing for the following year. Despite this seemingly contradictory action, the new government continued to support the two targets of sending 300,000 students from Japan and hosting the same number of international students to study in Japan by 2020.

After regaining its position as the ruling party in the December 2012 general election, the Liberal Democratic Party formed a coalition government. The new government announced the Japan New Development Strategy in June 2013, which mentioned continued support for the 300,000 international student plan of 2008. But the strategy reduced the 2020 numerical target of Japanese students who study abroad from 300,000 to 120,000, with the rationale that the new target would double the 2010 number of approximately 60,000.

Bologna Process and Other European Influences

European higher education initiatives and reforms have heavily impacted many parts of the world. Japan is not an exception. The Japanese government has been a careful watcher of developments of higher education in Europe. The spirit and ideas of the Bologna Process, which partly stemmed from the Erasmus program, have influenced educational discourse within Japan. Almost all government documents on international higher education in Japan refer to developments in Europe. A variety of Bologna elements such as European Credit Transfer and Accumulation System (ECTS), Tuning[7], and double- and joint-degree programs have been models for Japanese higher education reforms.

Erasmus Program

The Erasmus program has been a model for Asia and the Pacific for a long time. University Mobility in Asia and the Pacific (UMAP), which was inspired by Erasmus, was created in 1993 as the first student mobility framework covering Asia. Japan, as one of its founding countries, led the expansion of the program over the years. In 2008, in addition to the 300,000 international student plan, another initiative modeled on Erasmus was launched by the Japanese government, which was called the Asian Erasmus initiative. In his speech in May 2008, Prime Minister Fukuda proposed Asian Erasmus to increase student mobility in Asia. This program was in line with the discussions at the Asia-Europe Meeting (ASEM) Conference of Ministers Responsible for Education held in Berlin in May 2008, which pushed for an increase in cross-border mobility from the European Union (EU) side (Fukuda, 2008). Asian Erasmus is a more government-involved and regionally narrower initiative than UMAP.

Following Fukuda's speech, MEXT commissioned a research project in 2008 focusing on the new policy. A field survey was conducted to collect data from eight countries in Asia as possible partners in the new initiative (Kamibeppu, 2009). Its final report suggested that the EU case was not automatically transferable to Asia due to different historical and political contexts. However, the report also suggested that the successful expansion of the European Higher Education Area into Eastern Europe and across the Ural Mountains indicates that the model might also accommodate the broad diversity of political and educational systems and conditions in Asia. It also proposed that Asia should not use contextual differences between Europe and Asian as an excuse for the difficulties in harmonization of higher education in the region, because Asia was still in the early stages of development, trying to move from setting up frameworks to implementing substantial mobility programs. It concluded that the first step is to have a dialog regularly among different countries and within each country to reveal similarities and differences and possibilities and challenges. The second step is for leading ASEAN Plus Three (ASEAN+3) countries concerned with a high level of student mobility to form an initial core group and eventually include other ASEAN countries on a trial-and-error basis, using the European developments as an example. It also noted that interregional cooperation is important to make Asian frameworks comparable to other regions.

Several developments occurred regarding student mobility in Asia after August 2009 when the Democratic Party of Japan took office. Prime Minister Yukio Hatoyama referred to the realization of the East Asian Community as one of his top priorities. In the joint press conference in October 2009, Mr. Hatoyama mentioned new initiatives for student exchange among Japan, South Korea, and China (Prime Minister's Office, 2009). The Asian Erasmus initiative in 2008 went through political changes in Japan and, combined with echoing ideas in ASEAN, gave rise to a tripartite (Japan, China, and South Korea) cooperation with inputs from other sources, including ministries and agencies. This enhanced (short-term) mobility in education and research was called Collective Action for Mobility Program of University Students in Asia (CAMPUS) Asia. The government provided funds for 10 university consortia in 2011 to implement the tripartite program for the following five years.

Bologna Process

Regarding the Bologna Process, Japanese higher education appears to have been influenced in multiple ways. The Bologna Process was first introduced into Japan through multiple channels (such as EU meetings and academic research) and gained slow but gradual recognition by the Japanese higher education community. Some policymaking and program implementation were inspired directly or indirectly by the Bologna model. Although Bologna was initially considered simply as something occurring on the other side of the Eurasian continent, MEXT paid particular attention to the Bologna Process for its discussion of internationalization of higher education in Japan. Almost all government documents on the internationalization of higher education refer to the developments in Europe: double- and joint-degree programs; student mobility; the harmonization of diploma, degrees, and credits; Tuning; and the Bologna "Stocktaking Report[8]."

The following section will describe and review the reactions to the variety of Bologna elements (three-cycle degree system; ECTS; qualification frameworks, learning outcomes, and employability; Tuning process) by the Japanese higher education community and offer some examples of direct or indirect effects of the process.

Specific Implications of the Bologna Process for Japan

First, the degree cycle has little impact on Japan, because the Japanese degree cycle (mostly four-year bachelor's degree) is already equivalent to Bologna's three-cycle (bachelor, master, and doctorate) system. In Japan, there is a discussion for formulating a new policy to allow students to earn bachelor's degrees in three years while maintaining the four-year bachelor's system, independent of Bologna.

Second, in terms of credit recognition (ECTS) and mobility, UMAP was created in 1993 modeled on Erasmus as aforementioned. UCTS (UMAP Credit Transfer Scheme) was also developed using ECTS as a model. But, the diffusion of UMAP and UCTS has been limited in Japanese HEIs. The subsequent CAMPUS Asia program now faces a tough political environment among the three participating nations (Japan, China, and South Korea), which might jeopardize further progress. Regarding double- and joint-degree programs, double-degree programs have been legalized, and joint-degree programs will soon be approved. Europe's dynamic Erasmus Mundus[9] program is certainly inspiring the Japanese higher education community to make possible both double- and joint-degree programs. Recently, MEXT began to join the activities of ASEAN, which is quite active and advanced in establishing frameworks (such as the ASEAN International Mobility for Students [AIMS] program by Southeast Asian Ministers of Education Organization Regional Centre for Higher Education and Development [SEAMEO RIHED], and the ASEAN University Network [AUN][10]) in order to increase student mobility between Japan and ASEAN, following the Bologna Process as a model. These ASEAN experiences have inspired Japan to create a student mobility framework as an East Asian Community including ASEAN+3 (China, South Korea, and Japan) and beyond (adding Australia, New Zealand, and India).

The causes of limited expansion of UMAP or CAMPUS Asia can be attributed to several reasons particular to Japanese higher education. In Japan, job hunting begins in the second semester of the junior year, sacrificing the most important academic mobility period. In addition, diversity is not necessarily celebrated or appreciated in largely homogeneous Japan. In many cases, mobility and double or joint degrees are considered extra or negative in Japan's job market, where a single bachelor's degree is valued. If job-seeking students have many mobility experiences, they are in many cases considered as unstable. Therefore, it would be natural for students to refrain from studying abroad, considering the costs and benefits (United States–Japan Conference on Cultural & Educational Interchange, 2013).

Third, there have been certain impacts in the field of qualification frameworks, learning outcomes, and employability. A national qualification framework has not yet been developed in Japan, but there has been a gradual paradigm shift in the definition of educational quality from input to outcome. There have been active discussions regarding learning outcomes and employability, with Bologna and Europe in mind. The UK system has been frequently referred to as a potential model for Japan. In 2010, the Science

Council of Japan released a report on quality assurance based on academic discipline in college education, acting on a request from MEXT. The council proposed a standards initiative, called Reference Standards, to assess and achieve learning outcomes in each academic discipline. This initiative took into account the UK system of Subject Benchmark Statements. Reference Standards is one of many proposals (such as Bachelor Skills, Workers' Basic Skills, and Employable Skills) from different sectors in Japan to better link college education and the labor market and to increase the mobility of the labor market. The impetus behind this influx of proposals is the very rigid Japanese recruitment system, which puts excessive emphasis on the students graduating from undergraduate programs. The motivation for this initiative comes from a growing demand by the private sector and society in general for more accountability from the higher education community, especially as admission procedures have loosened in response to a shrinking student population and ever increasing enrollment capacity. Globalization and global competition have also contributed to this growing demand.

Using a researcher-led and top-down process, the council delineated Reference Standards in more than 10 academic disciplines so far. Reference Standards consist of learning outcomes and competencies in each academic discipline, and as a "loose model" for Japanese HEIs, while the HEIs' diversity is respected. It is expected that Reference Standards will serve as major and clear criteria for employment, and that employers might shift their hiring paradigm from trainability to employability. This could help solve the current, very early, and very long job-hunting process, because HEIs would be providing the education students need to acquire such competencies, and employers would be reassured that the students would be meeting the employers' criteria by acquiring competencies through attaining an undergraduate college degree. The new paradigm would enable students to pursue academic study fully and study abroad in a more flexible manner. This would eventually contribute to eliminating employment discrimination against older graduates. The expectations are to ensure students that students gain employable skills during college years and to make certain that students move from college to work under explicit and transparent hiring standards.

Regarding promoting learning outcomes for Japanese HEIs, the Tuning Europe project (whose goal is mapping out learning outcomes and competencies) has received some attention. Some research groups recently began a Tuning Asia initiative at a small scale.

Do the European Schemes Work in the Japanese Context?

Student mobility is supposed to contribute to the development of learning outcomes, competencies, and the employability of students, according to the European experiences. But, the big question is, does it really work in Japan? In the Japanese employment system, employers put strong emphasis on students' trainability, and as a result, employers maintain a very high preference for hiring new graduates. Japanese recruiters (either from the private or public sector) have a strong preference for new graduates

(22–24 years range) because they fit well into the seniority-based pay scales and promotion patterns of the organizations. New graduates are wanted because they are young, fresh, flexible, trainable, and mendable. Therefore, hiring is not for particular positions, but for the organization as a whole. A traditional mechanism is established as a result of a long-standing alignment between the HEIs and industry. As previously mentioned, many students start their job hunting in the second semester of their junior year, resulting in losing focus on study on campus during the most important academic study period, and some continue to looking for jobs right up to graduation. This practice has contributed to the low mobility of the overall labor market. Job-seeking students in general, and human and social science students in particular, are evaluated based on vague hiring standards such as flexibility or harmony, because employers do not much expect them to have utilized the knowledge and skills they learned at college classrooms. In recent years, it has been reported that students give up study-abroad opportunities due to the very early and very long job-hunting process, especially since the economic and employment downturn. This mechanism makes it very difficult, if not impossible, to develop young professionals with global perspectives, which is considered to be an urgent issue from many sectors of the society. Thus, there is a discrepancy between the demand and supply of young college graduates with global perspectives.

In this context, most Japanese university students can focus on study essentially only for the first two years, and in the junior year, corporations gradually take over their lives. Students cannot afford to "miss the boat." There have been many attempts to end this type of early recruitment, but they have been in vain. It appears that universities and faculty members feel helpless about this peculiar landscape. College has many dimensions, and while international experience is important to nurture their competencies, it is not a requirement. Study abroad is exciting and useful, but not indispensable for their lives. The value of international mobility experience is compromised in Japan due to the current employment conditions.

Conclusion

Erasmus and the Bologna Process have thus impacted the discussions on internationalization of higher education in Japan in terms of both cooperation and competition with Europe. Japan has learned from an array of alignments and harmonization under the Bologna Process, which has set some emerging "global" trends and standards. Japan could not afford to overlook this crucial trend. Joint programs such as Erasmus Mundus have also contributed to mutual internationalization (e.g., foreign language skill improvement) and quality improvement (e.g., clearer connection between learning outcomes and employability) by making participating education programs comparable and transparent.

In contrast, the European Higher Education Area has been recognized as a competitor to Japan, especially in the Asian student market. Rather than directly borrowing Bologna ideas, European examples tend to be considered in terms of how Japan can take leadership in these areas in Asia as a growing student market and as a region moving towards the harmonization of higher education. It appears the Japanese government fears that powerful European universities will expand their links and their cooperation with Asian counterparts, to the detriment of Japan's position in Asia (e.g., the case of Vietnam), and that Japanese universities will lose their edge in education and research in the international marketplace. Overall, Japan has used lessons learned from Europe, effectively allowing it to assume a leadership position within the higher education landscape in Asia.

REFERENCES

Central Council on Education. (2003). *Aratana ryugakusei seisaku no tenkai nitsuite* [Implementing new international student policy]. Tokyo, Japan: Central Council on Education.

Central Council on Education. (2008). *Minutes of nine meetings of the International Student Special Sub-committee of the University Committee in Central Council on Education.* Tokyo, Japan: Central Council on Education.

Fukuda, Y. (2008, May). *When the Pacific Ocean becomes an "inland sea": Five pledges to a future Asia that "acts together."* Speech by H.E. Mr. Yasuo Fukuda, Prime Minister of Japan, at the 14th International Conference on the Future of Asia, Tokyo, Japan. Ministry of Foreign Affairs. Retrieved from http://www.mofa.go.jp/region/asia-paci/speech0805-2.html

Goodman, R. (2007). The concept of Kokusaika and Japanese educational reform, *Globalisation, Societies and Education, 5*(1), 53–70.

Horie, M. (2002). The internationalisation of higher education in Japan in the 1990s: A reconsideration. *Higher Education, 43*, 65–84.

Japan Student Services Organization (JASSO). (2013). International students in Japan 2013. Retrieved from http://www.jasso.go.jp/statistics/intl_student/data13_e.html.

Kamibeppu, T. (2009). *Ajia taiheiyo ni okeru daigakukan koryu to no kakudai* [Towards the expansion of inter-university cooperation in Asia and the Pacific]. MEXT Pilot Research Project for University Reform Promotion (2008). Tokyo, Japan: MEXT.

Ministry of Education, Culture, Sports, Science and Technology (MEXT). (2008). *Outline of the student exchange system: Study in Japan and abroad.* Tokyo, Japan: MEXT.

Pokarier, C. (2010). Japanese higher education: Seeking adaptive efficiency in a mature sector. In C. Findlay & W. Tierney (Eds.), *Globalisation and tertiary education in the Asia-Pacific: The changing nature of a dynamic market* (pp. 255–283), Singapore: World Scientific.

Prime Minister's Office. (2009). Joint Press Conference by Prime Minister Yukio Hatoyama of Japan, Premier Wen Jiabao of the People's Republic of China and President Lee Myung-bak of the South Korea following the Second Japan–China–South Korea Trilateral Summit Meeting. Retrieved from http://japan.kantei.go.jp/hatoyama/statement/200910/10JCKkyoudou_e.html

Shiraishi, K. (2006). *Ryugakuseisu no hensen to nyukan seisaku kara miru ryugakusei juman'nin keikaku* [100,000 international student plan from the viewpoint of the changes of the number of international students and immigration policies]. Tokyo, Japan: Asian Students Cultural Association.

United States–Japan Conference on Cultural & Educational Interchange. (2013). *CULCON education task force report*. Tokyo, Japan.

Yonezawa, A., Akiba, H., & Horiuchi, D. (2013). Japanese university leaders' perceptions of internationalisation: The role of government in review and support. In T. Coverdale-Jones (Ed.), *Transnational higher education in the Asian context*, (pp. 15–31). Basingstoke, UK: Palgrave Macmillan.

NOTES

[1] A European Union (EU) student exchange program run from 1987 to 2013. Now it is part of new EU program called "Erasmus+" (2014-2020). With close to 3 million students participating, the Erasmus Program is considered the most successful student exchange program in the world.

[2] In the government's documents, "international student" is defined as a student from a foreign country who is receiving education at any Japanese university, graduate school, junior college, college of technology, professional training college, or university preparatory courses, and who resides in Japan under "college student" visa status, as defined in Annexed Table 1 of the Immigration Control and Refugee Recognition Act (Japan Student Services Organization [JASSO], 2013). University preparatory courses are offered to those who complete their secondary education before they reach 18 years old in an education system, so that they can be qualified to enter Japanese HEIs (The minimum age required for entrance is 18).

[3] "Short-term international student" is defined as a student from a foreign country who is receiving education in Japan for a period of one year or less. The purpose of the study is not necessarily to obtain a degree but rather to study at Japanese HEIs, to experience a different culture, or to improve Japanese language skills (JASSO, 2013).

[4] It absorbed the functions of the University Council in 2001.

[5] There has been a traditional emphasis to recruit students from developing countries partly using the budget of ODA (Official Development Assistance commonly known as "foreign aid" to assist developing countries).

[6] In 2014, MEXT started the Super Global University program as a successor of Global 30 program.

[7] "A faculty-driven process that identifies what a student should know and be able to do in a chosen discipline when a degree has been earned" (Tuning USA, retrieved from http://tuningusa.org/).

[8] Bologna Process, retrieved from http://www.ond.vlaanderen.be/hogeronderwijs/bologna/actionlines/stocktaking.htm.

[9] Erasmus Mundus is an international extension of the Erasmus Program. It began in 2004 aiming to enhance the quality of European higher education and to promote mutual understanding between peoples and cultures through graduate-level cooperation with non-EU countries. Like Erasmus, Erasmus Mundus became also part of new "Erasmus+" in 2014 (European Commission, retrieved from http://eacea.ec.europa.eu/erasmus_mundus/).

[10] Both of these programs were also inspired by Erasmus and Bologna models.

Chapter Eleven

The Role of Development Partners in Supporting Higher Education in Asia

Jouko Sarvi[1], Asian Development Bank, Philippines

Introduction

The dynamic development context in Asia provides both promising opportunities and complex challenges for higher education. The long, sustained period of economic growth in the region has resulted in a rapidly growing number of middle-income countries. By 2020, only two Asian countries are expected to remain low income (Asian Development Bank [ADB], 2014). However, many middle-income countries will struggle to advance their development unless they pursue reforms on several fronts, including making higher education more responsive to the human resource development needs of the economies. Carefully designed and timely investments in higher education in developing Asian countries will help them build high-income economies, with the innovation, knowledge, and technology needed to thrive in an interconnected, competitive world.

As higher education systems across Asia look ahead, they face four overarching challenges: (1) maintaining and improving higher education quality, even in the face of serious financial constraints; (2) increasing the relevance of curriculum and instruction at a time of rapid change in labor market needs; (3) increasing and better utilizing the financial resources available to higher education; and (4) balancing the continued expansion of access to higher education with greater attention to equitable access and inclusiveness of higher education to support inclusive development and economic growth (ADB, 2011).

This chapter discusses some of the drivers that are likely to increasingly influence the strategies and operational models in higher education development in Asia. It highlights the needs for shifting assistance strategies of development partners, such as the Asian Development Bank (ADB), that are supporting higher education institutions in their efforts to tackle the challenges and prepare for the future. The chapter draws on a series of studies on higher education financed by the ADB, as well as other studies.

Opportunities for Higher Education Development with a Wider Range of Contributors

The old distinctions between rich and poor countries, developed and developing countries, and development assistance providers and recipients are breaking down in Asia (Solheim, 2014). The composition of development financing is changing due to an increase in government resources and direct foreign investment and the emergence of private-sector organizations, corporate social responsibility programs, and foundations as sources of development financing (ADB, 2014). Thus, the region provides momentum for collaboration and partnerships, including in higher education development and financing, among a wider range of international, regional, and domestic contributors and opportunities to pursue innovative strategies and integration of a variety of operational models.

While more countries in Asia are advancing to middle-income status, each country has distinct development challenges and opportunities. Thus, support for higher education development will need to be sensitive to the differences and adjust strategic engagement accordingly. While lower-middle-income countries have relatively higher per-capita incomes than low-income countries, they share with low-income countries the broad challenges in tackling poverty and pursuing inclusive development and growth. Upper-middle-income countries generally are more advanced in human development fields, including experience collaborating with the private sector, and can attract diverse sources of finance. Overall, in comparison to low-income countries, middle-income countries have more advanced institutional systems and pool of expertise (ADB, 2014). Development partners supporting higher education development in the region will increasingly need to facilitate collaboration and partnership-building efforts among the expanding range of higher education contributors and stakeholders and to leverage know-how and financing and help customize the support in line with the capacities and needs of individual developing countries.

Inclusive Higher Education Can Help Tackle Inequalities

The phenomenal economic growth in Asia has been far from inclusive (ADB, 2012c, 2012e; Kanbur, Rhee, & Zhuang, 2014). Developing countries increasingly prioritize inclusive development, because they realize that large inequalities make it difficult to sustain economic growth and reduce the impact of economic growth on poverty reduction. Many countries face the risk of "middle-income trap"[2] unless they transform their economies, strengthen innovation, improve their human resource base, and decrease inequalities of opportunities (ADB, 2014; Kohli, Sharma, & Sood, 2011). This has implications also for higher education development, given that inequality in access to education, including higher education opportunities, is a key determinant in Asia of income inequality and widening disparities. Educated and skilled citizens can contribute to and benefit from economic growth, thus helping to make it inclusive.[3]

Developing Asian countries have made significant progress in raising enrollment rates in basic and secondary education. However, the low quality and completion rates at these levels continue to be a concern, especially with regard to readiness for higher learning among secondary education graduates. At the same time, and particularly fueled by the overall trend of middle-income economies, the demand is increasing for expanding opportunities and pathways for higher learning in the region to support human resource development and innovation for knowledge and technology—intensive sectors to help countries and economies move up the value chain. Providing higher education opportunities for marginalized and excluded groups is not only necessary for establishing a broad human resource base for advancing inclusive economic growth but also for achieving other equally important development goals in societies and the region as a whole. Asia makes a strong case for shifting the higher education development agenda from the narrow perspective of access to widening participation and pursuing inclusive higher education.

Sustainable Higher Education Development Requires Innovative Financing

Given that per-student costs in higher education are significantly higher than in lower education levels, developing countries with large student populations and limited public resources cannot feasibly expand higher education with public financing alone. The common strategies of mobilizing more financing through student tuition fees and through commercialization of research and private use of institutional facilities and staff have proven to be insufficient where demand for higher education has accelerated. Lessons learned from innovative financing mechanisms underline the importance of pursuing multiple sources of funding and a mix of supply- and demand-side mechanisms . This approach facilitates flexibility, which can be necessary when countries and institutions consider a response in the context of limited public resources and increasing demand for higher education, particularly when also keeping in mind the importance of not only improving but also sustaining quality in higher education (Salmi & Hauptman, 2006).

The rapid and substantial expansion of higher education enrollments in much of the Asian region, without concomitant increases in public financing for higher education, has led not only to expansion of private higher education institutions but also to "internal" privatization of public higher education institutions (ADB, 2012d, 2012h). Many higher education institutions have struggled with the privatization drive, as it can require considerable transformation of their governance structure and capacity for taking forward a range of development and fundraising strategies required to strengthen the sustainability of institutional resource base (ADB, 2012b, 2012d). An increasing number of universities in the region are facing financial difficulties and substantial levels of debt due to the reduction in public funding. Many public universities experiencing substantial resource squeeze have adopted the strategy of providing programs that are commonly termed "extension," "diploma," or "executive" courses to raise funds. However, this has often led to the diversification of teaching resources out of degree courses and increased risks that undermine the quality of the degrees (ADB, 2012d). Higher education institutions in Asian developing countries will increasingly need support from development partners to pursue innovative financing strategies that have proven effective for sustainable higher education development and to facilitate the sharing of their own lessons and knowledge on financing models, costs, and resource-mobilization strategies with others in the region.

Sustainable financing will require better strategies than those that merely shift costs, for example, shifting costs to students by increasing tuition fees. The student loan schemes that are common in developed countries face many obstacles in developing countries for various reasons, not least due to inefficient systems for recovery of the loans from students and the low motivation of commercial banks to partner in student loan scheme programs due to (at least perceived) high risk (ADB 2009). However, the expanding range of collaborators and contributors in higher education development and financing can provide opportunities for exploring the potential and feasibility to scale up innovative collaboration models for affordable, low-risk student loan schemes. Drawing on experience in, for example, microfinance loan schemes in other sectors, some philanthropic organizations (see Vittana.org) are pursuing innovative student loan product development and catalytic capital models to help establish feasible higher education student loan programs in countries, including in Asia, where conventional student loan schemes are not feasible.

While the so-called human capital contracts in education can be controversial ("Crowdfunding Students: Start Me Up," 2013), their potential to bring innovation and feasibility to student financing should be further explored in higher education development. Such approaches are pursued in collaboration with private sector and other labor market stakeholders. These approaches aim to reduce and spread the risks of student financing and strengthen the prospects of students being employed or establishing their own business after graduation. It also is critical in the region to link innovative higher education financing with equity in higher education provision: More attention is needed on financing models that support inclusive higher education by providing more opportunities for poor students and other disadvantaged students to pursue higher education studies (ADB, 2009, 2012d).

Demographic Trends Increase Pressure for Efficient Utilization of Technology in Higher Education Delivery

Demand projections for higher education over the longer term have often underestimated student population growth. Currently, some projections predict a somewhat diminishing demand for more student places in the long term in the region (ADB, 2011, 2012a). However, at least in the short to medium term, demographic trends in the region continue to increase the pressure to expand higher education enrollments and the need to increasingly utilize advanced educational technology. UNESCO's data indicate that the secondary education student population in Asia in 2012 was 338 million, and the tertiary education student population 105 million (UNESCO Institute for Statistics, 2014). In the light of some recent projections (e.g. ADB 2012a; British Council, 2012; Calderon, 2012), in the next decade more than 200 million Asian young people may be exploring higher education opportunities. Given the demographic trends, technology, while not a panacea, is increasingly in the nexus of balancing the quality, quantity, equity, and costs in higher education expansion in the region.

Delivery of higher education through distance education, including through videoconferencing and online technology, is common in some countries in Asia, expanding higher education opportunities for students in remote areas. Similarly, open universities have a long tradition in Asia of serving the higher education needs of a wider student population. Several universities are also pursuing mobile learning strategies and technology as media of delivery. In addition to the dedicated open universities or mixed-mode institutions delivering learning outside the confines of campuses, "virtual" or "cyber" universities are beginning to appear in the higher education landscape in Asia (ADB, 2012a). The emergence and potential of massive open online courses (MOOCs) are increasing pressure for universities to transform their institutional and organizational arrangements to provide virtual means of teaching and learning.

Advanced information and communications technology (ICT) and education technology can further expand opportunities for widening participation and inclusiveness in higher education, especially for disadvantaged and marginalized groups. These technologies can also improve cost efficiency. However, studies show that universities still mostly use technology to enhance traditional classroom teaching rather than to transform teaching design and delivery (ADB 2012a). The reluctance of universities to adopt a transformative approach can result in a significant increase in costs and other burdens; incremental adoption of educational technology within existing institutional structures actually can require more resources and the establishment of additional institutional layers (Bates & Sangra, 2011). As a result, universities are failing to respond to the learning needs of students who are increasingly turning to online resources and mobile devices to access information.

As ICT tools and capacities are continuously evolving, higher education leaders and institutions must continuously review the value of each new ICT advancement with regard to how it might enhance the institution. There is greater demand for development partners in the region to assist higher education leaders and institutions in establishing a holistic policy for better anticipation and utilization of advanced ICT.

Higher Education Contributes to Regional Economic Integration

As economies in the region have grown larger and more complex, they also have become more integrated through various forms of economic and social exchange. Higher education in Asia has an increasingly important role in human resource development; the movement of people, students, and the workforce; and regional economic integration. Thus, the demands are increasing for expanding and improving regional cooperation in higher education development. More opportunities for this exist in the region, which is home for some of the most advanced countries that have established themselves as leading regional hubs of education and have successful experiences to share in higher education development. Several Asian universities are climbing steadily upwards in global higher education rankings.

In particular, countries in Southeast Asia have pursued regional cooperation on harmonization of higher education by focusing on the comparability of degree programs, credit transfer system development, quality-assurance frameworks and standards, and faculty development for teaching and research, among others (ADB, 2008, 2012i, 2012f; Sarvi, 2011). Lessons learned in Southeast Asia can and should be embraced by other countries in Asia. As the rest of Asia moves forward, its demand for broad and deep cooperative frameworks in the region to facilitate the sharing of experiences and knowledge on important new and emerging development issues will increase and require continued attention.

More strategic discussion is called for on the development of higher education, and especially on how to balance the demand for establishing centers of excellence (which are necessary for strengthening the indigenous capacity for science and technology) with the demand for diversified networks of higher education institutions that are more responsive to diverse and evolving local labor markets. Other broad strategic issues include the role and extent of private higher education provision and higher education governance and financing reforms. Individual countries will need to find the right balance and model suitable for their context and needs, and they will have to adjust their strategic approach as their needs evolve.

Institutions' networks in higher education development are still very much limited to collaboration among national or other leading, well-resourced universities in the region. Other higher education institutions complain that they are left out. Regional cooperation and cross-border collaboration strategies and models should become more inclusive. They should increasingly focus on the needs and opportunities in countries to invest more on the expansion and diversification of higher education institutions that may not aspire to become major centers of excellence but that can have an important role to play as institutions that are closely linked with specific, niche development needs of local economies (ADB, 2012g). In this development area, demand is increasing for support from development partners. These partners provide assistance in the development of regional and cross-border platforms that effectively involve and facilitate collaboration and exchange of experiences among a wider range of higher education institutions.

Going Forward: Higher Education for the Future, Beyond the Horizon

Higher education undoubtedly supports aims that are broader than the development of human capital for supporting economic growth. However, at this time in Asia, for understandable reasons, economic growth is increasingly dominating deliberations on higher education development. As the rapid economic progress in the region has been accompanied by widening inequalities, the need to support inclusive development increasingly influences national and regional higher education development agendas. Demographic pressures also increase the demand for transformation of higher education in the region.

Responding to the demand, development partners' operations providing assistance and financing to higher education require a comprehensive scope covering a range of development aspects. The design of higher education projects financed by ADB include a number of intertwined components that focus on (1) improving policy formulation and regulatory frameworks for higher education; (2) establishing effective and functional governance structures, financial management, and quality-assurance systems; (3) enhancing relevance of course, curriculum, and teaching materials; (4) upgrading staff and teacher qualifications with appropriate postgraduate degrees by staff and faculty development programs; (5) improving the enabling environment, including for the utilization of ICT, for teaching and learning; (6) effectively targeting female students, poor students, students in remote areas and from ethnic minority groups, and other disadvantaged students, and supporting their study programs; and (7) facilitating timely participation of higher education institutions and their leaders and faculty in professional regional cooperation and cross-border collaboration networks and learning platforms.

Depending on the needs of individual developing countries, external support has specific priorities, including establishing and diversifying the services a network of a national university and provincial universities (the main focus and framework of ADB's support to higher education development, e.g., in Lao PDR), responding to the growing demand for both high level human resources and research and development capability in the context of country's industrial transformation (ADB's support to higher education in Vietnam, a country with rapidly evolving economy), providing assistance for the establishment of an enabling policy and regulatory environment for public–private partnerships in higher education (which is among the key strands of ADB's support to higher education in Mongolia), and providing financial and technical support for advanced technology for the delivery of higher education (ADB's support to modernizing distance education system of the University of the South Pacific network).

Asia continues to face challenges in reforming higher education, though there are also new opportunities. The region presents exciting prospects for collaboration and partnerships with a wider range of stakeholders through national, regional, and international platforms. The region and its partners are leveraging financing and, more importantly, know-how and innovative approaches that can help transform higher education well into the future. The Asian development context calls for new approaches that can support higher education development while anticipating issues that are currently beyond the horizon. It is important for development partners to strengthen their catalytic role to support these efforts, including helping to generate in-depth knowledge and understanding of the factors that may constrain innovation in higher education development in the region. Support is also important for formulating strategies and strengthening higher education institutions' capacity to creatively overcome the constraints.

The annual Asian Higher Education Leaders Summit, which is organized jointly by the University of Hong Kong and the Asian Development Bank, focuses on the importance of innovation in higher education development. Summit participants include current and future leaders of higher education institutions from developing countries in the region. The summit vision captures the direction of higher education development in the region:

> "With few exceptions, almost all jurisdictions in Asia are engaged in higher education development or reform. They are not about making up for a deficit and catching up with the rest of the world. They are creating a future of their own."[4]

REFERENCES

Asian Development Bank (ADB). (2008). *Education and skills: Strategies for accelerated development in Asia and the Pacific.* Manila, Philippines.

Asian Development Bank (ADB). (2009). *Good practice in cost sharing and financing in higher education.* Manila, Philippines.

Asian Development Bank (ADB). (2011). Higher education across Asia: An overview of issues and strategies. *Higher Education in Dynamic Asia: Study Reports.* Manila, Philippines.

Asian Development Bank (ADB). (2012a). Access without equity? Finding a better balance in higher education in Asia. *Higher Education in Dynamic Asia: Study Reports.* Manila, Philippines.

Asian Development Bank (ADB). (2012b). Administration and governance of higher education in Asia: Patterns and implications. *Higher Education in Dynamic Asia: Study Reports.* Manila, Philippines.

Asian Development Bank (ADB). (2012c). *Asian development outlook 2012: Confronting rising inequality in Asia.* Manila, Philippines.

Asian Development Bank (ADB). (2012d). Counting the cost: Financing Asian higher education for inclusive growth. *Higher Education in Dynamic Asia: Study Reports.* Manila, Philippines.

Asian Development Bank (ADB). (2012e). *Framework of inclusive growth indicators 2012: Key indicators for Asia and the Pacific special supplement.* Manila, Philippines.

Asian Development Bank (ADB). (2012f). Improving instructional quality: Focus on faculty development. *Higher Education in Dynamic Asia: Study Reports.* Manila, Philippines.

Asian Development Bank (ADB). (2012g). Improving transitions from school to university to workplace. *Higher Education in Dynamic Asia: Study Reports.* Manila, Philippines.

Asian Development Bank (ADB). (2012h). Private higher education across Asia: Expanding access, searching for quality. *Higher Education in Dynamic Asia: Study Reports.* Manila, Philippines.

Asian Development Bank (ADB). (2012i). Regional cooperation and cross-border collaboration in higher education in Asia: Ensuring that everyone wins. *Higher Education in Dynamic Asia: Study Reports.* Manila, Philippines.

Asian Development Bank (ADB). (2014). *Midterm review of Strategy 2020: Meeting the challenges of a transforming Asia and Pacific.* Manila, Philippines.

Bates, A. W., & Sangra, A. (2011). *Managing technology in higher education: Strategies for transforming teaching and learning.* San Francisco, CA: Jossey-Bass.

British Council. (2012). *The shape of things to come: Higher education global trends and emerging opportunities to 2020.* Retrieved from http://www.britishcouncil.org/sites/britishcouncil.uk2/files/ the_shape_of_things_to_come_-_higher_education_global_trends_and_emerging_opportunities_to_2020.pdf

Calderon, A. (2012). Massification continues to transform higher education. *University World News,* issue no. 237. Retrieved from http://www.universityworldnews.com/article.php?story=20120831155341147

Crowdfunding students: Start me up. (2013, June 15). *The Economist.* Retrieved from http://www.economist.com/news/finance-and-economics/21579490-helping-youngsters-sell-stakes-their-future-start-me-up

Kanbur, R., Rhee, C., & Zhuang, J. (2014). *Inequality in Asia and the Pacific: Trends, drivers and policy implications.* ADB. Manila, Philippines.

Kohli, H., Sharma, A., & Sood, A. (2011) Conclusion: Cost of missing the Asian century. In H. Kohli, A. Sharma, & A. Sood. (Eds.), *Asia 2050: Realizing the Asian century.* ADB. Manila, Philippines.

Salmi, J. & Hauptman, A. (2006). Innovations in Tertiary Education Financing: A Comparative Evaluation of Allocation Mechanisms. Working Paper Series, Number 4. The World Bank. Washington, D.C.

Sarvi, J. (2011). Cross-border collaboration for inclusive and sustainable higher education: Searching for priorities. In R. Sakamoto & D. Chapman (Eds.), *Cross-border partnerships in higher education: Strategies and issues.* New York, NY: Routledge.

Solheim, E. (2014). Asia rising—and faster than expected. *Asian Development Blog.* Retrieved from http://blogs.adb.org/blog/asia-rising-and-faster-expected

UNESCO Institute of Statistics. (2014). *UIS database.* Retrieved from http://data.uis.unesco.org/Index.aspx?DataSetCode=EDULIT_DS&popupcustomise=true&lang=en

NOTES

[1] The author is Practice Leader for Education at the Asian Development Bank. The views expressed in this chapter are those of the author and do not necessarily reflect the views and policies of ADB's management, Board of Directors, or the governments they represent.

[2] The middle-income trap refers a development stage in which countries are unable to compete with low-income, low-wage economies in manufactured exports and with advanced economies in high-skill innovations. Such countries cannot make a timely transition from resource-driven growth, with low-cost labor and capital, to productivity-driven growth.

[3] "Inclusive economic growth" is defined as growth with equality of opportunity.

[4] Asian Higher Education Leaders Summit, 2014. Brochure.

About the Contributors

Doria Abdullah is a doctoral candidate from the UTM Perdana School of Science, Technology, and Innovation Policy and academic fellow for Universiti Teknologi Malaysia (UTM). She is involved in various research and consultation projects concerning internationalization of Malaysian higher education. Her dissertation focuses on design of national higher education policies that would enhance the study and living experiences of international students.

Philip G. Altbach is research professor and director of the Center for International Higher Education at Boston College. He was Fulbright Research Professor at the University of Bombay. He has received the Houlihan award from NAFSA. His involvement with Indian higher education extends for almost a half-century. He is author of *Student Politics in Bombay, Publishing in India: An Analysis* and coeditor of *Higher Education Reform in India. A Half-Century of Indian Higher Education: Essays by Philip G. Altbach,* was edited by Pawan Agarwal.

Mohd Ismail Abd Aziz is the deputy vice chancellor (Student Affairs and Alumni) at Universiti Teknologi Malaysia (UTM) and the head of Critical Agenda Project (Internationalization), Department of Higher Education, Ministry of Education Malaysia. He holds a PhD from City University, London in Control Engineering; a MSc degree (Mathematics of Control Systems) from Loughborough University, United Kingdom; and a BSc degree (Applied Mathematics and Computer Science) from University of New South Wales, Australia. He is an applied mathematician specializing in dynamic optimization methods and its applications. His other research interest is internationalization of higher education, with a focus on policies and operational frameworks in operationalizing internationalization activities in individual institutions. He has held various administrative positions in UTM for more than 10 years ranging from head of Department for External Programs, Faculty of Science; deputy dean for School of Professional and Continuing Education (SPACE); and director for Office of International Affairs.

Rajika Bhandari is the deputy vice president for research and evaluation at the Institute of International Education. Dr. Bhandari provides strategic oversight of IIE's research and evaluation activities and leads two major research projects—Open Doors and Project Atlas—that measure international higher education mobility. She is a frequent speaker and author on the subject of student mobility and is the editor, most recently, of two books: *International Students and Global Mobility in Higher Education: National*

Trends and New Directions and *International India: A Turning Point in International Exchange With the U.S.* Before joining IIE, Dr. Bhandari was a senior researcher at MPR Associates, an educational research firm in California that provides research and evaluation services to the U.S. Department of Education. She also served as the assistant director for evaluation at the Mathematics and Science Education Network at the University of North Carolina at Chapel Hill. Dr. Bhandari holds a doctoral degree in psychology from North Carolina State University and a BA (Honors) in psychology from the University of Delhi, India.

Tan Eng Chye is deputy president (academic affairs) and provost of the National University of Singapore (NUS). He obtained his bachelor's degree in mathematics with first-class honors in 1985 at NUS and his PhD at Yale University in 1989. He oversees NUS' faculties and schools by providing strategic directions and setting academic policies. His responsibilities include admission policies and processes, educational quality assurance, budget and resource allocation for the faculties and schools, and the development and implementation of new educational initiatives. Professor Tan is also responsible for the appointment, promotion and tenure process, as well as the reward and incentive systems for academic staff.

Martin Hayden is Professor of Higher Education and Dean of Education at Southern Cross University in Australia. Over a long career, he has published extensively on all aspects of higher education policy and practice. Since 2005, he has been extensively engaged in research and consultancy in the Southeast Asian region. In 2011-12, he led a major project supported by the World Bank to develop a master plan for the higher education system in Vietnam. Over the past few years, he has also produced reports on higher education in Southeast Asia for the ADB, the EU, the OECD, the WB and the Australian Government.

Futao Huang is professor at the Research Institute for Higher Education, Hiroshima University, Japan. Before he came to Japan in 1999, he had taught at several Chinese universities. His major research fields are concerned with university curricular development, internationalization of higher education, including the internationalization of the academy, and a comparative study of higher education in East Asia with a focus on China and Japan. He has published widely in Chinese, English, and Japanese languages in many internationally recognized journals and domestic journals in both China and Japan. He is member of the Editorial Advisory Boards of *Higher Education* and *A Journal of Studies in International Education*.

Chaya Jain is an associate professor at Virginia State University and teaches public administration, political science, and economics to graduates and undergraduates. Previously, as public administration practitioner at state, local and federal governments, her focus was legislation, public policy and budgeting. An active community and professional service contributor, Jain serves on the executive board of the American Society for Public Administration's Section on International Comparative Administration. She earned her PhD in Public Policy and Administration and Master of Urban and Regional Planning from Virginia Commonwealth University, and MA in Geography with Merit from India. In 2012, Jain completed Harvard's Management Development Program.

Takao Kamibeppu is a professor in international education policy at Tokyo Jogakkan College in Japan. Previously, he worked at the Japanese Ministry of Education, Culture, Sports, Science & Technology (MEXT) in Tokyo and UNESCO in Bangkok in the field of international educational development and cooperation. He recently conducted research and published on internationalization of higher education in Asia, with particular country foci on Japan, Myanmar, Vietnam, and Bangladesh. He also served as a consultant for UNESCO, ASEAN, East Asia Summit, MEXT, and other organizations. He received an MA (intercultural management) from the School for International Training and a PhD (education policy) from the University of Maryland, College Park.

Jack Lee is an Assistant Professor at the Graduate School of Education, Nazarbayev University, Kazakhstan. His research focuses on international higher education and comparative education. Jack's research on education hubs was supported by a national fellowship from the Social Sciences and Humanities Research Council of Canada. He completed his doctorate at the Ontario Institute for Studies in Education of the University of Toronto. Previously, Jack developed and managed international education programs and intercultural training for domestic and international students, faculty, staff, and business executives at the University of British Columbia, Vancouver.

Alessia Lefébure serves as the director of the Alliance at Columbia University and is an adjunct professor at SIPA, the School of International and Public Affairs. An expert on global higher education and international affairs, she has been in charge of the academic and external relations with the Asia Pacific region at Sciences Po where she was the founder and director of the China Office in Beijing between 2001 and 2006, than as the director of the Centre for Asia and the Pacific between 2006 and 2011. She lectured and taught at Sciences Po in Paris and at Tsinghua University in Beijing on comparative higher education policies. Her most recent publication is a chapter in the book *China Innovation Inc.*, published in Paris by Presses de Sciences Po (2012), and in *Global Perspectives on International Joint and Double Degree Programs*, published in New York by IIE (2014). She is native of Italy, and completed her academic studies in Italy (LUISS, Rome), the United Kingdom (East Anglia University), and France (Sciences Po). She is the recipient of awards from the German Marshall Fund of the U.S. and the French American Foundation.

Miguel Lim is an EU-Marie Curie Doctoral Fellow at Aarhus University, Denmark, where he works on global university rankings and audit culture in higher education. He was previously executive director of the Global Public Policy Network Secretariat, a partnership between Columbia University, the National University of Singapore, the London School of Economics, and Sciences Po-Paris. He has worked for the Asia Pacific Center at Sciences Po and taught at the London School of Economics.

Pham Thi Ly is widely experienced with both the public and the private sectors of higher education in Vietnam. She is Dean of the Research Program at IEI, Vietnam National University-HCMC, and Director of Center for Higher Education Evaluation and Research at Nguyen Tat Thanh University. She was a Fulbright Scholar in 2008. Since then, been an active contributor to higher education policy discussion in Vietnam and abroad. Her works on educational policy, higher education governance and international education are widely published. For more information, please visit her website: www.lypham.net.

Kishore Mahbubani has had the good fortune of enjoying a career in government and, at the same time, in writing extensively on public issues. He was with the Singapore Foreign Service for 33 years (1971-2004). He was Permanent Secretary at the Foreign Ministry from 1993 to 1998. Currently, he is the Dean of the Lee Kuan Yew School of Public Policy (NUS). In the world of ideas he has spoken and published globally. His latest book, *The Great Convergence: Asia, the West, and the Logic of One World*, was selected by the Financial Times as one of the best books of 2013. Most recently, he was selected by Prospect magazine as one of the top 50 world thinkers for 2014.

Simon Marginson is professor of International Higher Education at the Institute of Education in London, UK. He is joint editor-in-chief of *Higher Education* and the 2014 Clark Kerr Lecturer at the University of California. Marginson works on new concepts and theories, and he explores the explanatory power of existing social theories, in order to better understand higher education and international education in the context of globalization. He is also focused on problems of policy, markets, and public and private goods in higher education. He draws on comparative state analysis, qualitative research techniques, and international agency data sets. Recent publications concern global competition, strategy, and the positioning of systems and institutions; university rankings; national and global public goods; cross-border student security; intercultural education; student self-formation in international education; and higher education in East Asia. His latest books are *Higher Education in Vietnam* (with eight co-authors) and *The Age of STEM: Educational Policy and Practice Across the World in Science, Technology, Engineering and Mathematics* (co-edited with Brigid Freeman and Russell Tytler).

Jouko Sarvi is practice leader for education at the Asian Development Bank (ADB). He oversees ADB's policy and strategy for supporting developing countries in Asia and the Pacific in improving education and skills for the future. He leads ADB's studies and knowledge sharing on good practice and innovation in education and coordinates ADB's external partnerships in the sector. He is the convener of ADB's high level international education conferences, and represents ADB in global and regional education events. He has served in boards and other strategic steering bodies of several international interagency organizations and partnerships. Mr. Sarvi has extensive experience in international development cooperation in education also in Africa, Middle East, and the Balkans.

IIE Information and Resources

THE CENTER FOR INTERNATIONAL PARTNERSHIPS IN HIGHER EDUCATION

The IIE Center for International Partnerships in Higher Education draws on IIE's wide-ranging network of more than 1,100 colleges and universities and extensive expertise in international education to provide administrators, policymakers, and practitioners with the resources and connections to develop and sustain partnerships around the world. Major initiatives of the Center are the International Academic Partnerships Program and the IIE Global Partner Service. The Center also produces timely policy research and convenes international education leaders in conferences and workshops.

WEBSITE: www.iie.org/cip

THE CENTER FOR ACADEMIC MOBILITY RESEARCH

The IIE Center for Academic Mobility Research brings together the Institute's in-house research expertise with leading minds from around the world to conduct and disseminate timely and relevant research and policy analysis in the field of international student and faculty mobility. The Center provides applied research and program evaluation services to domestic and international governmental agencies, nongovernmental organizations, corporations, and foundations. The Center's in-depth books and reports, including the well-known *Open Doors Report on International Educational Exchange*, supported by the U.S. Department of State, are key reference resources. In addition, the Center's policy papers and snapshot surveys capture trends in the changing landscape of international education.

WEBSITE: www.iie.org/mobility

RECENT IIE PAPERS

IIE Papers address the changing landscape of international education, offering timely snapshots of critical issues in the field.

- Charting New Pathways to Higher Education (2014)
- Syrian University Students and Scholars in Turkey, Lebanon, and Jordan (2014)
- What Will it Take to Double Study Abroad? (2014)
- U.S. Students in China: Meeting the Goals of the 100,000 Strong Initiative (2013)
- Expanding U.S. Study Abroad to Brazil: A Guide for Institutions (2012)
- Models for U.S. Study Abroad to Indonesia (2012)
- Learn by Doing: Expanding International Internships/Work Abroad Opportunities for U.S. STEM Students (2012)
- English-Taught Master's Programs in Europe: New Findings on Supply and Demand (2012)

- Expanding U.S. Study Abroad to India: A Guide for Institutions (July 2011)
- Evaluating and Measuring the Impact of Citizen Diplomacy: Current State and Future Directions (July 2011)
- Building Sustainable U.S.-Ethiopian University Partnerships: Findings from a Conference (July 2011)

WEBSITE: www.iie.org/publications

IIE/AIFS FOUNDATION GLOBAL EDUCATION RESEARCH REPORTS

This series of books explores the most pressing and underresearched issues affecting international education policy today.

- *Women in the Global Economy: Leading Social Change* (2013)
- *Latin America's New Knowledge Economy: Higher Education, Government, and International Collaboration* (2013)
- *Developing Strategic International Partnerships: Models for Initiating and Sustaining Innovative Institutional Linkages* (2011)
- *Who Goes Where and Why? An Overview and Analysis of Global Educational Mobility* (2011)
- *Innovation through Education: Building the Knowledge Economy in the Middle East* (2010)
- *International India: A Turning Point in Educational Exchange with the U.S.* (2010)
- *Higher Education on the Move: New Developments in Global Mobility* (2009)
- *U.S.-China Educational Exchange: Perspectives on a Growing Partnership* (2008)

WEBSITE: www.iie.org/gerr

IIE Web Resources

GENERATION STUDY ABROAD
Generation Study Abroad is a five-year IIE initiative to double the number of U.S. college students studying abroad by the end of the decade. IIE actively seeks new partners and resources to achieve this goal.

WEBSITE: www.generationstudyabroad.org

IIEPASSPORT.ORG
This free online search engine lists nearly 10,000 study abroad programs worldwide and provides advisers with hands-on tools to counsel students and promote study abroad.

WEBSITE: www.iiepassport.org

STUDY ABROAD FUNDING
This valuable funding resource helps U.S. students find funding for study abroad programs.

WEBSITE: www.studyabroadfunding.org

FUNDING FOR UNITED STATES STUDY
This directory offers the most relevant data on hundreds of fellowships, grants, paid internships, and scholarships for study in the United States.

WEBSITE: www.fundingusstudy.org

INTENSIVE ENGLISH USA
Comprehensive reference with more than 500 accredited English language programs in the United States.

WEBSITE: www.intensiveenglishusa.org

FULBRIGHT PROGRAMS FOR U.S. STUDENTS
The Fulbright U.S. Student Program equips future American leaders with the skills they need to thrive in an increasingly global environment by providing funding for one academic year of study or research abroad, to be conducted after graduation from an accredited university.

SPONSOR: U.S. Department of State, Bureau of Educational and Cultural Affairs
WEBSITE: http://us.fulbrightonline.org

FULBRIGHT PROGRAMS FOR U.S. SCHOLARS
The traditional Fulbright Scholar Program sends hundreds of U.S. faculty and professionals abroad each year. Grantees lecture and conduct research in a wide variety of academic and professional fields.

SPONSOR: U.S. Department of State, Bureau of Educational and Cultural Affairs
WEBSITE: www.cies.org

Programs of the AIFS Foundation

The AIFS Foundation

The mission of the AIFS Foundation is to provide educational and cultural exchange opportunities to foster greater understanding among the people of the world. It seeks to fulfill this mission by organizing high-quality educational opportunities for students and providing grants to individuals and schools for participation in culturally enriching educational programs.

WEBSITE: www.aifsfoundation.org

ACADEMIC YEAR IN AMERICA (AYA)

Each year, AYA brings nearly 1,000 high school students from around the world to the United States. They come for the school year to live with American families and attend local high schools, learning about American culture and sharing their own languages and customs with their host families.

WEBSITE: www.academicyear.org

FUTURE LEADERS EXCHANGE PROGRAM (FLEX)

Established in 1992 under the FREEDOM Support Act and administered by the U.S. Department of State's Bureau of Educational and Cultural Affairs, FLEX encourages long-lasting peace and mutual understanding between the United States and the countries of Eurasia.

YOUTH EXCHANGE AND STUDY PROGRAM (YES)

Since 2002, this U.S. Department of State high school exchange program has enabled students from predominantly Muslim countries to learn about American society and values, acquire leadership skills, and help educate Americans about their countries and cultures.

Programs of the American Institute For Foreign Study

American Institute For Foreign Study
The AIFS mission is to enrich the lives of young people throughout the world by providing them with educational and cultural exchange programs of the highest possible quality.

WEBSITE: www.aifs.com

AIFS COLLEGE STUDY ABROAD
AIFS is a leading provider of study abroad programs for college students. Students can study abroad for a summer, semester, or academic year in 17 countries around the world. Faculty-led and customized programs are also offered.

WEBSITE: www.aifsabroad.com

AMERICAN COUNCIL FOR INTERNATIONAL STUDIES (ACIS)
For more than 30 years, ACIS has helped students and their teachers discover the world through premier travel and education. Teachers can choose destinations throughout Europe, the Americas, and Asia.

WEBSITE: www.acis.com

AU PAIR IN AMERICA
Au Pair in America makes it possible for nearly 4,000 eager and skilled young adults from around the world to join American families and help care for their children during a mutually rewarding, yearlong cultural exchange experience.

WEBSITE: www.aupairinamerica.com

CAMP AMERICA
Each summer, Camp America brings nearly 6,000 young people from around the world to the United States to work as camp counselors and camp staff.

WEBSITE: www.campamerica.aifs.com

CULTURAL INSURANCE SERVICES INTERNATIONAL (CISI)
CISI is the leading provider of study abroad and international student insurance coverage. Since 1992, CISI has insured more than 1 million international students and cultural exchange participants worldwide.

WEBSITE: www.culturalinsurance.com

SUMMER INSTITUTE FOR THE GIFTED (SIG)

SIG is a three-week academic, recreational, and social summer program for gifted and talented students. Students from around the world in grades 4 through 11 can participate in SIG Residential programs offered at university campuses across the country including Bryn Mawr College, Emory University, Princeton University, UC Berkeley, UCLA, University of Chicago, University of Miami, Vassar College, and Yale University. Day, part-time, on-line and Saturday programs are also offered. SIG operates under the National Society for the Gifted and the Talented (NSGT), which is a nonprofit 501(c)3 organization.

WEBSITE: www.giftedstudy.org

AIFS Information and Resources

The following resources are available for download at www.aifsabroad.com/advisors/publications.asp

- Student Guide to Study Abroad and Career Development
- Diversity in International Education Summary Report
- The Gender Gap in Post-Secondary Study Abroad: Understanding and Marketing to Male Students
- Study Abroad: A 21st Century Perspective, Vol I
- Study Abroad: A 21st Century Perspective, Vol II: The Changing Landscape
- Innocents at Home Redux—The Continuing Challenge to America's Future
- Impact on Education Abroad on Career Development, Vol. I
- Impact on Education Abroad on Career Development: Four Community College Case Studies, Vol. II